Marine Raiders

On the Cover: Photographed by a U.S. photographer embedded with Edson's Raiders during WWII, members of a machine gun team pose for cameras on Guadalcanal, 1942. First Lieutenant Lee N. Minier, one of four Raiders featured in this book, lies on the ground stretched out behind his machine gun at the Raider camp dubbed Coconut Grove. *Courtesy Minier family collection.*

MARINE RAIDERS

THE TRUE STORY OF THE LEGENDARY WWII BATTALIONS

CAROLE ENGLE AVRIETT

Foreword by Joseph C. Shusko, Lt. Col. USMC (Ret.)
Honorary WWII Raider

REGNERY
HISTORY
Washington, D.C.

Regnery History™ is a trademark of Salem Communications Holding Corporation
Regnery® is a registered trademark and its colophon is a trademark of Salem Communications Holding Corporation

Cataloging-in-Publication data on file with the Library of Congress

ISBN: 978-1-68451-304-8
Library of Congress Control Number: 2020953035

First trade paperback edition published 2022

Published in the United States by
Regnery History, an Imprint of
Regnery Publishing
A Division of Salem Media Group
Washington, D.C.
www.Regnery.com

Manufactured in the United States of America

10 9 8 7 6 5 4 3 2 1

Books are available in quantity for promotional or premium use. For information on discounts and terms, please visit our website: www.Regnery.com.

To all Marine Raiders past, present, and future...

"Thank you" doesn't seem enough.

CONTENTS

Foreword

Ronald Reagan once said, "Some people spend their entire lifetime wondering if they made a difference to this world.... Marines don't have that problem." I joined the United States Marine Corps back in 1975, when it wasn't very fashionable to don the uniform, following in my father's footsteps. My six brothers also became Marines—we were a military family to the core. I served proudly in many billets, bases, and stations all around the world, visiting over seventy countries in the art of supporting and defending our Constitution. Hopefully I have made a difference during my service.

I recently retired after spending over forty faithful years in and around the United States Marine Corps. I would do it all over again if given the opportunity. I retired as the director of the Marine Corps Martial Arts Program in 2019, an assignment that was one of the highlights of my career. In this role, I not only met dozens of great American patriots actively serving in the Marines; I also got to meet those special Marine veterans who served in a legendary Marine unit in World War II. They were called the Marine Raiders, and they definitely made a difference.

From 2002 to 2003, I had the distinct pleasure of meeting a World War II Raider for the first time. His name was Ken O'Donnell, and he served with the 4th Battalion of Marine Raiders. He loved telling me he served under President Roosevelt's son, then his battalion's commanding officer. He was so humble yet so dignified. The stories he told left me eager to learn more about these unbelievable men, these heroes of our great nation.

Ken took me in to the Raider Association and made me feel like I belonged. Thanks to Ken, I was invited to their annual reunions, where I met many other Raiders. I reciprocated by pushing to name our new building in their honor: Raider Hall, the home of the Marine Corps Martial Arts Center of Excellence.

With the name change, Raiders started to come out of the woodwork to donate artifacts and mementos from their service. The Raiders were so thrilled about their "new home" that they thought it should host their reunions. As their new host, I met more Raiders and heard more and more stories that enthralled me from men like "Horse Collar" Smith, Chuck Meacham, Howard Berg, Archie Rackerby, "Mudhole" Merrill, and many, many more. These were men who were recognized around the world as members of the first elite fighting force in the Marine Corps, known for their physical endurance, their martial artistry, their patriotism, their professionalism, and the pride they had for serving as Marines.

Every year, thousands of people descend upon Raider Hall, coming from all over the globe to see what has become the unofficial Raider "museum." They don't come to see today's Marines; they come to read about the Marine Raiders of yesteryear.

I have been honored and privileged to be friends with members of our Raider Family for the past eighteen years. In that time, I have come to know and respect these men who sacrificed so much during and after World War II—men who, even after deploying to fight the evil powers of those years, came back home to build this great nation. Men who returned home to finish high school, go to college, get their master's, marry their sweethearts and start families, become doctors and lawyers, policemen and firemen. In my experience, Tom Brokaw was absolutely right to call them the "Greatest Generation."

Those hard-charging Raiders convinced our then commandant, General Amos, to change the name of the Corps Special Operations Organization, commonly known as MARSOC, to the "Raiders." MARSOC Marines were the "elite" fighting force serving as special operators for our country, just like the Raiders of World War II once had. The legacy of those gallant warriors of the past will never be forgotten, and our newest Raider Battalions carrying on the rich traditions will make sure that they continue to strike fear in the hearts of our country's enemies.

I am, and always will be, an ardent admirer of these fellow warriors.

Semper Fidelis
Joe "Marine" Shusko, USMC (Ret.)
Honorary WWII Raider
Marine Always

Author's Note

John the Apostle penned these words in the last verse of his Gospel:

> Jesus did many other things. If every one of them were written down, I suppose that even the whole world would not have room for the books that would be written.

In writing about our heroes of World War II, in particular these magnificent Marine Raiders, I too can appreciate John's lament.

Prologue

The whole world changed in the days following the "day of infamy." Though the winds of war had been blowing for many months, America was caught woefully unprepared. The country that would become the arsenal of democracy was undermanned, under-equipped, and under-supplied for war.

Activity spread nationwide as America woke up to what was going on in the world. Every industry was transformed to meet the needs of the war effort. The year coming to a close had seen more than 3 million cars manufactured in the United States. Only 139 more cars would be built nationwide over the remaining course of the war. Chrysler would produce fuselages; General Motors, airplane engines, guns, and tanks; and the Ford Motor Company at its vast Willow Run plant in Ypsilanti, Michigan, would produce B-24 Liberators—long range bombers with 1,550,000 parts each, much more complicated than the 15,000 parts per car. Yet, miraculously, one enormous plane would come off the line every 63 minutes.

The United States' commercial production machine had morphed into American wartime production, an entirely different beast. The eye of a sleeping giant had suddenly snapped open.

Yet as fiercely as this historically unprecedented manufacturing growth had ignited, an even more formidable force loomed on the horizon. Thousands upon thousands of American citizens volunteered to defend their country. America's industrial might was complemented by the commitment of her sons to their country's cause. Young men from across the country made the difficult decision to volunteer for the military effort. Both eyes of the slumbering giant had opened wide.

This is the story—plain and simple—of four of those young men. All four woke up one morning living in a country that had been attacked and decided to fight to protect her. When they went off to war, they wanted to be with the best. To their way of thinking, that was the Marines, and they found themselves, along with a few hundred others, marked by destiny to become part of a special-forces group called the Raiders. The configuration—four separate battalions—would form a single family of special forces within the Marine Corps. Yet each Raider Battalion developed a bit of its own persona, colored by the amazingly unique leaders who sired and led each. These four young men with contrasting backgrounds and widely varied personalities would join one of each of the four legendary battalions—altogether different siblings in the Raider family, but blood brothers nonetheless.

The Raiders' heroics would rock the world. Their fierce hand-to-hand combat tactics showed crack, veteran Japanese troops that these Americans were also fierce warriors. Their early Pacific successes would give their own discouraged country something to cheer. They would take part in battles whose names would forever brush elbows with the pinnacles of Marine Corps history at Tripoli, Montezuma, and Belleau Wood. They would be heralded in magazines, newspapers, and books worldwide—and often photographed. They carried special knives including thin, wicked blades known as stilettos. They had their own patches, penned their own songs, and even invoked their own unique calls, like "Saddle Up!" and

"Gung Ho!"—the title Hollywood would use in the '40s for a wildly popular movie based on their exploits.

But these special forces—as a separate group—wouldn't last long. The World War II Raiders were like shooting stars: short-lived and magnificent. The group would be disbanded after just twenty months. Yet their legacy stretches across generations, and their deeds will be remembered as long as mankind endures.

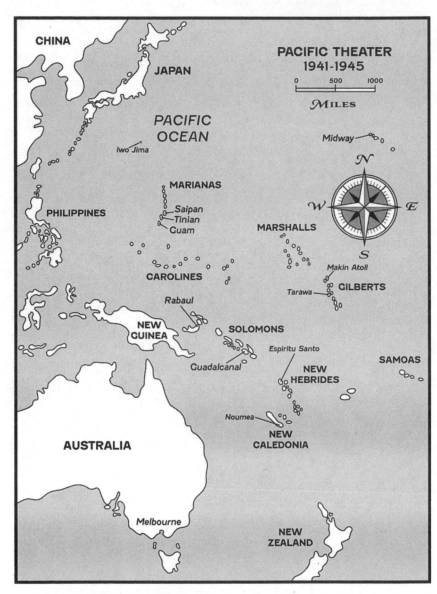

1. Overview of WWII Pacific Theater: 1941–1945

CHAPTER I

Boys Become Men

The Factory Guard
December 15, 1941

Ever since Pearl Harbor, an unmistakable sense of urgency permeated every aspect of rifle production at Ilion, New York's Remington Arms factory. Each worker strained to examine metal parts that much more carefully, while craftsmen sanded whiskey-colored walnut stocks with heightened concentration. Any particular '03 Springfield rifle could wind up in France or on an island in the Pacific. Chances were that rifle would be the only thing protecting an American soldier from death.

It had only been a few days since the Japanese bombed Pearl Harbor, but the U.S. government had already asked Remington Arms for 134,000 M1903 Springfield bolt-action rifles. Soon, however, it would raise that order to 308,000, before raising it again to 508,000. In short measure, target production would stand at a rate of 2,000 rifles a day.

It was mid-morning when the 6'2" Remington security guard moved with long, confident strides across the noisy factory floor toward the break room.

"Hey, Lee," called out one of the munitions workers with a wave of his hand. "Here, look at this beauty," he said and tossed over a brand-new Springfield.

The twenty-four-year-old deftly caught and raised the rifle to his shoulder in one easy swoop. Its whiskey-colored stock, so silky smooth, felt almost cool to the touch. He stared down the sight.

Lee Minier was no stranger to firearms. He had hunted since he was a boy and loved being outdoors. In high school, his natural athletic ability had elevated him to captain the school baseball and basketball teams. Perhaps his strength and agility was inherited from his father, who was once courted by the renowned Chicago White Sox of the '20s.

Though Lee was known for his competitive spirit, he also possessed the mellowest baritone voice of anyone in the church choir. With a pleasant, open face and a high forehead, he looked straight at people. He was honest and calm, though his eyes betrayed an ever-present, fun-loving stripe. Everyone liked Lee Minier.

"She's a beauty alright," grinned Lee, returning the firearm to the table.

The seasoned gunsmith looked down, giving it one last swipe with an oil cloth, then glanced up at the rugged guard before him. "These are different times," he said soberly.

"Yes, they are—they are that indeed," returned the young man, and continued his walk toward the break room.

Once settled at a commissary table, Lee rubbed a thumb across one side of his coffee mug, then fingered a cigarette. All the morning newspapers heralded a surging tide sweeping across the country: "Recruiting Offices Amazed at Sunday's Crowds," the New York Times headline read; "Recruitment Numbers Grow Ever Stronger," said another. Many of his friends had already enlisted.

Lee leaned back in his chair. The Depression years had hit hard. His family was no exception. When his parents were engaged, his father, Pat, had received an offer to play for the Chicago White Sox. His mother, Jolette McGrew, presented his father with an ultimatum: play ball or marry her. That way Pat would be positioned to take over her father's banks. George "Pat" Minier became a banker and was operating several banks until the Great Crash of 1929. Though he was able to pay back money lost from his banks, it took until the late 1940s.

Like so many families during the Depression, the magnitude of loss overwhelmed the Miniers, who struggled to feed and care for their four children. To help out, his father's sister, Clara Minier Swayne, took in one of the young boys. As she had no children of her own, Lee was the only child his aunt ever raised; she proved a loving surrogate, and he never forgot her kindness.

During his early twenties, the young man's personal finances in Pearl, Illinois, deteriorated. He quit college and headed east to Prospect, New York, where jobs in the late '30s were more available. However, the move had other upsides. It brought him closer to his own mother, who, after separating from his father, had returned to her original home in Prospect some years before.

Lee's other three siblings had also migrated to Prospect. It was the first time in years he and his mother, his brothers, and his sister had spent time together. Being reunited was undeniably fulfilling—it made separating again that much more difficult to imagine.

But there was another reason that Lee was happy to be in New York. Her name was Marjorie Robinson—called Marge for short. A lovely, petite young woman, she lived across the street from his mother in Prospect. She frequented the bridge table at his mother's home, where the two met and hit it off immediately. Lee knew he wanted to marry Marge one day.

He sipped his coffee, contemplating things, his usually smooth forehead contorted into deep furrows. His thoughts returned to what the gunsmith had just said: "These are different times."

Work at the arms factory was crucial. Of this Lee was certain. But he wanted to do more. The conscientious young man burned with a sense of wounded national pride, just like most people did. He couldn't exactly define the feeling in his chest, but he knew he wanted to be *there*, wherever that was, and play his small part in the war to get America back on her feet.

...And he knew that if he was going to fight, he wanted to go as a Marine.

Lee crushed out his cigarette, which had lain idle in his fingers. This afternoon, he would give his two weeks' notice at Remington Arms Factory. More importantly, on the way home he would stop to talk it over with the recruiter. He rested his chin in his left hand. A good feeling surged through him.

"Sometimes you just have to make the tough decision," Lee thought to himself. This was one.

January 7, 1942

A fresh dusting of snow overnight had softened the hard-edged Art Deco features of New York Railroad Station in Syracuse, New York. Now, in the freezing dawn hours, hundreds of young men steadily poured into the noisy terminal—one month to the day since the bombing of Pearl Harbor. They hurriedly lugged their small suitcases, duffle bags, and satchels into the station. They waited around, shuffling to keep warm. Many said their final good-byes to family members and girlfriends before boarding their trains.

Lee Minier had spent Christmas and New Year's Eve in Prospect. He'd soaked in family time with his mother, his sister Mary, brother Hugh, and his other family members. But he especially relished his time with his sweetheart, Marge.

When they could carve out moments to be alone, Lee and Marge talked of the future, what that might look like. They debated marriage. Lee felt it wouldn't be fair to Marge to marry before leaving, though many of his friends had married their girlfriends just prior to shipping out. Nonetheless, there was a clear understanding between them—they were a couple even though not formally engaged. And when he returned home, they would tie the knot.

Now Lee sat alone on one of the station's benches mulling over the wonderful holidays in Prospect. The past couple of days had been a whirlwind of enlistment activities in Syracuse. With pen in hand, he bent over to address and sign a small, preprinted postcard. One had been given to him and to all the others by military enlistment personnel. The moment had arrived; the unknown stretched before Lee Minier. But no matter what the future might hold, he would greet it as a member of the United States Marines.

The High School Junior

Roy Merrill, the Chief of Police of Mesa, Arizona, had a decision to make. He studied his good-looking, muscular son, who at that moment was passionately pleading his case. Kenny had been a handful his whole life. It had been tough for both of them.

When a devastating outbreak of typhoid fever swept across most of the southwestern United States in the early 1930s, Tilly Merrill and her oldest daughter, Jetta, both succumbed to the illness. The sudden tragedy left her husband, Roy, alone with five other children to raise.

Standing over the fresh graves, the new widower made a critical decision. He would take his then seven-year-old son, Kenny, the most rambunctious and mischievous of the bunch, to live with his sister and her husband in San Pedro, California. He needed some time to sort things out. After borrowing a used Oldsmobile touring car from a friend, Roy packed up his spirited son, dressed as usual in overalls with his one pair of shoes, and headed out.

The unlikely series of events would lead the youngster, Kenneth Henry Merrill, to spend time with his aunt's son, J.T., a sailor in the Navy. When three submarines moored in San Diego Harbor later that summer, J.T. asked if Kenny would like to go onboard a sub. Kenny answered with an instant, loud whoop of excitement.

Wide-eyed with anticipation, the eight-year-old boy half-ran, half-skipped his way from dock to submarine, scurried up and down its ladders, darted through the narrow passages, and rubbed his hands across the cold, slick torpedoes. Kenny was mesmerized by the trappings of a real-life sub and chattered non-stop about the experience for days. As he himself would later say, "It was really something."

And in one of life's stunning coincidences, this same submarine, the USS *Nautilus*, would play a key role in his life some nine years later. The three submarines moored in San Diego Harbor that joyous day when he darted around them at will had been the USS *Nautilus*, the USS *Argonaut*, and the USS *Narwhal*. These ships later would play vital roles in transporting Marine special forces to critical battles in the South Pacific. And the USS *Nautilus* herself would carry seventeen-year-old Kenny Merrill, along with his fellow Marines, to one of the first engagements in the South Pacific—one that would go down in the annals of Marine history.

But no one in Kenny's family could have possibly known what his future held. They were just trying to keep him alive and out of trouble. After his mother died, Kenny was bounced from one family to another until he finally settled in—to some degree—with his oldest brother, Chick. At one point, after Kenny was picked up by the local police, Chick decided to just let Kenny cool his heels in jail for a day or two.

Once Ken entered high school, however, the physicality of football suited him to a tee. He proved himself a worthy defensive lineman for the Globe High School Tigers, Globe, Arizona. At 5'10" and a muscular 185 pounds, he enjoyed being hit—and hitting back.

Then came December 7, 1941: the end of football season, and the beginning of war.

Now, Chief Roy Merrill had a decision to make. He continued to gaze at his son while Kenny argued with gusto—imploring his dad to grant his request.

"I want to go, but I don't want to go in the Army or the Navy. I want to get in there where we can get the fighting done," said Kenny to his father. "I want to go as a Marine—they're the first fighting and the toughest."

Because of his age, however, the Marines wouldn't take him without parental consent. Kenny had just turned seventeen three months before. So Kenny begged his father to sign the papers necessary for him to enlist in the Corps.

Finally, Roy Merrill gave his answer, laced with a condition. "Well, son, I'll sign for you if you promise me one thing— that when the war is over you'll go back and finish your high school."

"Okay," said Kenny, "I promise you I will."

So that was it. On January 2, 1942, Kenneth Henry Merrill left for boot camp in San Diego, California, assigned to Platoon Number 33. Six months of high school ROTC had equipped Ken with the basics of arms drills, marksmanship, and marching. The course helped him transition fairly quickly into military training.

Unlike some recruits, however, who needed time to adjust to the rigors of boot camp, the energetic young teenager thrived in the demanding, structured environment. Completely comfortable in his own skin, the belligerent sergeants didn't intimidate him. He took it all in stride and never lost his sense of humor. He was accustomed to tough conditions and being bounced around, and he adapted quickly—even relished the rough-and-tumble life.

Kenny Merrill had found a home in the Marine Corps.

The College Grad

Born at noon on July 31, 1920, Archibald Boyd Rackerby grew into his name. By his mid-teens, he was well over six feet tall and was interested in everything. He began selling magazines and encyclopedias— *Saturday Evening Post*, *Ladies Home Journal*, and *Colliers*, among others—when he was eleven years old for spending money. In high school, he organized a ski club, learned photographic developing, printing, and enlarging, edited the year book, joined the rifle club, worked in his father's Wheel and Brake Shop, and built sets for drama productions. He restored cars, took flying lessons from the U.S. government's Pilot Training Program, panned for gold, and paid his own way for a two-year degree from Yuba College. At Yuba, Rackerby established a weekly newspaper, learned French and German, and worked as a sportswriter for a local paper to help put him through the program. He could type ninety words per minute, a skill that would serve him well in the service.

In April 1941, he decided to join the Marine Corps. Having recently graduated from college, Rackerby thought joining the Marines would give him the chance to see the world. His mother, throughout his life, had always spoken highly of the Marines. As a young woman, she had been a clerk in the Navy, working in Washington, D.C. When she played her piano, which was almost daily, she played the "Marines' Hymn." It rubbed off on his psyche: he never considered any other military service. Both his brothers also joined the United States Marine Corps.

There was only one problem: Archibald Boyd Rackerby was rejected by the Marine Corps. He was 6'3" tall but weighed only 138 pounds. The recruiter told him to gain 17 pounds and come back. But after the bombing of Pearl Harbor, Archie knew they would probably take him, regardless of how skinny he was. He was right.

On Sunday, December 7, just hours after the attack on Pearl Harbor, Archie quit his job and raced his 1935 Pontiac sedan to San Francisco to enlist. By the time he made it to the recruitment offices, thousands of young men were already lined up to serve their country. It took hours to reach an officer.

After some waiting, he made it to the officer's desk and enlisted to join the Marines. He received his papers and was told that he would be sworn in after the holidays and returned home.

On December 26, 1941, Archie filled an old leather valise with some clothes, kissed his mother goodbye, shook his father's hand, and walked over to the bus stop to go to Sacramento and the Marine Corps recruiting office. He was on his way to fulfilling his dream of becoming a Marine.

The Lumberjack Farm Boy

Edwin Roger Blomberg walked briskly through the snow-covered field at dawn toward his uncle George Swanson's farm. It was New Year's Day, 1942. The clear air was freezing cold. Ed pulled the collar of his peacoat high around his face, then dug his hands deep into his pockets. The quiet settled like a handmade quilt over the land—a countryside filled with memories of family, work, and commitment since his birth in a log house twenty-one years past.

As he continued along the path, he thought about what these fields and forests represented—his heritage and its traditions. Both sides of his family had immigrated from Sweden, living and owning property in this area of Wisconsin since the mid-1800s. His mother's family had built a large frame house on the highest point in the state, and his grandpa, Anders Johan Blomberg, had purchased a piece of land nearby shortly after arriving in America.

Ed thought about the courage it must have taken to make such life-altering decisions. Grandpa Blomberg had left Daretorp, Sweden, in 1880 with his wife and four children, coming to the United States to escape religious persecution. Anders, through the influence of a coworker, had become a practicing and devoted member of the Baptist Church—much to the chagrin of Sweden's Lutheran authorities. They harassed Ed's grandfather, hindering his ability to work as a stonemason.

The Blombergs decided to sail for America for its promise of religious freedom. Among their luggage was a small worker's bag. In it were a mallet, hammer, metal straightedge, and a small set of wedges—all hand tools, symbols of a physically demanding trade. Anders was a master stonemason—in fact, he had learned the difficult and exacting technique of dry-laid stonework. He was certain that he could establish a lucrative business in the United States.

After arriving in the States, the Blombergs boarded the Soo Line Railroad for Wisconsin to see their newly purchased piece of land. When the train came to a stop, it wasn't because of a station call. It was because there was no more track. Anders's wife, now pregnant with their fifth child, climbed down from the train, found a nearby tree stump, sat down, and cried her eyes dry.

When Anders was able to pull his wife to her feet with his strong arms, the family traveled down a wagon trail. At the end was a small logging town, Ogema. Further down the path, they discovered their newly purchased land with only a two-story log house on the property—far less built-out than they had been told.

It was not what they had expected. Anders thought they had purchased an established farm complete with barns and other outbuildings. But they had arrived in America. And, without looking back, they began to build their new life.

Anders and his wife had eleven children, many of whom would go on to have large families of their own. Ed's parents, George and Lillian Blomberg, had fourteen children, of which Ed was the third.

Most of the young Blomberg men remained in the Ogema area, which quickly became one of the largest Swedish communities in the United States. Ed and his brothers often worked for other family members in the area, helping them with the farming tasks that required strong young men.

On this New Year's Day, wonderful memories flitted across his mind as he walked along the familiar land. He thought of all the heart-warming times that he had shared with his family in these parts: taking open sleigh rides through the forests at Christmas time to his grand-parents' house, helping his Pa with logging chores, get-togethers with aunts and uncles and cousins for picnics and celebrations. It was a wonderful place to grow up.

At that moment he happened to glance sideways and spotted several fair-sized stones lining a small creek bed. Somehow the stones reminded him of his grandpa—not just his trade as a stonemason, but also his strength, physical as well as spiritual. Grandpa had been a fairly short man but was amazingly strong, especially in his hands. Ed had inherited his strength—he could climb a tree trunk using only the strength of his arms and legs to push himself upward. But he was taller—tallest, in fact, of all his siblings and most of his cousins.

He had walked this path to his uncle's house, passing through forests and around lakes, more times than he could count. Today was different. It was the first time he had ever experienced conflicting thoughts about helping a family member.

They had heard the news of December 7, 1941, like most Americans, over the radio. The Blombergs had just recently acquired electricity. That this would be the first thing they heard seemed remarkable.

Ed had immediately applied to enlist. As proud as they all were of their Swedish heritage, their homeland had been attacked—this land that they loved.

He waited but heard nothing back. In the meantime, his widowered Uncle George had taken seriously ill, bedridden from an old logging injury. Ed's help around the farm was desperately needed. He consented to lend a hand, though reluctantly. The young Wisconsinite wanted to do his part in the nation's crisis, but family was important. His uncle needed him as soon as possible. Entry into the war would have to wait a few months.

But Ed Blomberg's time would come. And when it did, he would find himself in what some military historians have labeled one of the best-trained units of Marine warriors to ever take to the field of battle. Ed Blomberg would become a member of the 4th Marine Raider Battalion.

The Commandant of the United States Marine Corps
Washington, D.C., January 7, 1942

While young men all over the country struggled with personal decisions about going off to fight, Major General Thomas Holcomb, commandant of the Marine Corps, faced his own pressing dilemma. On this Wednesday, January 7, 1942, Holcomb stood at a bay window of his residence at Marine Barracks in Washington, D.C., and stared out over the parade grounds. The stately three-and-a-half-story mansion had been home to Marine commandants since 1801, when Thomas Jefferson and Lieutenant Colonel William Ward Burrows chose the site for a Marine post.

This morning, Holcomb's attention was divided by two major dilemmas. The Marine Corps had a pressing need for not one but two field-ready infantry divisions. At the time President Roosevelt declared a state of war, the Marines were unable to put even one full infantry division (approximately nineteen thousand men) in the field, much less a second. Initial plans called for bringing the existing 1st Marine Division to full complement by mid-1942. At the same time, a new 2nd Marine Division was to be organized and trained on the West Coast. Most assuredly, this meant that the veterans and "Old Salts"—those who had fought in the Banana Wars and in the Caribbean—would be called upon to help mold and train the extreme influx of newcomers as the Corps grew to fighting strength.

In accord with his reputation as a master administrator, Major General Holcomb knew his resources were stretched tight. Getting a single combat-ready division to sea was one thing; putting together a second division from scratch was quite another.

Solving this problem would have been exacting enough, but Holcomb found himself distracted by a second issue—one that emanated from the highest levels of the White House.

Holcomb had recently returned from meetings with Secretary of the Navy Frank Knox. In those meetings, Knox indicated that both President Roosevelt and Prime Minister Winston Churchill of Great Britain were strongly in favor of forming commando-like strike units. They envisioned these specially trained troops employed for swift raids against Japanese outposts in the Pacific.

Both statesmen, and particularly the president, were impressed by the exploits of British Commandos in Europe. They each felt that similar successes could be effected against the Japanese with analogous small fighting units.

Just a few days prior to Holcomb's meetings with Secretary Knox, a personal memorandum had reached the Executive Offices concerning the subject of commandos. It was marked top secret, prepared by William J. Donovan, newly named head of the Office of the Coordinator of Information, an early forerunner of the Office of Strategic Services (OSS), which in turn was a precursor to the CIA.

Dubbed "Wild Bill," Donovan is known as the father of modern American espionage.

The intelligence officer was a close confidant of President Roosevelt and enjoyed direct access to the president's ear. In his top secret memorandum, Donovan proposed forming guerilla bands of small commando units, much like President Roosevelt would later discuss with Churchill. The Marine Corps was the logical home for such commando units. Independent and separate from the Army and Navy, with troops already trained in small-scale unit operations, the Corps fit the bill very nicely.

The idea wasn't altogether new to the commandant of the Marine Corps. As early as 1935, the Corps had officially produced the Tentative Landing Manual, outlining amphibious landing maneuvers for small groups. Several units were already training to perfect these techniques and develop an amphibious program.

Commandant Holcomb wasn't worried about developing the guerilla force; he was worried about who would lead it. Holcomb had received a memorandum from Admiral Ernest J. King, commander in chief of the U.S. Fleet, informing him that the proposed Marine Corps would be trained by British Commandos.

That worried Holcomb. It was one thing for the Marine Corps to develop and train special forces; it was quite another for this group to be led by an outsider. Outside leadership of Marines was where Holcomb drew the line. Plus, all signs seemed to indicate that William J. Donovan would be that leader—the head of an intelligence organization, not a Marine.

The pressure was great. In a personal letter to his friend at *Time*, Samuel Meek, Holcomb expressed his apprehensions: "The Donovan affair is still uppermost in mind. I am terrified that I may be forced to take this man. I feel it would be the worst slap in the face the Marine Corps ever was given because it involves bringing an outsider in to the Marine Corps as a leader in our own specialty, that is, amphibious operations.... It will be bitterly resented by our personnel."

With some crafty maneuvers and the help of top naval brass, Holcomb was able to ensure that the new force would remain under his auspices. But one significant decision remained: What should these new special forces be named?

Holcomb had several suggestions to choose from. Some thought the new force should have the fairly conventional name of the Commando Battalions or the Guerilla Battalions; others wanted to name the group the more creative Shock Battalions or Destroyer Battalions. Holcomb didn't find any of those suggestions fitting for Marines. He kept looking for the name that would eventually strike fear in enemy hearts and evoke a special sense of pride and purpose both in and out of the Marine Corps: thus the Raiders were born.

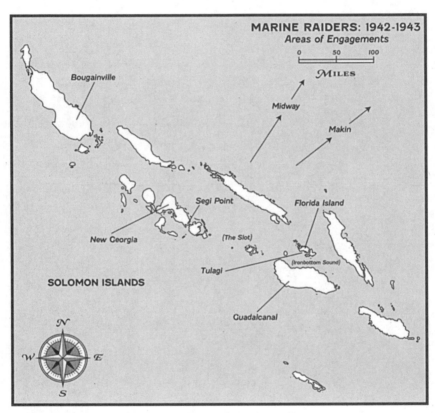

2. Primary areas of engagement for Raiders during WWII

CHAPTER II

Edson's Raiders

On February 16, 1942, Marine Corps commandant Thomas Holcomb officially activated the first of the new special forces units, designated the 1st Marine Raider Battalion. The unit was to be stationed on the East Coast at Quantico, Virginia, with Lieutenant Colonel Merritt "Red Mike" Edson tapped as its commander. Three days later, the commandant activated the 2nd Marine Raider Battalion, to be based in San Diego with Lieutenant Colonel Evans Fordyce Carlson for a commander. In the months to follow, two new sister Raider Battalions, the 3rd and 4th Raiders, would also be formed. Each of the battalions initially contained about eight hundred men.

The commanders chosen to train and lead these new Raiders boasted larger-than-life personalities and tremendous talent. Raider leadership was composed of some of the most unique, charismatic officers to ever marshal troops. In a testament to the importance of their leaders' personalities, some battalions would come to be known by their commanders' names.

Though he may not have possessed the appearance of a warrior, Merritt Edson was the obvious choice to lead the 1st Raiders. He personified the age-old warning against judging a book by its cover.

Edson had arrived at Quantico several months prior to the formation of the Raiders as a 5'7", slightly overweight Marine officer. He was delighted to leave his relatively sedentary job at Headquarters Marine Corps for more "hands-on" duty.

On the day of his arrival, June 7, 1941, the forty-four-year-old lieutenant colonel was introduced to the men at his current duty station— one of the battalions of the 5th Marine Regiment. Merritt Edson's quiet voice was not much more than a hoarse whisper. His officers and non-commanding officers (NCOs) needed to lean forward just to catch what he was saying. Most of the assembled group were fully aware of his reputation and received his arrival with a mixture of curiosity and unease. They all might have been surprised to learn that Edson's family tree didn't boast any military ancestors, something that was often found among the highest rungs of the officer class in those days.

Merritt Austin Edson was born on April 25, 1897, in Rutland, Vermont, the son and grandson of farmers. Reared in Chester, a picturesque New England village and gateway to the Green Mountains, Merritt grew up with an appreciation of the outdoors coupled with a farmer's work ethic.

As a young man, he left Chester for two years of college at the University of Vermont. There, Edson joined the Vermont National Guard and saw duty in Texas on the Mexican border. This was his first real taste of the military, and it agreed with him. After returning to college later that year, he decided to join the Marine Corps Reserves in June 1917. In the fall of that same year, he was commissioned as a second lieutenant in the Marine Corps.

It wasn't long before Edson had established himself as an expert marksman. Hunting had been a passion since his early childhood, so it wasn't too surprising that he was a good shot. He competed and earned a spot on the Marine Rifle Team in spring 1921. That year they defeated Army. Edson soon enjoyed a hero's reputation as a member of a National Championship Rifle Team, especially since marksmanship was earning a cult-like status throughout the Corps. He would go on to captain these

Marine rifle teams, winning four straight national championships in a row. His expertise became a trademark, and he would utilize these talents to mentor his Raiders in what he considered a signature element of fighting—marksmanship.

In the late '20s, Edson experienced combat that would teach him some of the most critical lessons of his career—and prepare him for what he would later face with his Raiders in the Pacific. In the jungles of Central America and Nicaragua, the then captain led his men up and down the Coco River, chasing marauding bands of Sandinistas, named for their leader, Augusto Sandino. Edson was not the only one to learn from these early engagements. Many other Marines who fought in these jungles would later ply their seasoned skills in training young World War II Raiders.

Central America, however, wasn't the only place Merritt Edson gleaned valuable knowledge that would assist him in his later life. He arrived in Shanghai on July 7, 1937, the day after the Japanese launched a war with China. His early experience in the Asian theater gave him valuable insight into Japanese battle methods.

When Edson returned from China, he became a proponent for increased emphasis on amphibious warfare and tactics. Now with his duties at Quantico, he commenced working with vintage World War I transports refitted for use in carrying troops for amphibious landings, known as APDs (high-speed transports; AP for "transport," D for "destroyer"). In the coming war years, these "heroic" little ships would play an invaluable role transporting troops—especially the Raiders.

When Commandant Holcomb decided to form the Raiders, Merritt Edson was his first choice to lead one of the two new Raider Battalions. Edson possessed all the qualifications. He was skilled as a marksman and experienced in guerrilla warfare, having led successful raiding-type patrols. He had been to China and had firsthand knowledge of Japanese tactics. And, of equal importance, he was familiar with the APDs which would be used in Raider landings.

Despite his slight stature and smaller-than-usual head that always made his helmet look too big, Edson gained the respect of those who served under him. Most would say his piercing blue eyes were his most memorable feature, as it was said that his stare could wither a man. And though Red Mike, his lasting nickname after sporting a bright red beard while fighting in Central America, might not have looked the part, he would soon earn the lasting respect of all those who knew and served with him. Well-known war correspondent Richard Tregaskis, who would later spend time embedded with 1st Raiders on Guadalcanal, described him this way: "He was the bravest, the most effective killing machine I met in fifteen years as a war correspondent."

Though Edson would go on to have a storied career, complete with a two-star generalship and a Medal of Honor, for now his job was to establish the most efficient and well-trained special forces unit possible for amphibious landings, mostly at night, on Japanese-held islands in the South Pacific.

The "Old Breed"

The Marine base at Quantico, Virginia, had been designated the site for the assembly and training of the 1st Raider Battalion. The site also headquartered the 1st Marine Division—the designation for the large, regular Marine group in the Corps.

Marine One, as this larger group was sometimes called, possessed a large number of what was generally known as the "Old Breed." These veteran Marines had seen service and action overseas in the '20s and '30s. Commanded by the recently appointed Brigadier General Alexander Archer Vandegrift, Marine One was soon to be the mainstay of America's first Pacific offensive. The Raiders, on the other hand, would be given smaller assignments—but of no less importance.

The Old Breed were a tough and hardened lot. Their presence played a crucial role in importing knowledge and spirit to the rapidly growing Corps. But for Red Mike, they represented a reservoir of seasoned warriors whom he could tap to begin training the type of fighter he envisioned for the Raiders. Edson's assistant commander, Samuel Griffith, would later describe the inveterate bunch as a "motley crew" of rough-and-tumble soldiers known for their unvarnished machismo. They boasted long disciplinary records, smoked bad cigars, drank cheap booze, gambled, and stayed away from chapel ("the God Box") unless forced to go. They had served around the world and had developed the tastes and survival instincts common to the men of the world's great port cities. They were tough as nails and had the fighting skills to back it up—with many boasting expert badges in a variety of combat areas.

Once Edson received formal orders to create the 1st Marine Raider Battalion, he siphoned off as many of the Old Breed as he could to help him train his young Raiders. These were the people he needed to create the special Raider spirit, the "elite of the elite." And while Edson's pilfering of talent from Marine ranks didn't engender the goodwill of his fellow commanders, it was key to the success of the force he was charged with crafting. This particularly bedeviled the newly appointed commander of Marine One, General Alexander Vandegrift, who had his hands full creating not one but two full divisions. And as time progressed, few in the Corps remained neutral to the Raiders: they were either loved, loathed, or envied.

Edson recruited Raiders through a uniform but laborious selection process. Marines had to volunteer to join the new force, knowing full well that the hardship and adversity would be severe. Then, after volunteering, candidates faced a personal interview process. Edson was looking for Marines who showed poise, intelligence, and character. Raiders needed to be motivated and independent yet capable of working with a team. The standards were high, but Edson knew they needed to be if his crack troops were going to succeed.

Soon after arriving at Quantico, Lee Minier would volunteer for the Raiders. Rumors swirled around base about the special forces group forming under Lieutenant Colonel Merritt Edson. The rumors piqued his interest, so he decided to interview—what did he have to lose?

After volunteering, Lee would soon be called to the one-story brick building where Edson's staff was conducting interviews. As Lee sat in the waiting room, he wondered what the "ole man," as the Marines on base affectionately referred to Edson, would be like. Many recruits had already formed their opinion about the colonel from base scuttlebutt. Edson had won a reputation for being hard-nosed, emotionless, and tough as nails. But Lee's thoughts soon drifted off to his own kin, two of whom had been soldiers in the American Revolution.

"I guess Miniers have never backed off from a fight worth fighting," Lee smiled to himself. His musings about his ancestry were abruptly curtailed when a door down the hall swung open forcefully. An older, gaunt-looking master sergeant barked out, "Private Minier?"

Lee came smartly to attention and followed the sergeant into a small office where two officers sat behind a large desk sorting through papers. There was a third man, much shorter than Lee, standing quietly over by the window smoking a cigarette. The two officers behind the desk directed him to sit down and began the interview.

First, they asked general information questions—where he was from, what was his family like—friendly questions concerning background and growing up. Lee had never been uncomfortable meeting new people, even senior officers. The conversation was serious but affable.

Then they turned to more specific questions. Why had he joined the Marines, and what had he heard about the Raiders? Lee continued in his usual pleasant manner, relating what he had heard—that the outfit sounded like it would be involved in places where it could make a difference in the war effort. And he, Lee, wanted to contribute whatever he could.

Lee knew instinctively that the man standing in the corner was Lieutenant Colonel Merritt Edson. Now, without so much as a nod, the two men got up from their chairs, and the colonel sat down in front of the private.

Lee made a mental note of the colonel's economy of motion. Though Edson had been smoking a cigarette, he hardly moved his hands and arms, and didn't shuffle his feet. He moved slowly and deliberately, and it amazed Lee. Now the gimlet-eyed Edson sat quietly behind the desk, sizing up Lee.

"Private Minier," Lt. Colonel Edson began, "I see you've made excellent marks as a rifleman."

"Thank you, sir," said Lee.

"That's one of my main areas of concern. We need only the best, most committed men in 1st Raider Battalion—and those who can use a rifle."

"Yes, sir," replied Lee, quietly.

"Our mission will be one that'll require everything you've got; it will test us to the limit," he went on. "It'll be tough fighting."

"Yes, sir," replied Lee.

Then, with little warning and absolutely no change in his voice or his penetrating stare, Edson asked the young man a question that Lee never thought anyone would ask him.

"Could you slip up behind a Jap, grab him, and slit his throat?" Edson asked in a voice that was little more than a whisper, the cadence of the words slow and modulated.

For the first time since the interview began, Lee paused. It took him a few moments to absorb the question.

Years later, Samuel Griffith, second-in-command to Edson, would recall asking that question to every Marine who had volunteered to be a Raider. "A Marine was carefully scrutinized and measured as he gave his responses. No hotheads, no false bravado, no pseudo-patriots wanted here. Just men who could function as cool killing machines and realize that [it] was their job to do."

Lee, likewise, never turned away from Edson's gaze; finally, the quiet question received an equally quiet answer. "Yes, sir," returned Lee, "I believe I could do that."

Almost imperceptibly, a hint of a slight smile pulled at one corner of Edson's mouth. It came to be a well-known characteristic of Red Mike. Some would say it usually meant, "Somebody is going to be killed."

"Welcome to the Raiders," said Lieutenant Colonel Edson. He stood up and extended his hand to Lee Minier, the newest member of 1st Marine Raider Battalion.

Lee often wrote home and was quick to send a letter announcing his new status—one of the first young men in Marine Corps history to be selected as a Raider. But thanks to the publicity regimen the Raiders would be exposed to, even Americans who didn't have a Marine son selected for the elite unit would learn of the new outfit.

On Tuesday, February 24, 1942, Lieutenant Colonel Edson led a contingent of 10 officers and 244 troops to New York City. There, a jubilant parade celebrated these young men, a grand event for the Raiders and the people of New York City. The Marine band played, the crowds cheered, and the Raiders proudly marched up Fifth Avenue. They stayed at the St. Regis and didn't have to buy their own libations anywhere—such was the patriotic outpouring of all New York City. Lee enjoyed the celebrations, but like his fellow Marines, was eager to get to fighting. He didn't sign up to be a Raider for the parties, after all.

A Dangerous Training

Edson, with his executive officer Samuel Griffith, was determined to create the best-trained fighters who were highly skilled in hand-to-hand combat and as proficient maneuvering through hostile environments at night as in daytime. Edson and Griffith both knew full well that the Japanese were experts in these forms of combat and that the Raiders would need to be extremely skilled hand-to-hand fighters in order to survive.

To instill the level of prowess he desired, Red Mike relied on any and all who had previous experience, such as the Old Breed. And in hand-to-hand combat, he could think of none better to train his young warriors than the man who possessed the reputation of being the best close-quarters combatant on the planet, the retired Marine Anthony Biddle, who was sixty-five years old.

On the day Biddle arrived, Edson ordered a group of his Raiders to fix bayonets to their rifles without a leather protective sheath. Raider Captain "Jumping Joe" Chambers, wild and woolly himself—possibly an inherited trait, since he was related on his mother's side to the infamous Valentine Hatfield, patriarch of the Hatfield Clan notorious for feuding with the McCoys—gives his eyewitness account of what happened next.

"Biddle crouched barehanded and nimble-footed within the circle of Raiders engaging him with bare bayonets," writes Chambers, "and he disarmed them all."

Though much older than his students, Biddle was still a skilled fighter. He would train the Raiders in his unique set of skills and insisted on proficiency in knife fighting. Some would say later that many among them displayed a talent for knife throwing that could rival the great knife throwers of the P. T. Barnum Circus.

Knife fighting was a preserve of British Commandos, and the Marines who trained with them in the months just prior to the United States' officially entering the war brought it back home. Samuel Griffith, Edson's second-in-command, was one of those Marines and understood the importance of familiarizing oneself with the blade. One knife in particular became a trademark of the Raiders, especially at the beginning of World War II: the thin, wicked knife known as a stiletto.

The double-edged blade on a stiletto measured about seven inches long and was ideally suited for silent killing. It was manufactured by Camillus Cutlery and modeled after the Fairbairn-Sykes design. British Commandos found their light weight and needle-sharp points ideal for stealth. Raiders appreciated their usage but found them susceptible to the wet jungle environs of the South Pacific. Furthermore, you couldn't pry open a can of beans with one without bending the tip.

The Ka-Bar knife, a long, sturdy, Bowie-style blade, became a favorite. It could accommodate camp-style jobs—opening rations, cutting tent pegs, even digging foxholes if necessary—plus, it could also get the job done in hand-to-hand combat.

Some Raiders used both, hanging a Ka-Bar knife encased in a leather sheath from their belts while slipping the smaller, more delicate stiletto just behind it. Better to have choices—one never knew when the need might arise.

CHAPTER III

Gung Ho

Three days after Marine commandant Thomas Holcomb activated 1st Marine Raider Battalion, he activated 2nd Marine Raider Battalion. Holcomb looked no further for a leader than recently reinstated Marine Corps officer Evans Carlson, seven days shy of his forty-sixth birthday. With 1st Raider Battalion training on the East Coast, 2nd Raider Battalion would train on the West Coast.

Roughly a year apart in age, Merritt Edson and Evans Carlson had both spent their boyhood years in Vermont. And that's about where their similarities ended.

The first time Evans Fordyce Carlson ran away from home, he was twelve years old. His mother, Joetta Carlson, pleaded with her husband, a well-known Congregationalist minister, to intervene. Their son returned home after three weeks. Two years later, however, he ran away again—this time permanently.

"It's no one's fault," said the elder Carlson, attempting to console his wife. "Evans is a good boy. But his spirit is restless. There won't be peace for him or us until he breaks away."

The fourteen-year-old worked on a farm for a while, then for the Rutland Railroad. After two years out on his own with no more than the clothes on his back and a small volume of Ralph Waldo Emerson poetry in his pocket—which he carried throughout his life—Evans decided to join the Army to see the world.

On November 6, 1912, the adventure he craved began. Lying about his age to circumvent the Army's minimum age requirement of twenty-one and obviously possessing an impressive air of confidence, the sixteen-year-old joined as a private. In three months, he found himself helping install guns on the island of Corregidor in the Philippines.

Five years later, when the United States entered World War I in Europe, the Army commissioned Carlson a second lieutenant. By year's end, he was promoted to captain. In two years, however, Carlson resigned from the Army to work with the California Packing Company. Perhaps the "restless spirit" his father had identified early on in his brilliant, non-conforming son prompted the decision.

Whatever the reason, it took only a couple of years for him to realize that he had made a mistake. And after the Army declined his readmission unless he accepted a reduced rank, Carlson turned to the United States Marines. In April 1922, Carlson enlisted as a private; before the end of that year, he was pinned with a single gold bar, the simple hardware of a second lieutenant.

"Well, I'm back—in the service," he wrote to his father. "And believe me, I'm so happy I'm almost moved to tears. Lord, I've fought off the desire to get back into the harness.... [But] my heart is in the service—and here I must stay."

During the next several years of his career, a series of three major events, all revolving around tours of duty and personal travel, shaped Evans Carlson's philosophy of command. In fact, they would define his entire life, most especially his involvement in World War II.

Like most Westerners of the period, Evans Carlson knew little of Chinese culture and history. What he found on his first tour of duty there beginning in 1927, however, fascinated him and would continue to do so as long as he lived. Merritt "Red Mike" Edson also served in China during this period. However, both men absorbed and processed their Chinese experiences differently.

Despite rebelling against school as a boy, Carlson had a fondness for classroom-style instruction. When he first arrived in China, severe disciplinary problems plagued the unit. Immediately, he began a series of meetings meant to raise the level of awareness among the Marines. He shared in depth his knowledge—and respect—for the Chinese. Later, in Nicaragua, he would employ similar teaching techniques. As was so often the case during Carlson's life, he seemed destined to encounter the top leaders and influential people of the day. So it was that on this second tour of duty, Carlson forged friendships many in the military would consider suspicious. None, however, raised more eyebrows than his association with Mao Tse-tung.

Through lengthy conversations with Mao, Carlson learned the military leader's philosophy of warfare, which focused primarily on guerrilla tactics, to combat the Japanese. Relying heavily on stratagems from Chinese military strategist Sun Tzu as outlined in his book, *The Art of War*, Mao adapted a formula of three basic ingredients: (a) speedy strikes by (b) highly maneuverable forces against (c) points of weakest resistance.

So Carlson could observe these tactics firsthand, Mao contacted his top military aide, General Chu Teh. The general arranged for the Yankee Marine to accompany the 8th Route Army, an elite communist fighting force, on an epic 1,000-mile trek into the hinterlands of China.

Of Chu Teh, Carlson would later write that the Chinese general shared all the rigors of warfare with his men and "was loved by every man in his army." Carlson compared his kindness to Robert E. Lee, his tenacity to Ulysses S. Grant, and his humanity to Abraham Lincoln.

From 1930 to 1933, in between trips to China, the Marine Corps sent Carlson and other young officers and troops to Nicaragua. Tours in Nicaragua were like stepping back in time. The environment was more like the Wild West than a modern battlefield, complete with wooden barracks secured by long, wooden slabs across the doors, roving bands of marauders, and native scouts who were often guerrilla spies. Samuel Griffith, who later served as Merritt Edson's executive officer in 1st Raider Battalion, said that as a young officer he had total responsibility and had to rely on his own judgment and cunning to survive. "I think I learned more in the fourteen months that I was in Nicaragua—I learned a hell of a lot about men and animals and the country."

Carlson was no different. When he arrived in-country, seven Marine officers had already been killed by the Nicaraguan troops they were leading. This was attributed in large part to their handling native troops with disdain and a refusal to understand local customs. Carlson determined to approach the Nicaraguan troops with a different attitude. He learned Spanish in order to communicate directly with them and sought to learn whatever he could about their customs and beliefs. He thought this would build connections between the command and the men.

The fighting was mostly done with small bands of guerrillas, who would come down out of the hills and mountains and attack quickly and ferociously, then retreat. Carlson adapted by utilizing similar-style tactics with smaller groups of Marines through the thick jungles and streams crisscrossing the wild countryside. It proved to be the perfect training ground for his later fighting in very similar terrain in the South Pacific. And it was especially advantageous as a precursor for training Raiders. Though malignant malaria would make it impossible for Carlson to complete his duties and send him home after just a few months, the experience would shape his worldview for years to come.

In 1935, the third major tour of duty in the life of Evans Fordyce Carlson may have been, when all is said and done, the most influential of all. This pivotal and decisive event in his life came when the young officer was sent as part of a security detail to a small Southern town in Georgia. Here, in the middle of nowhere, a friendship began that would last the rest of his life—and which would impact his career, his decisions, and perhaps even his military judgment in the field. He was assigned as second-in-command of a personal security detail at

Warm Springs, Georgia, to the president of the United States, Franklin Delano Roosevelt.

The president took an immediate liking to the affable young officer who had met with Mao Tse-tung in China, had fought Sandino's guerrillas in Nicaragua, and quoted Emerson's romantic, transcendental poetry. Their friendship developed quickly, as did a close relationship with the president's son, James "Jimmy" Roosevelt. It would be an important, lifelong relationship for all three. President Roosevelt gained a trusted counselor outside the political arena to report news, ideas, and opinions about a variety of current events, especially pertaining to Asia. Carlson chose Jimmy Roosevelt as his executive officer to serve beside him in the Pacific. For most anyone at that time, to have a personal relationship with FDR would have been heady. But for a high school dropout from the hills of Vermont who had run away from home at the age of fourteen, it must have been monumental.

After Carlson's last military tour of duty in the Orient, he returned to the States with a burning desire to express his ideas and views on China, and especially the threat posed by Imperial Japan. Carlson's relationships with high-profile communist leaders had caused heartburn for most high-ranking Marine Corps officials for several years. Now, the more he spoke out, the more it became untenable for the Marine Corps. Carlson himself realized it would be impossible to continue speaking and lecturing on the subject while still an officer, so he submitted his resignation on April 30, 1939.

For the remainder of that year and throughout 1940, Carlson spoke around the United States in radio programs, lecture halls, and civic groups about his views—political and geostrategic. Carlson urged Americans to take the Japanese threat seriously. In addition, he wrote two books, *Twin Stars of China* and *The Chinese Army*, which discussed China's communist revolution and China's military organization. He also revisited China at his own expense and became convinced that Japan intended to carry their war to the world, predicting an attack on the United States at some point in 1941.

During his return trip to the United States from China, he stopped in the Philippines to meet with Douglas MacArthur. The general listened politely as the ex-Marine major urged him to train a guerrilla force to combat Japanese forces that he, Carlson, was certain would come to the Philippines eventually. MacArthur thanked him for "dropping by"— then ignored every word while showing him the door.

Once Carlson returned to the States, he knew from all the signs that war with Japan would come sooner or later. Carlson felt it his duty to get back on board to help in any way he could. One can only imagine the rolling of eyes and even outrage among fellow officers at his request to rejoin the Marine Corps. Merritt "Red Mike" Edson himself was particularly incensed and raised the most objections.

As the years progressed, many would consider Merritt Edson a Marine's Marine. Some went so far as to call him a poster child for the Corps. Evans Carlson, on the other hand, stirred many pots with his open admiration for China's governing philosophy and military training. Traditionalists within the Corps didn't hesitate to use the word "maverick," or worse, "communist sympathizer," when talking about Carlson. Nonetheless, he had many supporters and admirers, who included none other than FDR himself. While Edson was quiet and outwardly emotionless, Carlson was open and talkative, quickly becoming a favorite of reporters and Hollywood. The 1943 hit movie *Gung Ho!*, starring Randolph Scott and Robert Mitchum, was based loosely on 2nd Raider Battalion exploits. Carlson served briefly as a consultant on the set during filming— something he enjoyed immensely.

But now, in April 1941, Carlson was reinstated as a major in the Marine Corps—his talents outweighing his controversial statements and associations. As noted Carlson biographer, John Wukovits says, "Carlson was again with the Marines, this time fortified by a guiding philosophy that he hoped to implement. Fashioned by a New England childhood and influenced by events in Nicaragua and China, Carlson now needed a vehicle through which he could test his theories." Having a good friend in high places would only help him accomplish that goal.

Despite the enormous differences between the two commanders of 1st Raider Battalion and 2nd Raider Battalion, both men would find avenues within the Corps for expressions of their deepest-held convictions on leadership, organization, training, and development of esprit during a time of world war. And though a rivalry would come to exist between the members of "Edson's Raiders" and "Carlson's Raiders," the individual courage and heroism of each man was never in doubt.

For the first few weeks, the Marine recruits in San Diego lived in 8-man tents. Almost immediately, however, base scuttlebutt buzzed with talk of a new group forming—a "catch me/kill me" outfit—they were called Raiders. Teenager Kenny Merrill was eager to learn more.

"Hey," he asked one of his tent buddies. "What have you heard about that new outfit—that Raider group? I heard they're asking for volunteers."

"Naw. I ain't looking into that—those guys lookin' to get killed before they get started," his tent buddy said.

When one of Ken's sergeants heard he was thinking of volunteering for the Raiders, he took Kenny to the post exchange (PX) and bought some beer. Then he sat down to talk with the boy—really to persuade him not to seek to join the Raiders.

"Hey, you get out there, you'll get your old butt shot off, you know," said the sergeant.

"Yeah, probably," chuckled Kenny. "But Sarge, that's what I want to do—become a Raider."

Ken had already heard about the 2nd Marine Raider Battalion and their leaders. First, Lt. Colonel Carlson had a reputation for being a great guy with experience and influence in high places. Of course, everyone had heard who his executive officer was—none other than the son of the president of the United States, Major James "Jimmy" Roosevelt himself.

The next time Raider staff sounded a call for volunteers, Ken and ten other guys raised their hands. The eleven young men were loaded in trucks and taken to newly acquired campgrounds north of San Diego. Upon their arrival, they were directed to a large, makeshift building. Once inside, two long tables about twenty feet apart on either side of the room served as registration and interview stations amid the bustle of dozens of young recruits, older sergeants, and an assortment of officers.

At one table, surrounded by staff, sat Lieutenant Colonel Evans Carlson, interviewing one recruit after another. He had an open but somber manner. At the other table, also surrounded by Marine personnel, sat a tall, thin, pleasant-looking young man wearing large spectacles and tennis shoes to accommodate his flat feet—Major James "Jimmy" Roosevelt.

It was Ken's turn to be interviewed. A sergeant escorted him to the table where the man with large spectacles sat at ease occasionally chatting with those around him. Out of the eleven young men in his group of volunteers, Ken was the only one chosen by the president's son that day. The young, spunky, good-looking boy, barely seventeen years old, was now officially a Marine Raider—a member of Carlson's Raiders, to be exact.

Once Lt. Colonel Carlson satisfied himself with interviewing Raider volunteers, he immediately saddled up his new special forces unit and led them to their new home. They marched to Jacques Farm, a newly acquired tract of land located a few miles southeast of Camp Elliott that had once been a 10,000-acre working farm. No evidence remained, however, of its former usage except a large, filthy chicken coop. Carlson promptly detailed a clean-up crew to transform the building into a mess hall.

The surrounding countryside, which at one time may have been fertile with crops, was now rocky, barren, and dotted with the occasional cactus. Mountains loomed far in the distance—the Raiders would soon learn just how far.

As soon as the Raiders had erected their pup tents on the farm property, Carlson called the entire battalion to a meeting. These get-togethers would characterize his leadership style throughout their training and the entire time he commanded Marine Raiders.

"Ahoy, Raiders!" Carlson heralded, giving the new battalion a hearty welcome. His first order of business was to explain the concept of the "Gung Ho" spirit. "It's our ability to work together, to cooperate," began Carlson. "It's imperative to understand this spirit; it is even more imperative to apply it to daily accounts, no matter how unimportant they might seem."

Young Kenny Merrill listened intently as the colonel explained the words.

"'Gung' is a Chinese word meaning 'work,' and 'ho' means 'harmony,'" Carlson continued. "So together they mean 'work in harmony.' The 'Gung Ho' spirit is complete cooperation. It's a spirit of tolerance, cooperation, and equality—really democracy at work."

Carlson also explained in depth the history of China and Japan, their long conflict and relationship. He schooled them on things he had learned during his time spent in China—especially with the 8th Route Army, Mao Tse-tung's army. "I want you to know *why* you are fighting and *who* you are fighting," he told the men.

Though orders were expected to be followed, lines between officers and enlisted men were blurred. Carlson expected his officers to do everything the non-commissioned officers did. If the non-coms slept on the ground, so did the officers. Carlson snapped at an officer once who asked a private first class (PFC) to clean his weapon. "Do it yourself," demanded the commander.

All this had a tremendous effect on the entire group, but especially on Kenny, one of the youngest Raiders. He wanted to do his best for his country of course—but he especially wanted to do his best for this iconic man named Evans Carlson.

"Lord knows, I love him," Kenny told one of his tentmates. "And that goes for Jimmy too," continued the young Raider with a smile.

Raider training on the West Coast was as rigorous as on the East Coast. As Oscar Peatross, later a highly decorated two-star Marine general, would recount of his own Raider experiences:

We trained eighteen hours a day, seven days a week, completing a syllabus that covered everything from weapons training to physical conditioning; from armed and unarmed hand-to-hand combat to scouting and patrolling. We fired hundreds of rounds from all of our weapons and hiked hundreds of miles with full pack and equipment. Gradually, individuals were converted into units and an esprit was born—a "Gung Ho" spirit. Marines became Raiders—Carlson's Raiders.

Early one morning, Carlson asked his 2nd Raiders if they could see a particular mountain in the far distance. "Yes, sir," snapped everyone nearly in perfect unison.

"Well, saddle up! Because that's where we'll be tonight," he barked as he strode off on his way.

The day was particularly hot and muggy with a simmering desert sun blazing down on the column. Their packs were fully loaded, as were their ammo bandoliers and belts. But spirits were high as usual, and, though they were drenched in sweat, there really was little complaining— at least not any above mutterings here and there. The Old Man himself led the serpentine line, never letting up the rapid pace.

Occasionally, he would fall back to check on everyone. He almost always had a friendly word for Kenny Merrill. All the men knew how young he was, barely seventeen, and he was such a good-looking kid topped by a thick mop of hair.

Maybe Carlson saw something of himself in this spunky, good-natured kid, perhaps some of his own restless spirit that had always craved adventure. Perhaps looking at Kenny reminded the commander of his first trip to an unknown region—Corregidor. There were those who would say the young Merrill was his favorite. But on this particularly blazing day, it was the president's son who bestowed favor on Kenny.

They'd been marching for several hours. Besides all his other gear, Kenny shouldered a 32-pound machine gun that seemed to get heavier with every step. Every hour or so, when Carlson's hand went up, the men would stop and rest for five or ten minutes. Then Carlson would yell out, "Saddle up, Raiders!" and they were off again.

During one break at around noon, Kenny upended his canteen—bone dry. He looked around and spotted a small mud puddle next to a large rock. In Arizona, where he had grown up, any water in the desert is appreciated. Bending over on all fours, he began to lap it up—hands, face, tongue, and all in the brown water, nearly sucking it dry.

About that time Major Roosevelt—"Jimmy" to the men when out of earshot of the major—moved alongside the column of resting men. With eye glasses in hand, wiping his face with a handkerchief, the son of the president nearly stumbled over the kneeling young Raider with his face submerged in the puddle.

Barely catching himself before tumbling over, he immediately belched out a loud expletive. Drawing the attention of all nearby, he yelled out, still flustered, "Merrill! What in the hell are you doing down in that mud puddle?"

Kenny raised up on his knees. "I'm getting a drink of water, sir."

"Well, for God's sake, boy, get out of that hole!"

The Raiders who witnessed this incident got their belly laugh for the day. For his part, Roosevelt couldn't wait to share the story with Lt. Colonel Carlson. And young Kenny, one of the youngest Raiders in Marine history, earned a new nickname that would stick: he would be known as "Mudhole Merrill" until the day he died.

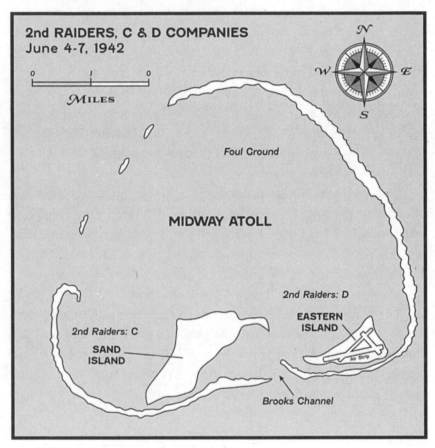

3. Midway Atoll: 2nd Raiders, Companies "C" & "D," reinforce Marines on Midway, arriving just days before the battle began on June 4, 1942.

CHAPTER IV

Beyond the Seas

The first few days—even hours—after the attack on Pearl Harbor were revealing. Within ten hours of bombing Pearl, Japan began the invasion of the Philippines. The following day Japan attacked Guam, which fell on December 10, 1941, just as Japanese Special Forces were landing without resistance on Makin Atoll in the Gilbert Islands. On December 23, Wake Island surrendered; Christmas Day, Hong Kong submitted; January 3, 1942, Manila went. On the twelfth, enemy forces invaded the East Indies...the twenty-third, New Britain and New Ireland, islands in the Bismarck Archipelago...the thirtieth, West Borneo. On February 8, in perhaps the most stunning event of all, the Japanese stormed into the supposedly impregnable British base of Singapore after surging down the Malay Peninsula with terrifying ease. Finally, a few weeks later, General MacArthur and his family left the Philippines by PT boat, and Bataan fell on April 9; Corregidor on May 6.

There was no mistaking their purpose. The Japanese fully intended to expand their Empire throughout the South Pacific. The U.S. military knew this would be the arena of war: an ocean that covered 63,800,000 square miles, more than the combined land mass of the entire Earth.

Specks of dirt—islands, islets, coral outcroppings, and atolls—would be the battlegrounds.

This is No Joke!

When reveille sounded earlier than usual at the Marine Raiders' barracks on April Fools' Day, 1942, Edson's Raiders awoke to a long line of passenger cars parked on the nearby railroad siding—their troop train. Anticipation morphed into reality. The real adventure was about to begin.

Even so, Lee Minier, along with most other of his fellow Raiders, wagered they were probably bound for Florida. There, heavy coastal surf would provide opportunity to perfect their rubber-boat landing techniques. With no official word about their final destination, this seemed highly plausible, especially since the troop train continued traveling south deep into Georgia.

However, when their direction suddenly turned due west, and a sign posting mileage to Birmingham, Alabama, flashed by the window, all bets were off. Though their final destination remained unknown, they could hardly have imagined places with exotic names such as Pua Pua, Nouméa, Tulagi, Tasimboko, the Matanikau, Enogai, or Bairoko.

Yet for the present, this augured adventure enough—traveling the entire United Sates from East Coast to West Coast by train. Most of these young Raiders had never crossed the Mississippi River. That massive and majestic water system, basically splitting the forty-eight states in half, defined a critical characteristic of the entire United States Marine Corps. Those recruits born on the east side of its banks automatically trained on the East Coast, primarily at Parris Island, Beaufort, South Carolina; those born to the west of the Mississippi trained on the West Coast in and around San Diego, California. It had been thus for decades and remains so today.

As their train cars rumbled on hour after hour, small groups of young men occupied themselves with cards, shooting craps, arm wrestling, writing letters, and exchanging stories of family and girlfriends. Once, when Lee picked his way down the center aisle, he encountered two Raiders singing. He stopped to harmonize, and before long a couple more had joined the vocalists. These initial choral forays eventually formed the nucleus for a singing group that would rise to star status among troops in the South Pacific. Lee's clear tenor voice became a favorite of all who heard him sing.

One of the newly discovered Raider songbirds was Thomas "Jinx" Powers. He would prove to be as much a free spirit when it came to following orders as he would show himself lionhearted in battle. And in the months to come, his singing would actually contribute to saving his life one dark night behind Japanese lines on the Solomon Islands. But that was in the future. For now, belting out Marine beer-drinking favorites, the bawdier the better, just helped pass the time.

When the troop train finally reached San Diego, California, the battalion received instructions to set up a temporary tent camp at the recruit depot. Recognizing their time would be short in this sailor-friendly town, the Raiders took full advantage of local bars and bistros. But many also worked to hone a skill as old as soldiering itself—scrounging.

And it so happened that a naive staffer left his jeep parked at dock's edge next to the USS *Zeilin* (AP9), a twenty-two-year-old transport, formerly the USS *President Jackson* but renamed in 1940 for Brigadier General Jacob Zeilin, sixth commandant of the Corps. It would carry 1st Marine Raider Battalion into the South Pacific. Some enterprising Raiders, spotting the unattended vehicle, lowered a net, pushed the jeep into it, and hoisted their prize onto the transport's deck. It wasn't until the ship was well underway that the mischief was discovered.

(Not to be outdone in subsequent months, 4th Marine Raider Battalion, the last and final Raider unit to be activated and deployed, would perfect this shore-to-ship technique in a stunt worthy of campfire legends. It would also give rise to an infamous nickname—Roosevelt and his Thousand Thieves, referring to Lieutenant Colonel James "Jimmy" Roosevelt, FDR's son, who would command the nearly one thousand members of 4th Marine Raider Battalion.)

For now, however, Monday, April 13, 1942, was memorable enough for the 1st Marine Raider Battalion—Edson's Raiders. At 0400, a particularly early reveille signaled that the time had come—time to get going, time to begin making a difference, time to fight. The Raiders were ready.

That morning was memorable for another reason unknown to anyone at the time—none of the four Marine Raider Battalions would ever return to their homeland as Raiders. All four battalions would be disbanded and folded into other divisions in a little more than eighteen months in the field…and the United States Marine Corps would not have their special forces units again—Raiders—until nearly seventy-five years later.

Lee Minier and other members of 1st Marine Raider Battalion loaded the last of their gear, weapons, and ammunition up the gang plank of the *Zeilin*. The group included 29 officers and 638 enlisted men. A rear echelon of 9 officers and 250 men led by the executive officer, Major Samuel Griffith, would catch up with them several weeks later.

After Lee had secured his equipment below in whatever cubbyhole could be found, he proceeded back up on deck to watch tugs slowly guide the transport ship from the harbor. Once out into open water, it joined up with the cruiser, the USS *Honolulu* (CL-48), and headed west.

Several days into the vast Pacific, any Raider who may have temporarily lost his sea legs had quickly regained them. The Raiders knew their leader though. And true to form, Red Mike wasted no time setting up a daily routine of brisk calisthenics and any other form of physical fitness protocol to help keep his Raiders in tip-top conditioning. They needed no prodding, and often these exercises turned into animated sparring matches. Several particularly feisty young men emerged as very good with their fists. Seizing the opportunity to enhance upon these contemporaneous one-on-one fisticuffs, Red Mike saw an opportunity. Out of these initial spontaneous forays, he instigated what became known as "smokers," all-out boxing matches that became a resounding favorite pastime among Raiders.

As the transport and her escort continued deep into the tepid South Pacific waters, a spate of submarine sightings kept away any boredom that have might set in. And on April 28, 1942, the *Zeilin* pulled into Pago Pago Harbor, Tutuila Island, American Samoa. It was around noon, and it was raining so hard that visibility was nil. The Raiders, eager to see their destination, would have to wait until the next day.

Lee fumbled in his pockets to locate a postcard, one of which had been given to each Marine upon leaving the States. Like the postcard in January, which had told of his acceptance into the Marine Corps, this one also had a blank for the addressee and a place to sign. And again, the preprinted message was poignantly simple: "Dear Mom, I have arrived safely at my destination beyond the seas."

Carlson's Journey

Eleven days after Edson's Raiders arrived in American Samoa, Carlson's Raiders boarded the USS *J. Franklin Bell* on May 8, 1942. The following morning, the transport left San Diego Harbor bound for Hawaii. The two newly-formed Raider Battalions would now be located in the Pacific, ready for deployment when needed. It had been barely five months since Japan's attack when the *Franklin Bell* steamed slowly into Pearl Harbor on May 18. Most Raiders stood on deck in stunned silence. No one aboard the transport was prepared for what they saw upon arrival in Hawaii.

Though the smoke and fire had cleared, the results of that terrifying "day of infamy" remained fully visible. Instead of Battleship Row, the men saw "battleship death row." Once proud American warships existed only in varying degrees of catastrophic wreckage. Some ships lay over on their sides, some bow-up, some stern-down. Everywhere the sights and sounds of repair crews filled the harbor as they busied themselves with the daunting task of restoration.

Mudhole stood next to his buddies, Joe Gifford and J. C. Green. They could hear the men around them hissing curses about the Japanese. The young Raider believed he would never forget what he saw that day as long as he lived. And if any of them needed additional motivation for what they came to the Pacific to do—take the war to the Japanese—none left Pearl Harbor that morning with an inkling of doubt.

The sheer scale of the damage was overwhelming: 6 battleships damaged, 2 destroyed; 3 cruisers and 3 destroyers damaged, and 5 auxiliary craft damaged or destroyed. Of Army and Navy aircraft, 159 were damaged and 169 destroyed.

Yet property losses could be replaced. The loss of life and limb was another matter. U.S. Navy, Army, and Marine Corps casualties totaled 2,403 killed and 1,176 wounded. That didn't include civilian causalities, not to mention damage to morale.

The rampant destruction left Mudhole somber as the Raiders disembarked and traveled along the main highway to their new base, Camp Catlin. It wasn't only the sight of Pearl Harbor, however, that created the subdued atmosphere. News had arrived that just two days before the Raiders had left San Diego, the brave men of 4th Marines, after a blistering 27-day siege, surrendered Corregidor, the island that guarded the entrance to Manila Bay in the Philippines. Only a month earlier, Bataan had surrendered to Japanese forces. Seventy-five thousand Filipino and American forces had been captured and were now living as Japanese POWs. There was simply no good news emanating out of the Pacific.

Once at Camp Catlin, Mudhole and the rest of the 2nd Raider Battalion hurried to set up their base camp. Meanwhile, Carlson and Roosevelt were directed to join an urgent, top secret meeting aboard a repair ship, the USS *Dixie*. They were to bring the commanders of "C" and "D" companies with them.

After being sworn to secrecy, the officers were told the reason they were assembled on the small ship. Two companies of Raiders would leave immediately for Midway Atoll to reinforce 6th Defense Battalion, already in place. Their mission: to help repel a Japanese landing force believed to be five to six thousand strong.

The situation at Midway was ominous, and the news that some Raiders would be expected to join in the fighting caused some dismay.

Someone in the meeting asked how long they were expected to hold out, given that they would be outnumbered at a ratio of approximately six to one, would have minimal ammunition, and little other support. The briefing officer's response was hardly encouraging: "To the last man and last bullet," he began, "but *if* our 'cheese-in-the-trap' plan works, and *if* the Japs go for the cheese [Midway], and *if* we sink their carriers, your chances of survival will increase."

The Raiders were being offered up as sacrificial lambs. And to make matters worse, the mission didn't match up with what they had been training to execute—commando-style raiding. Rather, they were now going to be used in a more conventional fashion, expected to hold an island that was essentially under siege. But they wouldn't complain. The company leaders understood that they had to do what was asked of them to advance the war effort and prepared to follow their orders as best they could.

The two Raider companies left for Midway on May 21, while Mudhole and the remainder of Carlson's Raiders continued training at Camp Catlin as planned. The two companies sailed aboard the USS *St. Louis*, a cruiser, and the USS *Case* and *Gwin*, two destroyers. By steaming at flank speed without zigzagging, the Raiders arrived at Midway just seventy-two hours later. Their appearance was rougher than usual thanks to having been at sea for most of the past month without much time on land. The Raiders left quite the impression on the American troops who had already staked out their defenses. Rumors rapidly spread among the American ranks not to approach a Raider from behind, or else risk a quick—and potentially lethal—response. The Raiders did nothing to discourage such scuttlebutt and relished their reputation as fearsome killers.

The atoll called Midway is just that: a small Pacific coral outcropping located midway between the continental United States to the east and the continent of Asia to the west. Its narrow ribbon of sand and coral forms a loose circle with two small islands and a fairly deep harbor inside. However, unlike most Pacific Islands, which were virtually anonymous at the beginning of World War II, Midway was already a well-known spot in the Pacific.

For over two decades, Pan American Airlines had utilized the larger island, called Sand Island, as a seaplane base. This allowed for refueling on regular routes from the United States to Singapore. These routes were flown primarily by clippers, seaplanes that lumbered along yet shortened the trip between continents from three weeks or more by ship to six or seven days by air. Besides developing a seaplane base on Sand Island, Pan Am maintained a terminal, warehouses, small storage facilities, a radio station, fuel tanks, and housing for airline personnel.

Midway's second island, known as Eastern Island, is considerably smaller. A 3-runway landing area occupies nearly all of its triangular-shaped land mass. By June 4, 107 military aircraft covered almost every square inch of the small island, of which 64 were Marine planes. Thirty-four of the Marine planes were dive bombers led by Major Lofton R. Henderson, a name that would earn great renown in the months of combat to come.

One company of Raiders was assigned to each island at Midway. "C" Company deployed to Sand Island, while "D" Company reinforced Eastern Island. They didn't have to wait long for fighting to break out. Shortly before 5:30 a.m. on June 4, barely ten days after arriving at Midway, a PBY patrol plane spotted the enemy fleet. Just twenty minutes later, radar on the island detected a large number of Japanese planes approaching. For well over an hour, Sand and Eastern Islands were lit up with exploding Japanese bombs, strafing planes, and returning gunfire from the ground.

One Raider later described the melee to fellow Raiders back in Hawaii: "During the Japanese attack (on Midway), all hands fought back with everything we had. Not just antiaircraft gunners but infantrymen, aircraft mechanics, ordnance men, cooks and bakers—literally all hands—fired at the enemy planes with whatever weapons they could lay their hands on: rifles, Browning automatic rifles, light machine guns, even .45-caliber pistols."

During the bombing, the determined defenders of Midway hosted an unexpected observer. Acclaimed Hollywood director John Ford had arrived on Sand Island just two days before the Japanese air attack. At the request of the Navy Department, Ford set up his cameras to produce a documentary on the upcoming battle. The director was well familiar with filming shoot-outs—cowboy-style, that is. He had already produced several Westerns with his favorite movie star, John Wayne. Now he would discover new heroes in the boys on Midway.

Ford later declared that he took one look at the young warriors and knew the war was won. "I have never seen a greater exhibition of courage and coolness under fire in my life," he recalled, "and I have seen some in my day. These kids were remarkable." Ford's film of the events on Midway won an Academy Award for Best Documentary of a Short Subject later that fall.

Within ten minutes of the sighting of Japanese planes headed toward Midway, Marine planes launched and began their attack on the Japanese fleet. Most of the Marine planes were older, slower, and vastly less maneuverable than the enemy Zeroes they met in the skies, but the Marine airmen took to the air anyway. They had no choice.

Major Lofton Henderson led the first wave of Douglas SBD Dauntless planes from Midway to apprehend the Japanese fleet. When he spotted the enemy carriers, he began his low dive toward them, leading the planes in his squadron. The Japanese Zeroes recognized him as the leader and concentrated their fire on his SBD. The enemy shells soon found their mark and flamed his right wing. But Henderson stubbornly ignored his burning aircraft and continued his dive. Though he ultimately crashed into the water without hitting the ship, his dauntless heroism inspired all who learned of it.

The cost of that day was agonizing. Of Major Henderson's group of sixteen SBDs, eleven did not return. Of Major Floyd B. "Red" Parks's group of twelve planes, nine failed to return. Six Navy torpedo bombers and four Army B-26s rigged with torpedoes had been shot down.

The naval battle had begun in earnest that same morning, June 4. By nightfall, the most severe fighting was over. Though the Americans sustained heavy losses, they had repelled the Japanese attackers. On June 6, Marshal Admiral Isoroku Yamamoto ordered his remaining ships to retreat. The Japanese suffered steeper casualties than the Americans, losing 4 aircraft carriers and a heavy cruiser, along with 3,000 men and nearly 300 aircraft. The Americans lost the *Yorktown* and *Hammann*, 145 aircraft, and approximately 360 servicemen. The Battle of Midway is considered by military historians as one of the most stunning and decisive victories in the annals of naval history. It was a pivotal engagement that marked a turn in American fortunes in the Pacific.

Meanwhile, back in Hawaii, the remaining Raiders of the 2nd Raider Battalion had continued their rigorous training schedule, though the dilemmas they faced were hardly as life-threatening. While their fellow Marines were fighting back the Japanese, the Raiders still on Hawaii were trying to sort things out with the local plantation owners.

The Raiders, training with low rations in the island heat, had taken a liking to Hawaii's native pineapples. The ripe fruit was there for the picking, and the Raiders had developed a taste for the citrusy delight. Plantation owners were peeved by the unauthorized addition to the Raider diet. They didn't consider that raiding their fields was part of the art of raiding for military purposes. Raider leadership spent more time than they preferred smoothing the ruffled feathers of irate local pineapple growers.

It wasn't just missing pineapples, however, that were the problem: Raiders were taking all sorts of goods from the local farmers. A rancher's cow disappeared here and there. Mudhole himself accidentally contributed to this dilemma, while ranchers became increasingly disgruntled, just like the pineapple growers.

Mudhole had been on watch most of the night with little sleep or food. Hawaii was on high alert for the possibility of Japanese infiltrators. A rustling in the bush abruptly brought him to attention. Mudhole called out, "Halt! Who goes there?" No response. The noise came closer. The Raider did all he knew to do: he fired into the bush. Then he hunkered down to await first light.

As dawn broke, a sergeant from his company stealthily approached to make sure he wasn't shot as well.

"What the hell are you doing?" he barked at Mudhole.

"Sir, I shot an infiltrator during the night," replied Mudhole.

"Mudhole, dammit!" yelled the sergeant. "You shot a cow!"

Sure enough, Mudhole had nailed a rancher's cow. He certainly didn't intend to kill a cow. But the Raiders enjoyed fresh meat that evening, seared over an open fire, compliments of the teenager, Mudhole, who would never live it down.

Toward the end of June, Mudhole and the remainder of 2nd Raiders boarded three APDs, the USS *Gregory*, USS *Little*, and USS *Colhoun*, and headed toward an "unannounced destination." In a few days, they landed on Midway and saw the aftermath of the ferocious battle firsthand. Destroyed buildings, pockmarked runways, and airplane debris were scattered all over Sand and Eastern Island. After two days, the Raiders reboarded the three APDs on June 28 and headed northward toward the Aleutians.

But shortly after their departure, the transports were ordered back to Hawaii. In six weeks, all of Carlson's Raiders would get a real taste of war—reinforcing Midway had only been an introduction. And their next deployment would be exactly the type of special forces commando-style raiding they had so diligently worked towards.

First Movements

While the 2nd Raider Battalion first saw the Pacific theater at the harrowing Midway, the 1st Raider Battalion first arrived at Pago Pago, a tropical paradise in American Samoa.

Pago Pago Harbor's naturally deep indigo waters could hold the largest ships built anywhere in the world. Encircled by thin strips of bleach-white sand, the lush jungle foliage rose nearly straight up on rugged mountains all around the harbor. Natives often referred to the volcanic island as the "Rock." The Marines called it by the native *pua pua*, meaning "stone"—or fudged the phrase as "pig." The sparkling tropical waters, jagged ridges, and towering mountains would be their new training ground for the next few weeks.

Once ashore, the sights and sounds of Pacific living mesmerized the men. It didn't take long for Samoan women to pass by in their colorful skirts and beads, many with bare breasts balancing large baskets on their heads. Raiders soon learned that they could continue striding forward with eyes cut sideways.

Upon arriving at the harbor, Edson ordered the men to march to a village named Leone some eighteen miles away. Once there, the Raiders pitched tents, organized a mess area, and established latrines. The commander was ready to begin graduate training—which he did with a vengeance. They would get their introduction to thick jungle foliage, intense heat, and stifling humidity. But they would learn soon enough that it was only an introduction compared to what they would discover elsewhere in the South Pacific.

The next several weeks were brutal, meant to bring the Raiders to knife-edge preparedness. They labored in Tutuila's rocky mountains and jagged cliffs and went on long hikes from one side of the island to the other and back again. They practiced marksmanship, night forays, and assorted ops. They studied and critiqued one another's movements in a bid to improve their capacity. Eight-man rubber boat exercises commenced immediately. The pounding Pacific surf gave the men a foretaste of the difficult landings ahead.

Once, when Edson gave the men a rare evening off, he met some of the officers stationed at the Samoan base for happy hour. As they chatted, the base commanding general joined them. The conversation eventually came around to talk of the Raiders.

"How are your boys doing?" the base commander asked Edson.

In an unusual moment of obvious pride, Red Mike told the group he was ready to put them up against anyone.

"Really?" said the general with a slight grin. "You think they're that good?"

"Well," said Edson quietly, with a grin of his own—one that he was becoming known for—"tell you what. I'll bet they can slip into your radar sight on that mountain top over there, and the men guarding it will never know."

Edson was referring to a top secret installation that was meant to provide an early warning for any enemy operations in the area. The radar was located on the most remote mountain ledge on the island, nearly inaccessible from all sides, with a large contingent of guards in addition to the radar operators themselves. The general immediately accepted the challenge.

Edson returned to his officers and told them his bet. Everybody chuckled with glee, ready for the dare. That same night, Edson charged his battalion commanders to choose the best group—though at this point almost anyone in 1st Raiders could have negotiated the mission. The squad was assembled and saddled up. It took hours to climb and traverse the rugged terrain.

But by the next morning, the Raiders had slipped undetected into the radar room on that high mountaintop. They left a calling card of a stiletto thrust in an obvious place and retreated back into the darkness. No one there had any idea until the next morning, when they discovered the thin, wicked Raider blade in plain sight.

The general gladly conceded defeat. "Your Raiders are really something," he remarked. "We are going to need them in this war." In response, Edson simply nodded with his thin, wry grin.

The beauty of the American Samoan scenery didn't mean that the Marines stationed there were on a cakewalk. Realistic drills could take a toll. Unfortunately, men were sometimes killed, even though not in combat.

During the intense weeks in the hot, wet climate while continually exposed to the elements, Lee and his Edson's Raider comrades recognized that the jungle represented a formidable enemy—perhaps as much as any two-legged foe. After just a few weeks in the boiling sun, constantly drenched in sweat, he began to notice itching in the folds and crevices all over his body. Soon, these spots turned into large, angry sores. Since they slept outside, the men never had relief from the dampness. In the months and years ahead, every Marine who fought in the Pacific came to understand that jungle fighting put real stress on the human body. Some paid a toll that would last a lifetime.

On July 3, the rear echelon under the command of Samuel Griffith finally sailed into Pago Pago Harbor on the USS *Heywood* (AP-12). Now, the entire 1st Raider Battalion was united once again.

The Raiders knew that the reunion meant their training was almost over. Soon, they surmised, they would be tasked with striking a blow on Japanese-held ground. After news of the enemy's defeat in the Battle of Midway, no one thought the Japanese would simply withdraw. On the contrary, the decisive trouncing to their navy and fighter pilots increased the Empire's resolve to deliver a return blow. The Japanese had begun planning and executing an ever-increasing penetration of the islands northeast of Australia and New Zealand.

Two days later on July 5, 1942, the complete 1st Marine Raider Battalion left Samoa. They sailed deeper into the South Pacific and arrived at Camp St. Louis in Nouméa, New Caledonia, on July 10. This French colonial island would serve as an advance training base for each engagement in the Solomon Islands and quickly became the main base of operations for the entire U.S. military in the Pacific Theater. Over the course of the war, the Raiders would spend a total of forty-five weeks here in three separate increments.

The 1st Raiders—Edson's Raiders—were drawing ever closer to their first taste of battle.

An Armada

Once they arrived in Nouméa, Lee and his fellow 1st Raiders knew they were ready. They felt physically fit, confident in their training, and aware of their skills. They knew how to use their rifles, machine guns, bayonets, and knives with aplomb. They had a noticeable swagger in their walk.

Early one morning in mid-July, after a particularly intense, all-night exercise, Red Mike assembled his Raiders:

"I'm ready to stack you men up alongside any other outfit in the world," he told them with open pride, even a hint of emotion. "The next time we pull this operation, it'll be for keeps," he continued, referring to their "capture" of the radar site on Samoa.

A few days later, Red Mike was given warning orders and told of an imminent amphibious operation. His Raiders would be attached to General Alexander Vandegrift, commander of the 1st Marine Division of the Marine Corps. Training was over; combat was about to begin.

Edson and his staff had done all they could to prepare their Raiders for combat against the Japanese. General Vandegrift, meanwhile, had spent several months hurriedly filling out a division—a task that required expanding ranks to nearly nineteen thousand men. To achieve a full division in abbreviated time required pulling Marines from multiple duty stations. As the general himself bristled, "We're scattered all over hell's half acre." When he was told that D-Day in the Pacific would be on August 1, Vandegrift lobbied vehemently for an extension, saying that his division was not ready for combat. He received one scant extra week.

The ground war in the Pacific was about to begin. As one historian would later write, "the unpracticed, unrehearsed, and poorly equipped 1st Marine Division was headed for its date with destiny." The Raiders, on the other hand, were destined to perform like superstars.

On July 24, converted transport ships, or APDs, arrived in Nouméa—the *Little, Colhoun, Gregory,* and *McKean.* When a fifth APD didn't make the rendezvous, a New Zealand ocean liner, the HMNZS *Monowai,* was commissioned to carry part of the 1st Marine Raider Battalion—primarily "E" Company, Lee's company.

Like many older ocean liners across the world that found service during World War II, this particular ship had been requisitioned by the Royal New Zealand Navy. She was refitted as an armed merchant cruiser with eight 6-inch guns, two 3-inch anti-aircraft guns and six 20-millimeter guns, plus machine guns and eight depth charges. In June 1942, she was also fitted with radar.

The vessel was manned by naval regulars, reservists, and merchant seamen, most of whom were New Zealanders. They were a friendly, obliging crew to the Raiders—supportive of them and their mission.

Leaving Nouméa on July 27, the ocean liner provided Lee and all of "E" Company Raiders with what could only be labeled luxury accommodations, at least by comparison to their previous jungle living. There was enough room to sleep inside—and even a few private baths. Ample storage areas allowed convenient stacking for "E" Company's gear, equipment, weapons, and machine guns. The dining hall's decorative wall panels, a carryover from the grandeur of its ocean liner days, made their chow mess line unusually pleasurable.

For Lee and several of his closest buddies, the spacious, empty lounge proved the greatest attraction. They discovered an upright piano underneath a tarp, perhaps overlooked in the rush to put to sea. Here, Lee and a handful of others spent enjoyable hours singing deep into the night. The group had come together in the past several weeks, mainly just to pass time engaged in some fun. But here in their fancy quarters, they really seemed to jell and develop their musical chemistry.

Someone mentioned they should think about a name for themselves. Suggestions poured forth; most had to be tamped down as too risqué. But finally one man in the group, Jinx Powers, suggested the "Singing Eight Balls." In Marine nomenclature, an "eight ball" was akin to a "goofball" or "screwup." The crooning Raiders liked it. The name stuck.

Lee, who held unopposed the baritone spot in the group, approved of the name. He was gaining a reputation for more than a superior singing voice. Though he could be forceful when necessary, he possessed a calm, steady nature that didn't give under pressure. He seldom raised his voice and kept his congenial attitude at every turn.

And so, as the Raiders headed into their first taste of battle, the Singing Eight Balls were officially formed. Most of the members were in "E" Company, and, in later months, when the Raiders would return to Nouméa for rest and recuperation, they served an important mission by entertaining the troops during amateur evening shows.

They had been at sea for several days when early one morning, before dawn, the ship steamed into heavier-than-normal seas. The strong rocking woke Lee, who, like many other Raiders, was having a hard time sleeping on the eve of what would be his first engagement. He decided to get some fresh air.

As he emerged out onto one of the long, narrow decks, he saw a few other Raiders already leaning against the railings. Unlike the raucous songfest the night before, the mood was somber. He slipped quietly along and found an empty spot. Each Raider stood in the pre-dawn darkness listening to his own thoughts and the rhythmic sound of powerful waves exploding against the ship's bow.

Shortly, the sky along the horizon began to lighten ever so slightly. Next, a deep purple line defined water from sky above. Someone spotted it.

"Hey, look out there!"

The shout broke above the sound of the waves, and all eyes followed the pointed finger. There, against a misty light, was the distinct form of a large ship. Everyone strained their eyes toward the lone silhouette.

But no sooner had they all spotted the ship than another seemed to materialize on the horizon. Then, a few minutes later, a third vessel appeared. Then another and another, all of certain United States origin. Now ten, then twenty, maybe thirty ships were in the anxious Raiders' field of vision. In just minutes, there were fifty or more. Slowly coming into view, they spread across the horizon, all facing the same direction.

The sight was the single most thrilling spectacle Lee had ever seen. He had never witnessed so many ships sailing together. The Raiders who witnessed it bristled with pride.

By nightfall, virtually every ship type in the U.S. Navy was represented. Almost eighty ships glided toward their destiny. The task force included air support built around the aircraft carriers *Saratoga*, *Enterprise*, and *Wasp* and the battleship *North Carolina*. A covering and bombardment force of cruisers and destroyers was present, as well as a minesweeper group. And on top of that, a transport group of nineteen transports and four APDs lined up, carrying almost twenty thousand Marines—a few more than the total strength of the Marine Corps three years earlier.

The arrival of the HMNZS *Monowai* brought the total number of Raiders participating in the first U.S. ground campaign of World War II to nearly nine hundred. It was a day of firsts: the first amphibious landing by U.S. forces since the Spanish American War in 1898, the first U.S. offensive engagement of World War II, and the first ground engagement with the Japanese.

And the presence of the Raiders would add another first to that list—the first special ops mission by the United States Military in World War II. Though the group would hardly exist for more than eighteen months, the Raiders would establish a foundational standard in training and exceptionalism for all future special forces throughout the U. S. military. They were the country's first special forces unit, but they would hardly be the last.

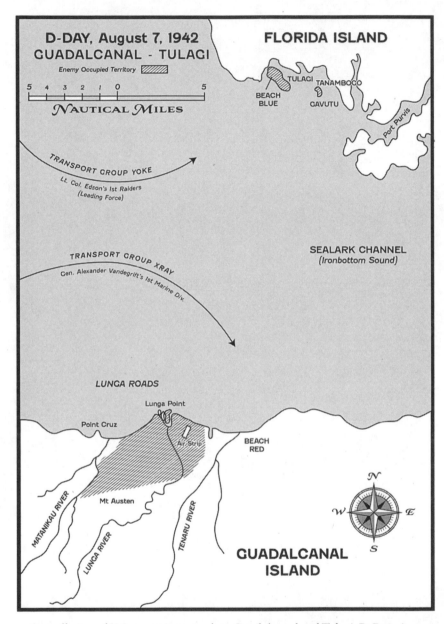

4. Overall view of U.S. troops' approach to Guadalcanal and Tulagi, D-Day, August 7, 1942

CHAPTER V

The Raiders Go to War

The Airstrip

It staggers credulity to compare its size with its importance. A mere six miles long by three miles wide—a few acres of sand on an island, itself a pinhead fewer than a hundred miles long by thirty wide in the vast Pacific. Yet the progress, perhaps even outcome, of the war with Japan rested largely on who controlled that small piece of flat real estate: an airstrip on Guadalcanal.

When the name "Solomon Islands" first surfaced—and all the more "Guadalcanal"—it sent military personnel scrambling for charts and maps. More than one commander was heard to mutter, "Where the hell is that?"

The six large islands and hundreds of tiny ones stretch like a string of pearls across 60,000 square miles of ocean. The British had established a protectorate in the Lower Solomons in the 1800s. By the early 1940s, there were 650 white settlers, mostly planters and missionaries, and 40 to 50 Europeans. Approximately 100,000 natives continued to live wild, secluded lives throughout the island chain. Most of these were ebony-skinned Melanesians with some 40 different dialects.

Headhunting was not unknown. But whether it was to raise a colonial flag, to establish a plantation, to conduct trade, to spread the word of God, or to get lost from the world, no person happened there accidentally.

So those who lived on Guadalcanal in 1942 knew it was only a matter of time before an invasion by Japanese forces. Because regardless of its remoteness, those who controlled the Solomon Islands could take control of Australia, New Zealand, and more. Establishing an airstrip there on Guadalcanal, on the only plain flat enough for a large airfield, would give Imperial Japan control of supply lines and dominance throughout the South Pacific.

As anticipated—and dreaded—during the night of April 31, 1942, a large Imperial Japanese convoy had sailed silently down the Slot between the islands of the Solomons and into Sealark Channel. Ferocious shelling began.

The next morning at 8:00 a.m., Japanese troops swarmed onto the small island of Tulagi. Within days, Japanese engineers had moved across the channel to Guadalcanal to begin preparing land and building an airstrip.

It was now clear to U.S. military strategists at the highest levels where their first major offensive ground engagement against Japan must take place—and what its objective would be: to occupy and control those eighteen square miles of dirt airstrip. It would take six months of bitter fighting to accomplish the mission.

The Marine Corps as a whole, with elements of the Army Air Corps alongside, would form the strong arm and fist for the task.

And the newly created 1st Raiders? They would make their formal debut as its brass knuckles.

Operation Watchtower

Shortly before 3:00 a.m. on August 7, 1942, exactly eight months to the day after the bombing of Pearl Harbor, the United States

Amphibious Task Force glided silently past the western edge of Guadalcanal. Code-named Operation Watchtower, the invasion of the
Japanese-occupied Solomon Islands was about to begin. Two days of
solid squalls and low-hanging clouds, near-perfect conditions for a
clandestine approach, allowed the large convoy to approach completely undetected.

Now turning eastward, the vessels carrying men, equipment, and
supplies slipped into the upper waters of Sealark Channel, which separated the 'Canal from Florida Island. Before long, these waters would be
known the world over as Ironbottom Sound, named for the untold dozens, if not hundreds, of Japanese and United States ships, planes, and
matériel—and men—that found an eternal resting place at the bottom
of its cobalt-blue waters.

Once the convoy turned south, it divided into two groups. The first,
named Group X-RAY, contained General Vandegrift's 1st Marine Division. Their landing site was designated Beach Red. Their mission: to
capture the unfinished airfield on Guadalcanal. The second group,
named Group YOKE, had two prongs: the 1st Parachute Battalion would
take the islets of Gavutu-Tanambogo, while the 1st Raiders in the lead
would seize Tulagi, supported by a unit from 5th Marines. Group
YOKE's landing site was designated Beach Blue.

The diminutive island of Tulagi, across the channel from Guadalcanal and just off the shores of Florida Island, measured only four thousand yards long and one thousand yards wide. At its southernmost tip,
the island narrowed to about three hundred yards. Compared to the steep
ridges at the northern end, the lovely southern area was relatively low
and hilly, with beautiful vistas of ocean and nearby islands. Nearly all
the island's build-out was concentrated here.

Though small in size, Tulagi served an important purpose. It had
long been headquarters to the Solomon Islands Protectorate and a Royal
Australian Navy seaplane base. Facilities included a residency for the
governor, several attractive one-story, island-style buildings for government personnel and other workers, a prison, hospital, radio station, and

numerous wharves. It also sported a 100-yard by 200-yard playing field and a 9-hole golf course complete with club house. One could imagine it wasn't too difficult for Japanese high command to decide where to billet their elite troops and commander once they took control of the Solomons.

Vandegrift knew this would probably be the toughest nut to crack during the initial invasion. Firstly, because of the particular Japanese troops stationed there—several hundred veteran Rikusentai of the 3rd Kure Special Naval Landing Force known for their fierce battle tactics. Secondly, because of the island's topography itself: a near-vertical ridge in the northern portion, extremely rugged and high, running two-thirds of the way down the center of the island. The southern third, located on smaller hills, would be easier to defend, especially with the shallow gulley separating the two areas.

Vandegrift needed the best, most combat-ready troops available to him for the difficult operation. He knew that group was Edson's Raiders, without question. He called upon the newly minted unit to lead the attack.

A First Mission

Lee stood cradling his machine gun in his arms on the deck of the *Colhoun*. He and the other 1st Raiders had checked and rechecked their weapons, distributed live ammo, and loaded their belts. Officers had reviewed their assignments. Now, in the early dawn light, he could make out the hulking landscape of Guadalcanal off the starboard side.

He looked the part of a commando. His helmet had strips of canvas tied to it, while camouflage paint darkened his face.

"This is no time for crooning," he thought as he spotted his Singing Eight Ball choirmates.

Despite the adrenaline's kicking in, Lee's mind remained clear and focused. His calm through the battles ahead would reassure the younger Raiders around him. At twenty-four, he was a few years older than most

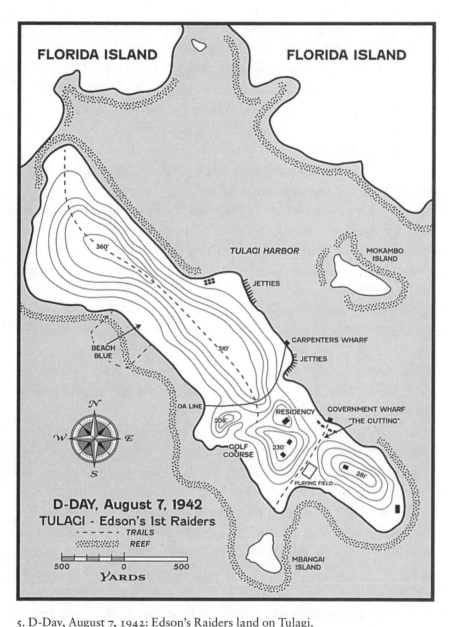

FLORIDA ISLAND

FLORIDA ISLAND

TULAGI HARBOR

MOKAMBO
ISLAND

360'

JETTIES

CARPENTERS WHARF

JETTIES

BEACH
BLUE

310'

OA LINE

RESIDENCY

GOVERNMENT WHARF
"THE CUTTING"

208'

230'

GOLF
COURSE

261'

PLAYING FIELD

N

W   *E*

S

D-DAY, August 7, 1942
TULAGI - Edson's 1st Raiders
- - - - - -   TRAILS
·········   REEF

MBANGAI
ISLAND

500   0   500
YARDS

5. D-Day, August 7, 1942: Edson's Raiders land on Tulagi.

of the other privates. He was mature, and his leadership qualities would be noticed by officers higher up the chain of command.

As the APDs *Colhoun* and *McKean* sailed into sight of Tulagi, their crews lowered the ramp-less, first-model Higgins boats into the tossing waves below. Raiders spider-crawled down the thick rope netting, each carrying seventy or more pounds of weapons and equipment. With several feet separating the end of the rope from a boat, Raiders would jump and crash into the bottom of the bobbing boat. Once the boat was full, the pilots gunned the engines and set off.

Like most South Pacific Islands, coral reefs ringed the perimeter of Tulagi, hiding just beneath the water's surface. At Beach Blue, a coral reef snagged Lee's Higgins boat some one hundred yards from shore. The packed-together men tumbled to their knees but quickly recovered. Each Raider threw one leg over the side before awkwardly plunging down into the tropical waters.

Once everyone found their footing in the deepwater reef, they lugged their way toward shore. A veteran sergeant who was there later said, "It was the 1st Marine Raider Battalion that led the assault on Tulagi, about [one thousand] lean, sinewy, superbly trained commando-type troops.... [A]rmaments included rifles, pistols, machine guns, mortars, bayonets, knives. Hand grenades hung from pack straps where they curved under armpits, and the chests of some of the men were crisscrossed with bandoliers. We must have looked mean enough to scare the balls off a brass monkey."

As soon as Lee reached the narrow beaches, he dropped quickly down to the sand to set up a machine gun position. The guy next to him muttered, "What the hell is this—a practice run? Why aren't they firing at us?"

It was a good question. The Marine landings had caught the crack Japanese soldiers completely flat-footed. They were hardly prepared to defend their posts, let alone the island. As a result, Edson's Raiders slipped in the back door of Tulagi with no casualties. But they would soon find that they were up against several hundred veteran Japanese troops, themselves special forces, who would not give up the island—or their lives—without exacting a heavy price from their opponents.

Landing on Tulagi

The element of surprise can help soldiers take an early advantage, but it only lasts as long as the enemy fails to recover. It didn't take long for the experienced Japanese troops in the Solomon Islands to regain their footing from the American sneak attack. Once they got organized, they started to fight like hell to defend Tulagi.

Once they had successfully landed on Tulagi, the Raiders planned to divide into two primary groups. One group would hit the beach and veer to the right, fanning out and working its way south down the beach. The other would press inland, crossing over the ridge that stood in the island's center, and work its way southward on the opposite side of the island. The pincer movement, the Marines hoped, would squeeze the Japanese to the southernmost tip of the tropical stronghold.

The group tasked with crossing the ridge soon learned some bad news. The ridge that intelligence had described as "steep-ish" was almost completely vertical. Dismayed but eager to push on, the Raiders stuck to their plan. They summited the ridge drenched in sweat, then descended the other side to begin working their way south.

Both groups had to fight back Japanese soldiers as they pushed down Tulagi's coasts. Pockets of riflemen, snipers, and machine gun nests hid in the island's dense vegetation, peppering the Raiders with gunfire. At around noon, Lee and most of 1st Raider Battalion were near the OA line—a line on the strategic map indicating each company's initial objective. Here the battalion would reorganize and prepare to continue the attack. Red Mike Edson had positioned the OA near a ridge overlooking the main structures of the Japanese outpost. He knew this is where the Japanese would dig in and where his Raiders would encounter the main fighting.

Over the course of the next eighteen hours, Edson's Raiders would learn four lessons about their enemy:

First, the Japanese were disciplined marksmen. Their snipers were patient and calculated and knew how to wait for just the right moment.

Second, Japanese would go underground when possible. Granted, the Japanese soldiers on Tulagi hardly burrowed as often as they would later in the war, but it was still the first time the Raiders had seen this unique tactic. And without the flamethrowers or grenade launchers that would later prove so useful to fighting cave warfare, these special forces would have to improvise to root out the enemy.

Third, the Japanese embraced nighttime as a weapon. The Raiders knew to expect this thanks to their leadership's time in China. But they still were surprised by the relentless onslaughts that the Japanese could launch at any moment of the day. Fighting the Japanese required constant vigilance, and Edson's Raiders first learned that on Tulagi.

The last thing the Raiders encountered on Tulagi was something that Americans couldn't have imagined: the incomprehensible policy of *gyokusai*—the Japanese soldier's commitment and desire to fight to the death or commit suicide. For Americans, perhaps nothing distinguished the Pacific War from that against the Germans more than this single factor.

Quite possibly the most important lesson the Raiders learned on Tulagi, however, was not about their enemy; rather, it was how to deal with taking casualties. Lee was close at hand when a platoon sergeant in his own company, "E" (Easy) Company, picked up the Browning machine gun from the hands of another gunner who had just been shot by a hidden sniper. The sergeant, Alexander Luke, twenty-six, had been a Marine for eight years and had actually served in the 4th Marines in Shanghai with now-Battalion CO Edson back in 1937.

Sergeant Luke's machine gun skills were greatly admired. He would shoot controlled bursts rather than continually firing. Lee had learned much from him.

As soon as Sergeant Luke picked up the Browning from his fallen comrade, he fell forward too. The sniper had struck again, hitting Luke between the eyes.

The fighting was unlike anything Lee had ever experienced. He wanted to stop, but he knew that he had to keep pushing forward in order to survive. The early combat at the foot of Tulagi's low hills was intense, with the Americans coming under fire from Japanese machine gunners and snipers dug into caves. But the later strife was just as bad when the Raiders made it to the makeshift town, the open environment now creating a chaotic battlefront.

As dusk descended on Tulagi on August 7, 1942, Lt. Colonel Merritt Edson informed his tired, weary Raiders to dig in for the night. The battalion had experienced mounting losses, especially among their officers. Two out of the five company commanders were badly wounded and out of action, while another had had a very close call with death. The troops were a bit rattled and needed a night to regroup.

The news of the loss of some of his best leadership hit Red Mike hard. He recognized the special qualities of the commanders he had lost. In due time, so would everyone else. By the end of the war in the Pacific, the three officers in question—Lew Walt, "Jumping Joe" Chambers, and Ken Bailey—would earn two Medals of Honor, two Navy Crosses, three Silver Stars, and seven Purple Hearts.

Checked by all of the first day's losses, Edson knew that the worst loomed ahead. He and Griffith both had thoroughly prepared the men, however, for what they could expect during the night from these enemy warriors they had fought all day. The Raiders were ready for any surprises the Japanese could now spring on them.

As black night descended, the Raiders dug in and waited. They had trained for this more times than they could count. Lee thought of how often, whether at Quantico, American Samoa, or Nouméa, the "Ole Man" had run them ragged all day only to make them traverse the same terrain at night. The dark changes everything, and Edson had trained his men to be able to navigate at night.

But the fighting didn't start with Lee and his fellow Raiders trying to find their way through a night fraught with enemies. It began with something that Edson and his officers had warned the men about: the "night campaign."

As the Raiders lay in their trenches, the Japanese began one of their most harrowing battle tactics. All at once, the Americans started to hear freakishly loud sounds everywhere: screaming, howling, unearthly screeches and groaning. They heard metal banging against metal and hands slapping weapons. Though he had been warned about the Japanese noise campaigns, Lee inadvertently recoiled. His eyes strained forward trying to pierce the darkness; he tightened his grip on the Browning machine gun. Every nerve and muscle in his body tensed.

Then, all of a sudden, the noise stopped as suddenly as it began. A serene quiet took over the island. None of the men around Lee said a word. Everyone waited. The nerve-racking "noise campaign" continued off and on for several hours.

Long after dark, around 10:30, the noise started once more. This time the ghoulish howls were accompanied by flesh and blood. The *banzai* attack commenced. Japanese troops ran at full speed like shadowy ghosts through trees, dense brush, and thick grass.

Lee and the other machine gunners opened fire with their rifles and machine guns. Exploding grenades lit up the night sky. Then, all of a sudden, the attack came to an abrupt halt—or so the Raiders thought. Other than a random pop here and there, they heard nothing but eerie silence for what seemed like an eternity. The serene pause only lasted a moment. Just a few minutes later, the Japanese began their light-speed attacks again, running at the American lines bent over and low to the ground like jackals.

"Here they come," yelled Lee to his assistant gunner as the assistant began feeding an ammo belt into the blasting weapon. The Japanese were screaming and howling in the flashes of fire, charging with drawn swords and raised knives. As one line of rushing soldiers fell, another group would take their place. Several Japanese soldiers tumbled down into some of the shallow fox holes, each time following with hand-to-hand combat against the Raiders. Two or three soldiers collapsed just in front and to the side of Lee's gun mount.

This attack would turn out to be the strongest of five attacks throughout the night. At one point, the Rikusentai penetrated deep into the Raiders, temporarily dividing "A" and "C" Companies. Several times during the night, smaller groups of Japanese infiltrated the Raiders' line in attempts to attack the Residency, Edson's command post. Half a dozen combatants managed to hide underneath the building's porch, killing three Marines before Raider grenades found their mark.

The Raiders managed to repulse each wave one way or another. Though the experience of a night attack was one of the most harrowing and disorienting American soldiers would face, Edson would dryly joke later that the attack on his command post in Tulagi was one of the few "exciting" moments of the Guadalcanal campaign.

As morning dawned on August 8, the sight of the death toll all around sobered the Raiders. Bodies were strewn everywhere, some piled on top of one another. Lee walked around; he could hardly believe what he was seeing. Then he saw Captain Lew Walt peering into a foxhole where Private First Class Eddie Ahrens lay quietly with his eyes closed. The 5'7" private was covered in blood and was dying. A dead Japanese officer lay flung across his legs; a Japanese sergeant lay beside him. Crumpled around his foxhole were thirteen other Japanese bodies. Eddie had been hit twice in the chest with bullets and speared several times with bayonets. As Captain Walt gathered the young man into his arms, the private whispered, "Captain, they tried to come over me last night, but I don't think they made it. Guess they didn't know I was a Marine Raider." Walt could only reply, "No, they didn't, Eddie; they didn't know." The story of the brave, defiant young Raider spread quickly through the troops.

Raiders gathered their dead and wounded and quickly went back to work. Everyone knew that the Japanese would regroup in order to begin their final defense in the rocky ravine at the southern tip.

The tough coral outcropping that gave form to the ravine was honeycombed with natural caves. Here, the defenders were relatively safe, for neither naval gunfire nor dive bombers could break through the tough rocky caverns.

U.S. troops had never faced a situation like this in previous conflicts. And for the present, flamethrowers were not available on Tulagi. Again, Raiders would have to improvise in order to clean out the remaining Rikusentai.

One of the true heroes of Raider history, Gunnery Sergeant Angus Goss, a Marine gunner who loved to blow things up, devised pole charges. As two demolition men crawled forward with the poles under smoke grenade cover, machine gunners supplied covering fire. Soon, the men were close enough to the cave openings to push the explosives inside. The mouth of the caves blasted shut, leaving their occupants trapped inside.

As Raiders pressed on with their dangerous work that day, they eliminated most pockets of remaining Japanese troops they found. By late afternoon, Edson felt confident enough to contact headquarters with a brief message: "Tulagi Island is secure."

In this first Pacific ground combat experience, the 1st Marine Raider Battalion had received their baptism of fire and had definitely been bloodied. There were ninety-eight Raider casualties from the assault on Tulagi—nearly 10 percent of the 1st Raider Battalion. Thirty-eight of those casualties were killed in action.

Lee's company, Easy Company, suffered disproportionately high numbers of losses among their non-commissioned officers. Lee was acquainted with all of the men lost from his unit—seven dead and seven severely wounded. It was a sobering reminder of the reality of war. The Japanese had made the Raiders pay dearly for each hard-fought yard of territory on the small island of Tulagi.

But the Imperial Special Forces also learned about the skill and power of the Marine Raiders in this first ground encounter in the Pacific theater. These young American commandos had been trained to the greatest degree possible by men dedicated to that cause. They were marksmen, and good ones at that. They didn't buckle during nighttime fighting, and they understood close-quarters combat. They did not back away from hand-to-hand combat.

Clearly, the Japanese had been caught off-guard when the Marines and Marine Raiders arrived on Guadalcanal and Tulagi. But they recovered quickly. Rear Admiral Gunichi Mikawa, commander of the Japanese 8th Fleet, formed a task force of seven cruisers and one destroyer. With the Admiral's flag aboard the heavy cruiser, *Chokai*, the Japanese headed at flank speed early on August 8 toward Guadalcanal.

During the dark early-morning hours of the tenth, the Japanese attack began. Within hours, they had blown holes in several American warships, inflicting the worst U.S. Navy defeat in history. The defeat forced American naval forces to withdraw, starting with the aircraft carriers but with transport ships soon following. Rations and supplies went with them, as did the heavy machinery required to build defensive positions on the island. The Marines were stuck on land without naval support.

General Vandegrift, knowing his Marines were already operating on a shoestring due to the hasty deployment, realized their predicament. For the next month, Marines on both Guadalcanal and Tulagi would feel the sharp pinch of insufficient supplies, most especially when it came to food and ammunition.

Nonetheless, the 1st Marine Raider Battalion had performed brilliantly on Tulagi—and they knew something about living off the land. Recognition of their courage and daring would soon be underscored: the United Sates Navy would name no fewer than twelve ships after the 1st Marine Raiders. The legend was beginning to grow.

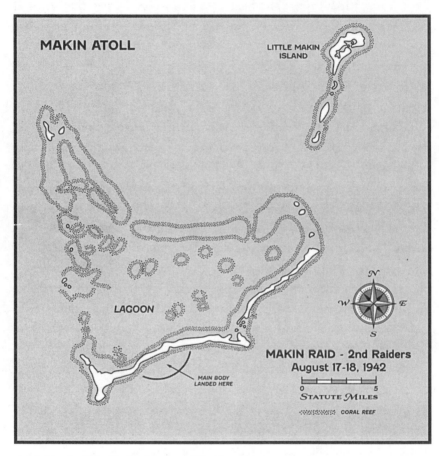

6. Makin Atoll Raid, Carlson's 2nd Raiders, August 17–18, 1942

CHAPTER VI

Taking Makin Atoll

While Lee Minier and Edson's 1st Raiders remained on Tulagi to watch for any stray Japanese or attempts to reinvade the small island, their sister battalion, 2nd Raiders, waited in Hawaii. Carlson's Raiders now geared up for another test.

While Midway had been their introduction to war, Makin would be 2nd Raiders' baptism of fire. As a battle, it was a landmark success for the Raiders—the first true commando-style raid at night in rubber boats from submarines. Yet the engagement would also spark lasting controversy and would eventually be punctuated by news of brutal executions. Nonetheless, in the battle's immediate aftermath, electrifying adulations of Raider heroics appeared in newspapers and magazines across the globe. Carlson's Raiders had earned a reputation as fearsome fighters.

The raid of Makin had been planned for a long time. During the summer of 1942, Admiral Chester Nimitz determined that a strike of some sort would be needed to divert Japanese attention away from Guadalcanal and Tulagi. He and his planners settled on Makin, and they decided that Carlson's Raiders were the perfect unit to execute the mission. On the same day that Edson's Raiders landed on Tulagi, Carlson's Raiders in Hawaii were given the green light for their first major mission. It would prove to be an example of the old adage: "If it can go wrong, it will go wrong."

The Raiders at Camp Catlin in Hawaii saddled up and headed out on August 7. All the Raiders quickly dressed in their standard issue khaki shirts and pants, which had been dyed black for the raid. Mudhole Merrill and Joe Gifford, his buddy in the one-man pup tent next to his, marched quietly with their gear stuffed in gunnysacks—helmets, packs, cartridge belts—out to the waiting convoy of trucks.

Once loaded, the trucks headed out of the cane fields east of Honolulu along the island's main highway to Pearl Harbor. There the USS *Nautilus* and the USS *Argonaut* awaited to take them to an "unnamed island." When Mudhole first saw these subs a few days earlier during rubber boat drills, he couldn't believe his eyes. They were the same submarines he had played on as a young boy in San Diego. Now, they would take him off to war.

"Hey—I was on this sub when I was a kid, did I tell you?" he said in muffled tones to anyone who would listen. "Yeah, you told us, Mudhole—about a million times," someone responded.

While other Raiders may have felt as if they were lowering themselves into an alien world, Mudhole gleefully clambered down the ladder. Some Raiders often received letters from home, but Mudhole's correspondence to and from family was spotty. Somehow this small coincidence emanating from a joyful moment during childhood gave the young seventeen-year-old a welcome touch of nostalgia. Grinning from ear to ear, he bounced from one compartment to another as if greeting an old friend.

The Raiders were told to stick, poke, or jam their gear anywhere they could find a spot. Mudhole found the perfect place in the area where he had once felt the silky coolness of torpedoes. Now only 6 remained on board to create as much space as possible for the crew of 9 officers and 88 enlisted submariners, plus the additional 87 Raiders of "B" Company. The other 134 Raiders of "A" Company loaded onto the *Argonaut,* which had more space.

Crews and Raiders of both submarines, however, were packed into compartments like sardines. Mudhole and Joe bunked next to each other in canvas slings about twelve inches apart, stacked four, five, sometimes six tiers high and three to four rows across with no space between.

"Joe, we're going to have to slide all the way out and then slide back in just to turn over!" said Mudhole.

"Yeah. Well, just don't wake me up when you do," barked Joe, slapping Mudhole on the back of the head.

When Mudhole first met Joe Gifford, he immediately latched on to the older Marine, especially when he learned Gifford was from Arizona too. To add to Joe's mystique, he had already seen duty in China. Mudhole admiringly called him a "4th Marine China Man." Joe was rugged as they come—stocky, muscular, with high cheekbones and gaunt cheeks—tough as nails. Joe had taken a liking to the feisty young teenager and kept an eye out for him.

As the two submarines glided out of Pearl Harbor at 9:00 a.m. on August 8, 1942, Lieutenant Colonel Evans Carlson informed his Raiders on the *Nautilus* of their destination. Per usual, he began with "Ahoy Raiders," though much reduced in volume. Major Jimmy Roosevelt supervised briefings on the *Argonaut*.

The "unnamed island," Carlson informed his Raiders, now had a designation—Makin Atoll. Its location in the northernmost part of the Gilbert Island Group had made it most attractive to Imperial Japan.

After the bombing of Pearl Harbor on December 7, 1941, Japan completed its smothering invasions of Guam, Wake Island, Singapore, Hong Kong, the Netherlands' East Indies, and the Philippines—victories all. Within a few short months, the Japanese further alarmed the United States and her allies by bombing Australia.

Besides these distressing activities, Japanese troops continued to land and occupy other strategically located islands or atolls. On December 10, 1941, around four hundred Japanese troops engulfed Makin (also called Butaritari). It represented Japan's easternmost possession.

These developments constituted reasons enough for growing concern. Now that the United States had invaded the Solomons, liberating Makin would also suffice as a much-needed diversion.

The 2nd Raider Battalion was about to enter World War II. Their mission actually represented a truer commando-style raid than their sister battalion, 1st Raiders, had negotiated on Tulagi: it would use rubber boats deployed from submarines at night; it was meant to be an extremely fast-moving raid—in and out within twenty-four hours—likely behind enemy lines; the Raiders would be traveling light, with limited heavy weapons to aid in maneuverability and quickness—all of this meant to startle and create maximum confusion on unsuspecting troops. Stealth and surprise were key.

The *Nautilus* continued on its intended course, submerging in the day, surfacing at night. With 184 men jammed into the *Nautilus*, nearly twice its intended capacity, duties had to be shared by crew and Raiders alike. Understandably, amenities such as the cramped lavatories would need to be organized and personally supervised. The commode required extra attention.

When the submarine was submerged, flushing the toilet was complicated. It necessitated a careful 17-step process with levers and buttons to assure water and contents didn't flow back into the bowl. The flush pressure was great—one misstep with the valves meant a discomforting accident.

When Major General Oscar Peatross later wrote his well-respected book of Raider events, *Bless 'em All*, he tells of the discussions he had on the *Nautilus* with the engineers. They decided a handful of Raiders should be selected and taught how to negotiate the flushing, then oversee that event. Mudhole Merrill, the teenager, had found his calling.

"You can call me the Sanitation Engineer," he told his buddies when the instruction class had ended. "And let me just say—don't spend too long in the head—there's plenty others waiting their turn."

Once he mastered the tricky sequence of levers and buttons, he soon learned how to give a little controlled squirt to any man who dawdled. More than one startled Raider or crewman exited pronto, grabbing up pants and dungarees, vehemently cussing at Mudhole, who would laugh uncontrollably.

"You should respect the Sanitation Engineer," he would yell down the passageway as they stormed away.

Most Raiders loved their beer and whiskey and were known to frequent as many bars as possible, whenever possible. Since a submarine carried only scant alcohol, and that reserved for an occasional "glass for the brass," a few Raiders decided to take matters into their own hands.

"Surely there's some alcohol somewhere on this boat," said one Raider. They concocted a drink known as a "Pink Lady," consisting of torpedo fuel and nothing else. "Hey—it's got alcohol," explained one Raider to another who shrugged his shoulders and downed a glass. Many were seen topside that evening after the submarine surfaced, bent over its sides.

As the *Nautilus* sailed westward, the equator and International Date Line drew ever closer. Several Raiders, including Mudhole's friend Joe Gifford, had crossed over both previously on prior Marine duty assignments. But for newcomers to the crossover, a ceremony conducted by U.S. Navy seamen at the Royal Court of the Realm of Neptune commemorated the event. Men were inducted into the fraternity with all manner of initiation rites, summoned by their very own certificate from "Davy Jones, Secretary to His Majesty" and "King Neptune, Ruler of the Raging Main."

Usually, however, nighttime was Mudhole's favorite for just that reason. The submarine would surface, and small groups of men were allowed topside for twenty to thirty minutes at a time. The fresh air was exhilarating—a welcome relief from the putrid smells below emanating from unbathed, sweaty adult men. The recirculated air was suffocating—so much so that when the captain allowed the smoking lamp lit the night before the raid, the men couldn't even get a match to flame since there was so little oxygen.

As the submarine sailed further into the expansive waters of the South Pacific, Joe stood topside one clear night with Mudhole. The stars seemed fiery—close enough to touch.

"See that small group of stars over there?" said Joe, pointing upward to seemingly endless heavens. A gentle breeze blew over them from across the sea. The only sounds were waves lapping against the sides of the *Nautilus* and the steady throbbing of diesel engines as she plowed forward.

"It's a cross!" exclaimed Mudhole.

"Yep—called the Southern Cross. See the four stars that form the cross? Then there's one tiny star to the right—all part of the same constellation," explained Joe. "You can't see that up north above the equator, except maybe in the Florida Keys sometimes."

Unbeknownst to the two Raiders standing together on the deck that night, these stars would soon form one of the most iconic symbols in the military. In a few short months, the Southern Cross would become the primary design element in a Marine patch to adorn uniforms for regular Marines in all divisions.

But it would also be the central design feature in another patch of equally historical proportions—the first-ever Marine Raider patch: a field of dark blue dotted by five stars representing the Southern Cross, with a death-skull embroidered on a red square buried in the cross's center—a patch that very few Raiders would ever wear on their uniforms during active duty.

Mudhole was silent for a while, head tilted back, staring straight up into the heavens. The Southern Cross (or Crux, as it is sometimes called), though the smallest constellation in the sky, was plainly visible. It blazed magnificently in the darkness.

Kenny knew about the Bible and God. His family went to church, but, as a typical seventeen-year-old, he had never been too enthusiastic about religion. Now, however, as he was about to enter battle, his thoughts turned heavenward.

"Keep me safe, Lord," was his simple prayer.

Murphy's Law at Makin

When the USS *Nautilus* and USS *Argonaut* finally reached their rendezvous point, both submarines surfaced at 3:00 a.m. on August 17, 1942.

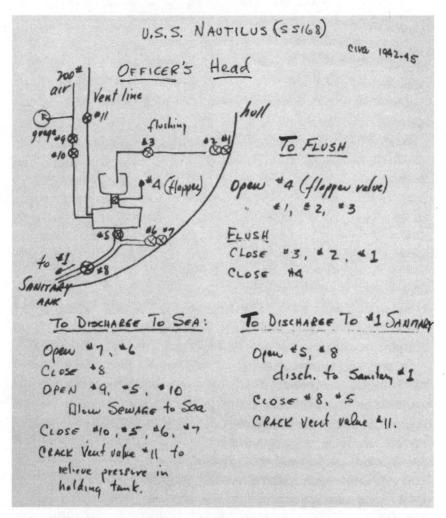

A sketch done by a crew member on the *Nautilus* shows the nineteen steps Mudhole Merrill mastered in order to flush the submarine's head—a tricky skill that earned him the title of Sanitation Engineer. *Courtesy Hal M. Winner.*

An unexpected squall raged through the night. Twenty-foot seas and driving rain tossed the submarines around like toothpicks.

The Raiders went about their business inside the subs with intense concentration and heightened awareness, but no panic. They collected their gear from all over the long vessels, moving quickly in what could only be described as controlled pandemonium. They exhibited a great deal of self-assurance despite the fact that most would be going into combat for the very first time.

Carlson and his officers went over last-minute instructions.

"We'll only be on the island twenty-four hours—quick in-and-out. We'll destroy installations, gather intel, take prisoners, create havoc. I promise you rice, raisins, wet blankets, and glory!" exclaimed Evans Carlson. The Raiders knew the drill.

"And remember—don't chamber your first round."

It had always been Carlson's final directive to his men during training. The element of surprise depended on the silent insertion of troops. Keeping the first chamber of your weapon empty lessened the chance of firing until necessary. It was critical to maintaining surprise.

They had practiced the rubber boat drills hundreds of times at Barber's Point in Hawaii. Each rubber boat crew of Carlson's Raiders had ten men. The senior man was the boat captain; then another was the outboard motor mechanic and usually the coxswain; another was the fuel man; another's duty was paddles; another was in charge of inflating the boat; and so on. Shorter men would be assigned the middle or back section, while taller men would sit up front.

Using this arrangement when they cast out from shore on the return, the taller men could keep the boat moving as they walked into deeper water, allowing shorter men behind them to crawl inside. This permitted the boat to be pulled further out into the water before the men began to paddle. As they would find out later that night, this practice would not make a hill-of-beans difference in the scheme of things. Second Raiders had practiced inflating boats, attaching outboard motors, pouring fuel into motors, tying down weapons and equipment inside the rubber boats, boarding their boats in correct positions, and getting paddles ready for assistance with steering. They had repeated these drills more times than they could count.

However, as Major General Oscar Peatross, a captain at the time of the landing, said later from personal experience of that night:

> Even under ideal conditions, the physical complexities of these procedures were immense, but with the hazards engendered by darkness and a wet, narrow pitching deck, the timing and coordination required easily surpassed that needed to control the movements in the rings of Ringling Bros. and Barnum & Bailey five-ring circus.

The original plan had, of course, called for a much less hectic debarkation—one where the rubber boats would rest on top of the submarine decks with men and equipment properly loaded. Then the subs would submerge while the rubber boats on top would simply float away. Because of the enormous wave swells, however, that debarkation was deemed impossible.

Despite the bad weather complications, most boat teams functioned unbelievably smoothly. Mudhole and his team wrestled with the nasty weather like all the others: wet hands, wet faces, slippery decks, mounting spray, all while waves of saltwater crashed mercilessly across the submarines' sides. When he emerged from below, it took him several seconds to find his balance in the severe rocking. Though extremely athletic, Mudhole struggled to stay upright.

His rubber boat team, however, knew their stuff. They quickly inflated their boat, mounted its motor, grappled to keep saltwater out while pouring fuel in, and secured equipment. Then they tossed their rubber boat over the leeward side, while one team member braced on deck holding the painter (rope tether) as tightly as he could.

Once the rubber craft hit the water, entering them became the next obstacle. Men waited until the boats were at the top of the swells, then jumped one at a time. They all realized that if they missed, they would go down into the deep—a most unpleasant thought, considering the amount of gear some carried.

After Mudhole's team entered the boat, every man sat in his assigned place: four on each side, one in front, and one in the rear. Each paddled violently to aid propulsion and steering.

Fortunately, their small outboard motor sputtered only briefly. They bounced upward, then plunged downward and away from the *Nautilus*. Surging waves propelled the rubber boat forward. Mudhole squinted through the driving rain. He thought he could make out two or three other boats close at hand.

With miraculous fortune, no one drowned that night. Only two rubber boats, loaded down with weapons, ammo, and medical supplies, jerked loose from the painters, or tender ropes, and disappeared into the darkness. As Raiders jumped down into the boats, several did miss in the pitching waters and went under. But other Raiders were alert and reached into the seas to save their teammates from drowning.

It seemed like an eternity, but it really took only a short while to cover the two thousand yards to shore. The incredibly strong waves helped propel them forward. Suddenly, ahead in the dark, a low, flat shoreline materialized. Mudhole's boat crew shoved into the sand before any of the others, though now many were quickly hitting the beaches on either side.

The next thing Mudhole Merrill knew, he was wading on the outer edges of Makin Atoll.

All up and down the narrow beach, shadowy forms of Raiders moved silently, pulling in rubber boats, hiding them in brush, retrieving weapons, setting up machine gun positions. No sounds other than the crashing breakers behind them could be heard. The first classic amphibious special forces raid by Marine Raiders at night in rubber boats from submarines had landed undetected.

…Until, breaking the silence, a rifle sounded off.

The resounding, loud crack emanated from somewhere along the Raider line—the unmistakable pop of an American rifle.

And not far off to his right, Mudhole heard the familiar voice of Lt. Colonel Carlson, at this moment swearing vehemently—the only time Mudhole had ever heard curse words leave his commander's lips. If any Japanese were around, they had just been alerted. In short order, the Raiders prepared to move quickly inward.

Meanwhile, a lone Japanese sentry sprinted towards his garrison headquarters as fast as he could. The enemy now knew the Americans had arrived.

Confusion Everywhere

Warrant Officer Kyuzaburo Kanemitsu of the Imperial Japanese Navy had occupied Makin Atoll for several weeks. Intelligence suggested his garrison consisted of between one hundred and two hundred Special Naval Landing Forces with a dozen or so support personnel in tow. As it turned out, Kanemitsu's forces numbered far closer to the lower end of that estimate. Lt. Colonel Evans Carlson, on the other hand, thought there were significantly more due to native scouting reports. He also believed more had landed during the actual engagement. Lack of accurate knowledge of enemy combatants would play a key role in significant decision-making as the battle wore on.

Kanemitsu's garrison, though they might have expected any invasion to come from the lagoon side of the island since the ocean side was so formidable, took no time in responding. Within thirty minutes after landing, Mudhole found himself in the middle of bullets whizzing and machine guns blasting from all sides.

And because of the great challenge of getting to shore during a blinding squall in pitch-black darkness, many of the Raider platoons were separated and scattered up and down the beach. Yet every Raider took it in stride. Pockets of men here and there grouped up to commence doing what they had been trained to do, even though at times it resembled a free-for-all. One Raider later said it reminded him of the Gunfight at the O.K. Corral.

As Raiders quickly moved inward, several platoons were fortunate to be intact. One platoon leader, Sergeant Clyde Thomason, led his platoon immediately through thick brush and crossed over a narrow dirt road. As they did, they encountered severe cross fire between two machine gun nests. His young platoon, momentarily stunned by the ferocity of bullets coming from different directions, couldn't determine where the enemy positions were located. Suddenly, Thomason realized he might lose his entire platoon unless they responded quickly.

The 6'4" Atlanta, Georgia, native stood up. With no thought of his own safety, he began to run up and down in front of his men to direct their fire. The Raiders positioned themselves under his instructions. Simultaneously, they began to open up on the machine gun nests and other riflemen hiding in the dense foliage.

For several crucial seconds, Thomason avoided the barrage of bullets directed towards him. Out in the open, he continued to encourage and guide his platoon. But he was too ripe a target.

Sergeant Clyde Thomason, for his courageous and unselfish actions, would be awarded posthumously the Medal of Honor. He would be the first enlisted Marine so decorated in World War II—a Marine Raider.

Kenny "Mudhole" Merrill came ashore lugging ammo lanyards with grenades hanging wherever possible, wearing a holstered .45 pistol, a stiletto, and a large Ka-Bar knife on his belt, and shouldering the tripod for his machine gunner, Corporal Leon R. "Chappie" Chapman. Both men immediately flattened on their bellies seconds before the shooting started.

Mudhole could hear bullets zipping all around them, digging up puffs of sand and debris, leaves and sticks.

When the two of them moved forward with several others, they came to the dirt road cutting north and south through the center of the skinny island. About two hundred yards ahead of them across the road, at least four machine gun nests suddenly hammered their group. Mudhole and Chappie rapidly responded with their machine gun. Revved up adrenaline helped Mudhole focus on keeping the ammo belt slightly raised up so that rounds fed without jamming.

But when they silenced one Japanese nest, it lasted only briefly. Just as quickly as an enemy was gunned down, other soldiers would take his place. Chappie's section leader, Corporal Edward Wygal, decided to crawl in from a different direction to lob a grenade.

Mudhole and Chappie kept the Japanese gunners pinned down while Wygal inched his way forward from one side and managed to get close enough to hurl a grenade. He then jumped on top and killed the survivors with his stiletto. Mudhole and Chappie had fired more than four hundred rounds of ammo before the nest was silenced once and for all. Wygal belly-crawled his way back into friendly territory. He would be awarded the Navy Cross for his courage that day.

The small group of Raiders drew deep breaths, but there was no time to stop. They continued to pick their way further south down the dirt road. Mudhole could see other Raiders cautiously inching their way along on the other side of the road. In a flash, a sniper from somewhere above fired a couple of rounds. They couldn't see him, but they knew he was somewhere up in one of the trees.

"Can you spot him?" Chappie whispered to Mudhole.

"Naw," said Mudhole squinting his eyes against the sun "Let's just spray the whole tree."

The staccato sounds of automatic fire lasted for several seconds. The palm fronds vibrated and fluttered as their bullets ripped through them. Then, a brief moment of silence.

Suddenly a loud crack boomed. An enormous bundle of foliage tumbled down through branches, bumped along the tree trunk, and landed in a heap at the bottom. Inside the ball of foliage was a dead Japanese sniper with leafy branches and coconuts tied all over his back and shoulders.

During the melee, Mudhole had watched one of his buddies across the road get pummeled by the machine gun fire. "Chappie, I'm gonna go get his shotgun—he don't need it anymore."

"Okay, but keep dodgin' them bullets," the corporal said back.

Sure enough, as soon as Mudhole started across the road, another enemy rifleman began firing. Mudhole dodged bullets all the way and reached the dead Raider. He could only look at his buddy a split second. The Raider had been shot multiple times in the chest, which lay wide-open. Mudhole grabbed the 12-gauge shotgun laying to one side. He took a deep breath and ran back across the road, bullets flying once more. He slid in by Chappie.

"Hey, Mudhole, why didn't you bring back the lanyard with the shells?"

"Chappie, that lanyard had blood all over it. I didn't wanna pick it up!"

"Well, how many shells you got in it?" pressed Chappie.

"Hell, I don't know," said Mudhole.

"You might fire and might not even have any shells. You better go back and get that lanyard," advised Chappie.

Mudhole hesitated, but he knew Chappie was right. He would need shells. So, once more, he ran back across the road, bullets flying from somewhere. He pulled and tugged at the blood-soaked lanyard wrapped around the dead Raider. Finally, it released, and he ran back to Chappie, who gave him a thumbs-up.

The seventeen-year-old sat still for a moment. He wiped his bloody hands across his pant legs, cleaning them as best he could.

Things were eerily quiet for the next few minutes, with no firing and no sign of movement anywhere. The small weapons group just held tight.

All of a sudden, out of nowhere, from further down the now isolated road came a lone Japanese, rifle slung over his shoulder, riding a bicycle.

"What the…" one Raider could be heard whispering close by.

Though he could never explain exactly why he did so, Mudhole suddenly jumped up and entered the road. He shot at the oncoming Japanese. He shot again and again and again. Finally, after numerous rounds, the man fell off his bicycle.

There was only one problem. The bicycle kept coming!

Mudhole continued to blast away at it. The riderless bicycle, some-way, somehow, kept rolling down the road straight toward Mudhole.

Though it was certainly split seconds in real time, it felt like an eternity. Finally, however, the bicycle veered off the road and crashed. It wasn't until that moment that Mudhole realized he was trembling violently all over. In later years, Mudhole would confess, "That damned bicycle scared the hell out of me!"

War sometimes unfolds with split-second extremes. That day on Makin, no sooner did the others realize Mudhole was okay than they burst into raucous, hysterical howling. As soon as Chappie could catch his breath, he gurgled out, "Mudhole, you just killed yourself a bicycle!"

A Day on Makin

Though a few lighthearted moments, such as finishing off a bicycle, punctuated tension that morning on Makin, Raider casualties mounted "at an alarming rate," remembers Captain (later Major General) Oscar Peatross. Carlson grew concerned. In addition, several village natives told him there might be as many as 350 combatants stationed on Makin. And, in the back of his mind, there also loomed the worrisome possibility of enemy reinforcements' arriving at any moment.

There was one other issue: Captain James "Jimmy" Roosevelt, the son of the president of the United States. Carlson had personally promised President Roosevelt and his wife, Eleanor, that he "would take good care of Jimmy," their oldest son and a close, personal friend of Carlson. To what extent this single situation rose above the others is hard to say. Taken together, however, it seemed to result in a tentativeness on Carlson's part, which, in hindsight, actually began during the landing. After establishing a well drawn-out plan for the beach invasion that morning for groups to disperse at various points over a reasonable distance, Carlson changed directives in the middle of the debarkation from the submarines. With the extreme difficulties caused by torrential rains and high seas, there were problems enough just getting away from the subs. When all finally made it ashore, the companies were intermingled, resulting in semi-chaos after landing. The accidental rifle discharge didn't help things. Then, one boat, under the command of Captain Peatross, again due to the difficulties posed by the storm, actually landed so far from the main body as to find itself behind enemy lines.

Later, as one platoon was maneuvering into place, Carlson changed his mind at the last minute to set up a "line of skirmishes." It wasn't the first time that day that Carlson had changed his mind after giving orders, nor would it be the last.

Shortly past mid-morning, it became evident the Japanese were preparing an all-out attack. Under the covering fire of snipers, machine guns, and grenade throwers, the Japanese spent several minutes yelling and shouting together. Then, after a quick moment of silence, two shrill notes from their bugler pierced the air. Immediately, a wave of infantrymen sprang up, charging full speed, yelling "*Banzai!*"

The Raiders, startled but not intimidated by the suddenness of the attack, held their fire until the charging soldiers were nearly on top of them. Then, they opened fire up and down the line. Most of the oncoming wave fell. Those soldiers that didn't regrouped behind their machine guns and snipers.

It wasn't long before a second *banzai* attack commenced with the same results. Most of the surging wave was eliminated by the steady, levelheaded Raiders.

The Raiders had barely recovered from these two attacks when they spotted a pair of Japanese reconnaissance planes circling overhead. As they had been trained, everyone dug in under the brush or logs, sat tight, and held their fire. The planes circled several times, then left.

Shortly past noon, twelve Japanese planes began bombing and strafing the area. With an average elevation of six feet above sea level on this South Pacific atoll, finding cover proved challenging. For the next hour and a half, Raiders dodged bombs and bullets but, fortunately, endured the raid relatively unscathed.

By this time it was mid-afternoon. Carlson alerted his Raiders to hold their position, not to advance or to continue to seek out the enemy—a defensive posture, in other words. To some that day, these orders seemed a tentative response.

When all had been quiet for a while except for random shots here and there, Raiders slowly gathered into small groups. Many were near Butaritari village, with its few structures, or close to the wharves, named On Chong's and King's. Others bartered with natives who brought coconuts in exchange for cigarettes. One or two pulled out small cameras like tourists.

They were all tired and hungry. Since the mission had called for them to be on the island for twelve or so hours, they each had brought one canteen of water and a food bar. Everyone knew that the selected departure time to leave Makin and return to the submarines was 7:30 p.m. And everyone knew that the departure would take place on the ocean side where they had landed and left their rubber boats.

But what transpired during the next twenty-four to thirty-six hours defies the imagination. The events would culminate in continuing controversy and tragedy, notoriety, and adulation that linger even today.

After the air raid, Mudhole and others around him continued to lie low, awaiting further orders. They heard random shots firing in the distance, but, for the most part, everything seemed to be settling down. Mudhole and his platoon commenced working their way back over the road dotted with what had been active enemy machine gun nests earlier. They were all silent now.

When he walked past the taro pit machine gun nest he and Chappie had pinned down with suppressing fire so Wygal could lob in a grenade, he stopped. The sight shocked him.

Though he had seen dozens of dead bodies scattered all among the breadfruit trees, salt-scrub brush, and coconut palms of the island, this vision still jolted him. At least a dozen, maybe more—it was hard to determine—Japanese lay in a tangled mass, a pile of disconnected legs and arms, guts and body parts. Flies and insects covered the entire taro pit. Around the edges, a couple of scrawny pigs gnawed vigorously.

The seventeen-year-old felt a severe wave of nausea come over him. He quickly looked away to keep from getting sick, then picked up his pace along the crushed coral road heading towards Butaritari village. Here and there, random pops could still be heard in the distance.

Shortly, he came into a small clearing with primitive structures, including a one-room schoolhouse and other simple, two-story buildings. A few Raiders sat in small groups, talking quietly, waiting for whatever was next. Island natives walked among them bartering coconuts for cigarettes.

Mudhole Merrill asked around if anyone had seen his friend, Joe Gifford. Everybody just shrugged or shook their heads. Mudhole was looking forward to seeing his friend Joe. It would be good to touch base with the older Raider after this first day of battle.

As Mudhole continued walking, he spotted a small, whitewashed church up the road on the other side of the clearing. He assumed it was the Catholic church that had been pointed out to them on the map of Makin when they prepared for their raid.

Mudhole was suddenly drawn to it. He wanted to go inside. Maybe it was curiosity to see inside, to look for souvenirs, or just to sit down out of the sun—away from it all. Whatever motivated him, he headed down the road. Once at the small church, he mounted its two steps and pushed open the wooden door.

As his eyes adjusted to the mellow, soft light inside, he saw a dozen or so rows of wooden pews on either side of the chapel. Closing the door behind, he gingerly tiptoed inside and slumped onto the first bench he came to.

Down front a simple, wooden altar stretched across the width of the nave. He saw two tables covered with white cloths. One table displayed a rough-hewn cross. On the other side stood a small pulpit.

Mudhole sat with his hands in his lap. At seventeen, he was at his prime both physically and mentally. Yet suddenly he felt exhausted. He had become a Raider just three months into his seventeenth year. He had wanted to be a Marine his entire life. And for the past seven and a half months, he had endured the most strenuous training program he could have ever imagined. He had marched fifty miles at a time fully loaded with equipment, almost daily. He could kick a can down the road with his .45 pistol and could fight a deadly fight with knives, bayonets, or his bare hands.

But nothing had prepared him for the terror of this first day of combat. Nothing could. Yesterday seemed an eternity away.

He looked down at his fingers. Several hours had passed since he pulled the blood-soaked ammo lanyard off his dead fellow Raider. Yet particles of dried, black blood still remained all over his hands.

Suddenly, a slight noise at the front of the church whipped him alert. Every muscle tensed. He dropped to his knees between the wooden benches and pulled out his .45. Slowly rising to a crouched position, Mudhole inched his way forward. He cautiously crept along, looking down each row of benches as he passed.

When he neared the altar rail, he heard a slight scuffling across the wooden floor. He rounded the altar where the cloth-covered table stood. Crouched down behind it was a Japanese soldier. The two just looked at each other for several moments.

Mudhole raised his weapon. "This isn't your day," he said, and fired into the man's chest several times. Then, he stood frozen, looking down at the curled-up, lifeless body and watching blood puddling over the floorboards.

He reached down and felt the man's jacket pocket—there was something in it. Gingerly, Mudhole pulled out a small, worn leather holder with two tiny pictures inside—one was a young woman, the other a much older-looking one. In an instant, their images framed what was probably a family waiting somewhere.

As he slowly turned to leave, Mudhole noticed a rosary, a long string of Catholic prayer beads, spread out on the table beside where the man lay. Mudhole grabbed it, spun around, and ran out of the church.

A Night of Horror

By 7:15 p.m., Raiders collected along the beach, pulling rubber boats out from underbrush and palm fronds. Since units had been intermingled most of the day, groups of seven or eight Raiders formed up around whatever rubber boat was nearest. A couple of wounded were loaded into each craft. Dr. Stephen Stigler, one of two physicians who had accompanied the raid, helped lift Sergeant Norman Lorenz into the first boat. The sergeant's wounds left him paralyzed. Corpsmen had tied him into a narrow litter for transporting. Dr. Stigler climbed in beside him.

"I'll stay right with you all the way," said Stigler, patting his patient's arm. "Don't you worry. We'll make it."

Lorenz gave him a weak thumbs-up—the only part of his body he was able to move.

It was high tide and dark. Intelligence planners of the raid had chosen this day and time for those reasons. Nighttime would increase their cover, and more water should help the rubber boats cross over the coral reefs with less difficulty. But the wind, perhaps due to lingering bands of the squall line from the previous night, furiously drove enormous waves toward shore. Further out, still larger walls of water surged above the coral shelf in rapid succession. Clouds completely covered a waxing moon. Only phosphorus could be made out in the dark, glowing against the black surface. The sounds of pounding waves, close at hand and beyond, were powerful and ominous.

At the shoreline, Raiders got their first taste of what was before them. The water here, though shallow, churned viciously. It whipped around their legs as they high-stepped into the surf. A desperate drama began to unfold.

Mudhole's group struggled to hold their rubber boat up high while maneuvering forward. When they got to shoulder-deep water, they fought to climb in.

Someone in a boat close by yelled out, "Shark!" Mudhole's heart jumped. He only heard the shout once, but it provided motivation. Now they climbed in and paddled with all their combined might.

Their rubber boat made it through the initial rollers, straining arms and shoulders to the max. But as they plunged into the larger breakers a little further out, the wave height was staggering. Sometimes, these water walls hovered high above them, then crashed down, filling the shallow boat. One Raider said later that they seemed twenty feet tall.

Mudhole removed his helmet, as did others, and furiously bailed. The next wave turned them sideways. They couldn't get turned back fast enough before the next wave hit, so over they tumbled. Mudhole could feel strong currents beneath the surface pulling at his legs from all directions.

After a struggle, the entire crew managed its way back onto the rubber boat's sides—but not before they had been driven back into shallow waters. They dragged their craft up onto the shore and collapsed where they stood.

After a few moments, one of the sergeants said, "Come on, Raiders. Saddle up!"

They started the punishing process all over. Another slab of water tilted them up. The craft stood on edge for a moment before crashing over. Men fought their way back up to the surface, sputtering and coughing. Once Mudhole got in, he reached down to help a Raider named William Pallesen who was still flailing in the water. He heaved Pallesen back in, who hastily nodded to Mudhole indicating he was okay.

All up and down the dark shore, the other rubber boats were having an equally difficult time. Occasionally, one or two might slip through the initial rollers only to meet up with the larger, angry breakers further out. They returned without shoes, shirts, even pants. The violent struggle had ripped clothes right off their bodies. All weapons, ammo, and any other equipment they might have had were torn away by the boiling waters. Raiders returned to shore completely exhausted.

After Mudhole and his crew stumbled back onto land for the third time, he noticed Pallesen was no longer with them. He asked the others, but no one had seen him. He began to feel a degree of panic rising. Furthermore, they had lost all their weapons and ammo. If the Japanese came, the Raiders would be unable to defend themselves. The submarines were out there waiting, but the Raiders were unable to reach them.

"Listen," one of his group huffed between gasps. "Count 'em. Let's count them waves—don't they get bigger, then smaller every seventh or eighth time—isn't it something like that?"

"I'll try anything," said another, forcing himself to get up.

They began to count. There did seem to be a pattern. After the seventh wave or so, they waited another two or three waves and thought they could see a lessening of height and strength.

"Okay. Let's do it," yelled the sergeant. "We don't stop this time—this is it!"

Back on shore, Carlson had chosen several Raiders as rearguard protection while others left the beach to attempt getting to the waiting submarines. One of those Raiders serving that function, Private First Class Ben Carson, later described the ruckus he witnessed that night from his ringside seat as the "most harrowing period of his life."

Mudhole had never paddled so hard in his life. His entire group did. They each knew this was probably their last effort. They were exhausted to the bone, but somehow they managed to get through the initial rollers.

"Paddle, Raiders, paddle!" someone yelled out above the crashing waves. Right next to them, a rubber boat suddenly veered sharply off to one side. Mudhole saw it spill into the sea. Amazingly, theirs stayed upright even as raging seas all around tried to swallow them whole. They wrestled against the ocean for what seemed like an eternity.

Then, all of a sudden, they had passed through the outer breakers. Though there were still swells, the water seemed incredibly calm in comparison to what the Raiders had just fought through. Not too far away, in the pale moonlight they could make out a dark form lying barely atop the water's surface. They rowed with all the strength they had left and finally pulled up to the side of a submarine.

Surrender? Yes. No. Maybe.

After five hours of grueling attempts to get off the beaches, eighty Raiders had made it to the waiting USS *Nautilus* and USS *Argonaut*. Miraculously, all the rubber boats carrying wounded made it.

Back on shore, Carlson looked over his exhausted men. Most lacked weapons or ammunition, many without clothes or shoes, all ripped away by the violent waves and currents. Now, they not only were aground, but they also had no way to defend themselves.

How many Japanese were on the island?

That had been the question all day long. Carlson and his Raiders arrived at Makin with intelligence reports that estimated the number of enemy troops between 100 and 250. After landing, natives told Carlson there might be as many as 350. During the day, two Japanese planes had attempted to land on the lagoon but were shot up by American machine gunners. Native scouts, however, informed Carlson they believed as many as 60 more troops disembarked before the planes exploded into flames. What to make of the reports?

Carlson thought back over the day's events. A series of unexpected circumstances framed their present situation, beginning early that morning with a chance, violent squall that wreaked havoc on their rubber boats' landings.

Then, the accidental weapons discharge as his 2nd Raiders came ashore. It had spoiled the element of surprise and alerted the Japanese of their presence.

Next, the morning's casualties began to soar well beyond what Carlson had anticipated.

To add to the confusion, island natives had reported higher-than-estimated numbers of enemy troops in the vicinity. That afternoon,

Carlson heard of the possible arrival of another additional 60 Japanese soldiers. (Two Japanese ships, a 33-hundred-ton transport, and a 1,000-ton gunboat had sailed into Makin Lagoon. Both were sunk by the submarines with only the "sheerest good luck," said Commodore Haines.)

But who knew when additional reinforcements might be arriving from Kwajalein? They most assuredly would; how soon was the question.

This freakish high tide with driving winds towards the atoll proved another obstacle to surmount. Mother Nature, not the Japanese, had trapped the Raiders on the beach.

And lastly, but certainly not least, there was the matter of the eldest son of the president of the United States. Did he, Carlson, want to be the one under whose command Jimmy Roosevelt lost his life? Especially considering he had promised his father, the president, and his mother, the first lady, that he himself would "look after" their son.

Carlson hesitated and second-guessed himself throughout the day. From the moment the Raiders landed to their departure from Makin, Carlson gave conflicting sets of orders and acted with great trepidation.

As to the numbers of troops—reports in later months would suggest that by mid-afternoon, there were probably fewer than two dozen Japanese combatants left on the entire island. The Raiders, with their courageous aplomb and highly skilled fighting techniques, had actually killed nearly the entire garrison. But Carlson didn't know that at the time.

Some suggest he could have sent out scouting patrols to have a look-see—certainly these Raiders were well-trained for such a mission. Or, as others have said, just listening to the vast difference in the sounds of warfare from morning to afternoon should have alerted him to the enemy's diminished force. By 4:00 p.m. only random shots here and there could be heard, presumably from lone snipers.

Regardless, the Japanese garrison commander, Warrant Officer Kanemitsu, had most certainly alerted the base on Kwajalein in the Marshall Islands. And, in fact, by 7:30 a.m. he had sent a message:

"Americans are here. We are dying." At some point, reinforcements would be arriving—perhaps in very large numbers.

Carlson himself evidently felt the situation was dire—dire enough to call a Gung Ho–style meeting. Around midnight, he gathered his officers and a few of his senior non-coms to talk over their situation.

Here is where things got squirrelly. To this day, a controversy remains—among some, a hotly contested one. Reports vary as to who attended this meeting, what was said, who said it, and what actions were taken afterwards. Even Raiders whose attendance can be documented disagree on what transpired.

Because at this midnight meeting, it appears someone raised the possibility of surrendering to the Japanese.

Some said Carlson himself raised the issue of surrendering and then left it up to the individuals, as was consistent with his democratic leadership style. Others claim someone else brought it up and was then encouraged to mention it to Carlson—or told to forget about such an absurd idea by others.

Some said there was a handwritten surrender note; others said there most definitely was not one. Still others said there was one but that it was not written in Carlson's handwriting and was signed with an illegible signature. This note was carried by two officers and given to a Japanese soldier, who presumably began the journey back to his garrison. On the way, he was shot by another Raider, who spotted him in the forest. Later, it appears that subsequent Japanese soldiers discovered his body—and also the surrender note—which then found its way to "Tokyo Rose," who used it as propaganda: the domino effect.

Many military historians have written their detailed research of testimonies, accounts, eyewitnesses, and opinions. Of those accounts from Raiders themselves, some believe that there was a surrender note; others vehemently insist Carlson would never have done such a thing— that he would have never surrendered regardless of circumstances. Some who were actually on Makin at the time retreated into silence on the incident when they returned home. They died without further comment. Among many, the controversy remains one of intense debate.

In the early morning hours before dawn on August 18, Carlson addressed the remaining 120 Raiders. Lieutenant LeFrançois, badly wounded himself and needing medical attention, later described the scene around them:

"...[They were] the most disheartened, forlorn, bloody, ragged, disarmed group of men it had ever been my experience to look upon. Their heads hung low, and despair frayed their spirits."

Carlson told the entire group that if anyone wanted to make another attempt at getting off the island, they had his permission. "Do it *now*," he said. He also told them he planned to stay with the wounded, then head to the lagoon side of the island at daybreak. He planned to use native canoes in another attempt to reach the submarines come nightfall on the eighteenth.

Then, Carlson pulled his executive officer, Major Jimmy Roosevelt, off to one side. "Jimmy, I want you to make another go at it—now," he told Roosevelt. "Don't wait." Roosevelt expressed his desire to remain with Carlson on the island and go out with him later that evening.

"No," said the commander. "Don't wait. That's an order."

Roosevelt knew it was futile to try to persuade Carlson further. He followed his commander's orders, though reluctantly.

Those Raiders that wanted to try again, which now included Roosevelt, pulled together the needed rubber boats. Shortly after, they began their ordeal back through the initial rollers, then to the high waves beyond. Boats turned over time and again.

Finally—astonishingly—fifty more Raiders were able to reach the submarines. As before, some didn't make it and had to return to shore. A total of seventy were now left behind on the island with Carlson.

The final boat that did manage to reach the submarines contained Roosevelt. As his rubber craft heaved to in the breaking dawn, suddenly a Japanese plane roared down out of nowhere. Sailors frantically pulled the men, including the president's son, up on board and down the hatch just as the submarine commander yelled out, "Dive! Dive!"

As news of the just-saved Raiders spread among the fortunate ones who had boarded the night before, so too did rumors of what was going on back on Makin—rumors of an attempt to surrender.

When Mudhole Merrill was told, he spit. "Why that's a bold-faced lie! Hell no, Carlson'd never do such a thing—he'd never surrender. And if there's somebody back there who set him up like that—and if I ever find out who did it—I'll kill the sonofabitch myself."

CHAPTER VII

The Raiders of Carlson's Ark

It would be impossible to pinpoint exactly why August 18 seemed to dawn brighter, but it did. Carlson's demeanor was more optimistic. By osmosis, so was the morale of his 2nd Raiders.

Jimmy Roosevelt had safely reached the USS *Argonaut*. Another fifty Raiders had also made it to the waiting submarines. Just seventy-two Raiders remained on Makin. And, with reports from a few of his men, it appeared increasingly possible that there might be considerably fewer Japanese on the island than previous estimates suggested.

Private First Class William McCall and others had decided to patrol around the wharf areas, through the underbrush, and along the central road. They reported back to Carlson that they had seen "no live Japs along the way, only dead ones."

Major General Oscar Peatross would later describe his commander as "intensely religious." Perhaps Carlson was thinking of an Old Testament verse he learned from his father, a devout Congregationalist minister—one that promises new mercies each morning from a Sovereign Lord. Whatever the reason, Carlson was noticeably buoyed the following morning. The renewed vigor resulted in constructive activity.

They moved the wounded to the lagoon side of Makin Island, closer to Government Wharf. The second doctor assigned to 2nd Raiders, Dr. William MacCracken, and his corpsmen had stayed behind to do what they could to keep the wounded alive until they could get off the island. Others, under Carlson's orders, destroyed a radio station, one thousand barrels of gasoline, and whatever else might be useful to enemy troops. The Japanese command post was ransacked. Raiders seized papers and documents for delivery to intelligence.

All through the day, natives emerged from their huts to offer assistance where they could. They brought coconut halves filled with coconut milk and small bananas. Other Raiders found cans of meat and dried fish among the Japanese supplies. Though not a feast, it helped stave off hunger, which had been building over the past thirty-six hours without anything to eat and just a few drops of water.

Others, who lacked shirts for their backs, found a variety of colorful garments at the trading post located at Stone Pier. Some who had lost nearly all their clothes in the surf were given bright, native sarongs which they wrapped around themselves with flare. After a bit of pillaging, a few even found men's silk underwear in floral patterns of blue and pink. By midday, many looked like pirates of the Pacific.

But there was always the tension of not knowing where a Japanese might be lurking among the foliage or in the trees. Sentries stationed and rotated all through the day keeping watch.

Carlson ordered the four rubber boats hauled across the island to the lagoon about three hundred yards away. After procuring an outrigger canoe, they tied the five craft together, with two rubber boats on either side of the canoe. Only two outboard motors were salvageable, and just one of those worked with any reliability.

Those who saw this makeshift "ark" would only shake their heads calling it the oddest-looking craft they had ever seen. It would be cramped for seventy-plus men, many of whom were wounded, but it would have to suffice.

Now, two hurdles still remained. They would have to locate the submarines at the new rendezvous point in absolute darkness. And they would have to escape the island before Japanese reinforcements arrived. By nightfall, Carlson and his Raiders were once more faced with the ocean before them and the possibility of Japanese on their coattails.

After dark all the Raiders squeezed into spaces that normally would hold no more than forty-five men. The wounded flattened in wherever they could. At 8:30 p.m., they shoved off Government Wharf and headed toward the lagoon entrance some three and a half miles to the west.

Even though these protected waters were calm, progress was painstakingly slow—fewer than two knots an hour. Once past the entrance and into the open ocean, it slowed even more. Exhausted men exerted what strength they had left to paddle. The waves were a strong opposing force but, fortunately, nothing compared to the previous night's breakers on the other side of the island.

The *Nautilus* and *Argonaut* waited less than a mile from the lagoon's entrance, yet it took the Raiders another hour to reach them. The submarine commanders understandably became increasingly antsy but had no intention of leaving until they loaded the remaining Raiders. Finally, after three hours of hard rowing and a stroke of luck—some would say divine guidance—Carlson's ark at last spotted a flashing light in the distance and returned it with the weak beam of the only handheld flashlight he had.

When the lookouts spotted the makeshift vessel bobbing up and down in the waters, they could hardly believe their eyes. Quickly, however, the sailors helped divide the wounded between the two submarines. Each now had a doctor aboard and could initiate surgeries immediately. Once every Raider had been pulled into one or the other of the waiting boats, the submariner captains gave orders: "Take her down...set a course for Pearl...rig for silent running."

A Tragic Discovery

The USS *Nautilus* and USS *Argonaut* ran silent all the way back to Hawaii. Officers and sergeants did the best they could to get an accounting for platoons. But because of the disjointed extraction from the island with three separate groups, an accurate head count couldn't be made until they reached Pearl Harbor. No one was certain who had made it back to the submarines and who hadn't.

Carlson had left fifty dollars with the native chief, Joseph William, to bury the eighteen dead Raiders. He was confident that if any were missing, it would not be more than one or two—and their deaths probably from drowning.

The mood on both submarines was somewhat subdued. The Raiders had battled enemies, both human and natural. But they were strong and resilient. Though thoroughly spent, they would recover quickly.

When Mudhole half-fell, half-slid down the ladder into the submarine that first night, he collapsed on his knees and whispered a prayer.

"Father, thank you for letting me get back alive," he muttered under his breath.

When he looked into the faces of his buddies, he wondered if his own face looked as haggard. Yet when the final group of Raiders boarded on the night of the eighteenth, they appeared even worse. He later heard someone say Carlson himself looked like he had aged ten years.

When they were given time to go topside, Mudhole saw no one exercising or gaming. It appeared everyone just wanted to rest. He didn't see his buddy, Joe Gifford, on the *Argonaut* either. He asked around, but no one could remember having seen him recently. Mudhole figured he was on the other submarine and would catch up with him once they got back to Hawaii.

On the route back, he resumed his duties as the Sanitation Engineer. He lacked, however, the exuberance he had shown on the way to Makin.

One night out on the deck getting some fresh air, he gazed upward. He just wanted to be alone. There was a cool breeze. His thoughts turned to the man in the church. It had happened so fast, yet he could remember the man's face clearly: he had the saddest expression—and a look of resignation. Mudhole wasn't sure he even had a weapon. In the years to come, he would think about that moment often.

Finally, the characteristic outlines of the Hawaiian Islands appeared, a warm and hospitable sight. The Raiders looked forward to hot showers and food. They were a motley-looking group, many of them wearing only a vague semblance of the uniforms they had left in. Most realized they had accomplished what they had been sent to do. But no estimation of what they had endured prepared them for what they were about to witness as their submarines glided into Pearl Harbor.

Coming topside they saw an enormous crowd of cheering supporters and well-wishers packed onto the docking area, waving flags, throwing confetti, carrying balloons. A military band played rousing, patriotic songs. Reporters armed with flashing cameras pushed into Carlson's Raiders. Every top brass on the island lined the docks, including Admiral Nimitz himself. He boarded the submarines with congratulatory speeches and smiles.

Mudhole stood in a borrowed T-shirt and ripped trousers. Others were in varying stages of undress. He looked at the Raider standing next to him draped in a native waist sarong. The crowds were cheering wildly for them.

"Can you believe this?" he asked no one in particular.

As submarines were tied off, the crowds became louder and louder, clapping and waving.

It soon became evident that these admiring fans were welcoming home heroes, men who were nothing short of celebrities. These American boys who had participated in a daring night raid and had succeeded in wiping out a Japanese garrison had destroyed most of the installations and any other thing that could be used for war, plus returned with intelligence.

In the coming days every newspaper in the country would herald Carlson's Raiders. Admittedly, Mudhole relished the limelight.

And America had been given something to cheer about: homegrown heroes—the Raiders. At that early point in the war, the country eagerly greeted any positive news.

Yet for the military, the celebratory mood would be short-lived. After docking and returning to Camp Catlin, the serious head-counting commenced. It was during these hours that a terrible tragedy reared its ugly head. Hard as it was to imagine, it appeared that thirteen Raiders were missing.

Mudhole realized when his buddy Joe Gifford didn't return to the pup tent next to his that Joe must be one of those missing Raiders.

Relatively quickly, one Raider thought to be missing was confirmed killed in action by his rifle team. In the weeks and months to follow, however, the fate of the other twelve would slowly come to light.

It appeared nine had remained stranded on the island. Though no records exist to determine exactly what transpired, the nine evidently met up sometime after the submarines had left Makin to return to Hawaii. Some reports claim they sought help from natives and that a priest provided a native outrigger. These nine then managed to leave the island in a desperate attempt to travel the two thousand miles back to Hawaii.

However, after only a few days at sea (some records indicate that date as August 24, 1942), they were picked up by a Japanese ship and taken to Kwajalein. There they were kept in tiny, filthy concrete-block cells. Several months later, Louis Zamperini (whose story is recounted in the memoir *Unbroken*), after being captured in a similar fashion, would be held in the same tiny cells. Before being transported to mainland Japan, Zamperini supposedly discovered the names of nine Marine Raiders scratched into the cell walls.

After being held on Kwajalein for two months, one of the natives observed a contingent of Japanese soldiers marching nine Americans, bound and shackled, into a small clearing in the jungle.

Here their captors placed a small table. Then, the soldiers forced each prisoner to bend over the table. A Japanese stood on one side of the table with a raised sword, another stood on the other side with a pistol. One by one, the nine Raiders were beheaded.

After the war, intelligence resources substantiated the reports of their beheadings in 1946. In 1947, Captain Yoshio Obara, then the local Japanese commander on Kwajalein, and Commander Hiusakichi Naiki, chief of military police on Kwajalein, were sentenced to ten years and five years in prison, respectively. Since authorization for these executions came directly from Admiral Koso Abe, commander of 6th Base Force at Kwajalein and wartime military governor of the Marshall Islands, Gilbert Islands, Nauru, Ocean and Wake Islands, he was tried in a military court and sentenced to death by hanging.

Years afterward—and as recently as the 1990s—expeditions have been sent to Kwajalein to recover the remains of the nine executed Raiders. None have never been found. Much speculation has entered into the discussion, including the possibility of cannibalism.

The remains of one Raider who was missing in action were found during later decades, bringing the total of those killed in action on Makin Atoll to nineteen. Two additional Makin Raiders, whose remains have never been found, are listed as missing in action to this day.

CHAPTER VIII

From Tulagi to the 'Canal

Meanwhile, as 2nd Raiders recuperated in Hawaii, 1st Raiders in Tulagi were told to "Saddle Up." They had remained there three weeks since securing the small island. It hadn't been a picnic. They were low on food and supplies since their ships hadn't had time to off-load these needed items before being chased away by incoming Japanese warships. Now 1st Raiders were ordered to the big island in the Solomons, known as Guadalcanal, just across the channel. Its name would soon be shortened to the 'Canal by most men who fought on it.

General Vandegrift had decided to transfer Edson's Raiders to bolster his defense perimeter at the Marine base. The perimeter protected perhaps the most critical piece of real estate up to this point in the South Pacific: the few flat acres of cleared land with a couple of long dirt runways. Elements of the 1st Marine Division (regular line Marine troops) had surprised the Japanese forces there on D-Day, August 7, as Lee Minier and 1st Raiders invaded Tulagi. The Marines had taken back the airfield held by a small number of Japanese troops.

The American military planners didn't think that Imperial forces would allow the Marines to control the airfield indefinitely. The Japanese needed the airfield to facilitate their plans of invading Australia, New Zealand, and New Guinea. Controlling the airfield meant their airplanes could assist in disrupting Allied supply lines to those countries, eventually cutting them off from the outside world.

To further complicate matters, the U.S. Navy had not been able to establish a presence in the waters of the Solomon Islands. Japanese reinforcements could land nearly unopposed at points surrounding Henderson Field. Dubbed the "Tokyo Express," Japanese transport ships hauled in supplies, equipment, and men around the clock to multiple areas in the Solomons.

What General Vandegrift knew, indeed what every military planner knew, was this: "We've taken it; they want it back." There were only two real questions: When would the "Tokyo Express" return to Guadalcanal to fight, and how many troops would it return with? That the Japanese would return was certain.

Turning to the Raiders for additional support might have raised concerns for General Vandegrift a few months prior. He had been wary of the Raider concept from the beginning. Edson's forays into the 1st Division to handpick the best officers and non-coms did nothing to endear the concept to a general already hard-pressed to fill out a battle-ready division.

Yet Edson and his Raiders had performed swiftly and executed decisively in the Tulagi campaign. The Raider performance undoubtedly impressed the general, who, with his planners, sought to shore up their position on Guadalcanal.

Consequently, on August 31 he ordered the transfer of the entire 1st Raider Battalion from the island of Tulagi across Sealark Channel to the big island of Guadalcanal.

Thus the pieces on the chessboard were falling into place. The fall of 1942 would go down in Raider history, indeed in Marine Corps history, as a season of spectacular engagements and events. The first was a 36-hour defensive battle so fierce and horrific it would forever be associated with the name of its commander: the Battle of Edson's Bloody Ridge. These months would also see a long patrol of over 30 days, again, forever to be known by the name of its commander as Carlson's Long Patrol. The extended patrol would put an end to any talk of tentative leadership that might have emanated from the events during the Makin Raid.

To top it off, rumors swirled about the possibility of two brand-new Raider Battalions, 3rd Raiders and 4th Raiders, to be formed and activated.

It appeared the Raiders' star status was rising at a meteoric rate and that these elite special forces would form a permanent part of the Marine Corps landscape. Destiny, however, would have other plans.

Heroic Little Ships

When Lee looked out across the sparkling waters of Tulagi Harbor, he saw a welcome sight. A small and familiar type of transport ship waited to take them across the channel to Guadalcanal.

The transfer of Raiders and other smaller specialty groups—such as the Marine parachutists—from one island to another involved the use of compact World War I destroyers rescued from mothball storage. They were labeled APDs, "AP" standing for transport (literally "auxiliary personnel") and "D" designating destroyer. One captain, when radioed from shore to explain what an APD was, had his radioman return the message, "all-purpose destroyer."

These older destroyers had seen service in the first world war, but most had been retired. Originally they had four smokestacks and flush decks, giving rise to their nicknames as "four-stackers" or "flush-deckers."

In order to transform them for troop carry, two of the stacks along with their boilers below had been removed to create more carrying space in the hull. And their flush decks proved ideal for exercising and daily calisthenics.

From the beginning of World War II, they were indeed "all-purpose destroyers." The small APDs saw service throughout the South Pacific, the Atlantic, or "wherever they sent [them]." General Merrill Twining would later describe them as "those heroic little ships." Another historian would call them the "workhorses" of the South Pacific campaigns, unsung heroes who time and again would meet the call of duty, often sacrificing everything.

But they were vulnerable. As part of their refitting to make room for troop and equipment loads, most of their torpedo tubes were removed as well as many of their deck guns. However, what they didn't have in actual armament, they made up for with the stout hearts of their courageous crews, who became beloved by the Raiders.

From all accounts, Marine Raiders as well as other smaller groups like the Marine parachutists cultivated close relationships with these hearty little ships and their accommodating crews. As Raiders poured over the ships' sides to take the fight to the enemy, the crews would cheer them on. Upon their return, Raiders found hot food and coffee waiting along with hearty welcomes. Seldom have particular ships been so closely associated with a military unit as the APDs and the Raiders.

No wonder that when tragedy struck, the Raiders grieved. On August 30, just as the last Raiders were debarking from the APD *Colhoun* onto Guadalcanal, air raid sirens blared.

Lee Minier was one of the last Raiders to debark that day. Friendly to everyone, he had become a favorite among the crew, always treating everyone with good-natured respect. As soon as he heard the sirens, he scrambled into the bushes and trees for cover. From a prone position in the dirt, he looked back across the channel and prayed for the small ship.

The *Colhoun* had immediately turned back in an attempt to reach the relative safety of Tulagi Harbor. But eighteen Japanese bombers—called Betties—swooped down, delivering their load. Four bombs made direct hits, with one bomb plummeting straight down one of the

Colhoun's smoke stacks. She sank within two minutes, taking down with her fifty-one of her crew, almost half her complement.

Lee couldn't believe his eyes. He had just stepped off that ship—and now he witnessed the loss of so many friends. He watched, helpless to do anything.

Unfortunately, only six days later another disaster would strike these "heroic little ships." Two companies of Raiders, under command of the executive officer Lieutenant Colonel Samuel Griffith, were shuttling back from a day-long combat patrol on Savo Island. Having found the island quiet, they returned to Guadalcanal and began unloading.

Back at command headquarters, Red Mike had received orders to leave for a raid on a Japanese supply depot located in the village of Tasimboko the following morning, September 8. He sent word to Griffith just to sit tight on board the APDs, the *Little* and the *Gregory*, since Griffith's two companies would be going on the raid also. However, these orders arrived late. The Raiders, nearly at the end of their off-loading, would wait and reboard early the next morning.

The captains of the two small transports then made a decision. They would take up patrol positions just offshore instead of traveling all the way back across Sealark Channel to Tulagi Harbor, since they needed to return first thing the following morning to reload Raiders.

During the dark night, large Japanese destroyers accidentally spotted the small, vulnerable transports. It didn't take the Japanese long to find their range and deliver fatal shells to both APDs.

The captains of the *Little* and *Gregory* reluctantly gave orders to abandon ship. During the melee, both captains were killed, along with many of their crews. Those sailors who did make it into the pitch-dark waters found themselves in the blinding glare of powerful searchlights on the Japanese destroyers. The helpless men became targets of depth charges and machine gunners who mowed them down mercilessly. The next morning, Marines from the beachhead rescued survivors, including seventy who were severely wounded.

The loss of these three APDs stunned the Raiders. More than that, when the surviving sailors relayed to them that the "Japanese ships deliberately tried to kill men in the water, it left the Raiders in a cold rage."

When Lee heard the news, he lowered his head with his hand on his helmet. Closing his eyes, he was beginning to understand something about war—nothing was ever guaranteed. Each second could spell disaster. He mourned for the brave crews he and all fellow Raiders had come to value so highly.

CHAPTER IX

Raiding Bandits

A Classic Raid: Tasimboko

Red Mike Edson returned from his visit to Division Command Post within the Marine perimeter around Henderson Field on September 7, 1942. No doubt he wore a look of satisfaction. As he walked past, most Raiders recognized the now familiar, fleeting grin that sometimes flashed across Edson's face. It usually meant they were headed into a fight and that "there'd be hell to pay."

General Alexander Vandegrift, commander of 1st Marine Division, and his operations officer Colonel Gerald "Jerry" Thomas were concerned about when and where the Japanese would attack Henderson Field. Protecting the twelve-mile perimeter around this valuable piece of real estate proved increasingly difficult. The "Tokyo Express" continued to deliver more troops and supplies to the island every night. Vandegrift's perimeter defenses were growing dangerously thin.

Intelligence reports indicated the Japanese had taken a deserted village called Tasimboko and were using it as a supply depot. The village was located some eighteen miles down the coast. It would be tricky to get there with a hastily formed flotilla because of the recent APD losses. An even bigger question was whether to siphon off the eight hundred highly trained Marine Raiders desperately needed to help secure the outer perimeter defense for a mission that might turn into a complete disaster.

On the other hand, if successful, Edson's Raiders might disrupt the Japanese buildup while gathering much-needed combat intelligence.

Once the possibility of such a raid was presented to Edson, he never wavered. This was a classic-style raid for commando units—quick in-and-out, traveling light and fast, disrupting, marauding, creating chaos, and gathering intel. This is what they had trained so vigorously for months to do.

He ordered his Raiders to be ready to saddle up early the next morning, September 8. And at 4:30 a.m., 1st Raiders began their sail to shore on the Higgins boats launched from transports and two tuna boats pressed into service. Upon landing the Raiders discovered row after row of literally hundreds and hundreds of neatly stacked soldiers' packs. Each contained new leather hobnailed hiking boots and five pounds of rice. But their owners were nowhere to be seen. General Kiyotake Kawaguchi's troops lurked somewhere in the thick jungle vegetation that stood before the Raiders—but where? That was the question.

The Raiders were on high alert. They stealthily began to fan out and work their way through the jungles toward the village of Tasimboko. Along the way they would come across a machine gun nest here and there, or a sniper hiding out in the trees. The scattered pockets of Japanese resistance couldn't resist the steady, aggressive pressure that the Raiders applied as they subdued their targets and made their way to the island's supply depot.

Sometime around noon, the forward platoon pushed through the jungle foliage to find themselves at the village. As other Raiders cleared past small pockets of rear-echelon Japanese defenders, they converged on the deserted village. Wherever Kawaguchi and his troops were, they were not found in the village in any great numbers. Those unfortunate ones who remained were immediately dispatched.

Fast pillaging began. Thousands of bags of rice were cut open, strewn over the ground, and ruined with either urine or gasoline. Canned goods—what wasn't stuffed into pants and shirt pockets for consumption later by hungry Raiders—clothing, and any equipment they found were all stacked into huge piles and torched. Some found dumps of valuable first-aid supplies—what couldn't be lugged to the beach for transport back to headquarters for their own use was also set ablaze.

Around 4:30 p.m., Red Mike radioed back to headquarters. "Am destroying Tasimboko and as much property as possible."

As Lee Minier carefully made his way back to the beach, he found himself walking alongside war correspondent Richard Tregaskis. The increasingly well-known war correspondent had accompanied the troops on their raid. He was carrying an army blanket pulled together like a sack.

"Looks like you've got some souvenirs," grinned Lee to Tregaskis.

"Came across these Japanese papers in one of the huts. The colonel said bring 'em. Looked like they might be important," the reporter said back to Lee.

And the documents turned out to be just that. By midnight Division Command would know Kawaguchi's order of battle and mission orders. The information helped shape the next few weeks favorably for the Raiders.

Though the Tasimboko Raid was a "perfect little raid," the engagement produced no Medal of Honor recipients, no ships named after any Raider, and no significant articles written about it back home.

Yet, one acclaimed military historian would label it the "...perfect spoiling attack, the ideal mission for the Raiders." During the raid, Kawaguchi lost four dozen crew-served weapons and a great deal of his reserve ammunition. These losses would greatly reduce the enemy's attacks against the airfield. And losing so much of his rations and medical supplies would turn Kawaguchi's subsequent retreat through the jungles into a trail of horror.

The aftermath struck a serious blow to Japanese logistics, fire support, and communications. However, the intelligence gathered had far more serious consequences: it uncovered details of upcoming Japanese movements. Finally, these losses affected the enemy's morale while further boosting that of the Raiders. These young U.S. warriors had defeated the Japanese yet again, and were "feasting [on] the fruits of victory"—literally.

But for any overlooked brilliance the Raiders may have suffered from the Tasimboko Raid, in four days Edson's Raiders would participate in a battle yielding accolades of lasting praise. These men would soon show what it means "to defend or to die"—and how legends are made.

Fortifying the Ridge

On the morning of September 10, Edson again ordered his Raiders to saddle up. They were to break camp at the Coconut Grove and move to a place he called "a rest area." Those Raiders nearest him when the order was issued noticed once again the ever-so-slight, inscrutable grin. Then a few saw him asking men to scrounge up any and all available barbed wire. Something was up; they knew it.

The 1st Raider Battalion's numbers were down. The recent weeks of combat and patrols had taken a toll. The jungle had not played favorites either. Many were suffering from the beginnings of malaria, dysentery, and other maladies related to jungle living, poor diet, and little sleep. For this deployment, Edson also called out 1st Marine Parachute Battalion, a unit who had suffered more casualties than his Raiders. The Para-Marines were now down to about two hundred men who could go into battle. Edson headed to the dubious "rest area" with approximately seven hundred men.

Their new home for the next five days would be a coral ridge located south of Henderson Field. One of many ridges on the island of Guadalcanal, it was located between the Lunga River on one side and the Tenaru River on the other. 1st Raider Executive Officer Samuel Griffith described it as a coral spine shaped like a swimming crocodile or hammerhead shark. It formed a gently curving "S" in a northeast-by-southwest orientation.

On top a dirt road striped its length, a feature troops would later appreciate.

The middle to southernmost sections were relatively high, with tropical jungles pressing up against its steep sides. At the northernmost point, the ridge began to slope downward and provided a spectacular view—and therefore a spectacular vantage point—of the prize: Henderson Field. A mere fifteen acres comprised the geographical feature Red Mike Edson marched his Raiders to. But that scant piece of real estate was the key to controlling the dirt airfield at its northern end. And the dirt airfield held the key of control not only for Guadalcanal but also the surrounding islands and waterways.

When Vandegrift had landed elements of his 1st Marine Division on August 7 (as Edson and the 1st Raiders were invading Tulagi), his Marines were met with relatively little resistance. Now they knew—many thanks to intelligence just gathered by Raiders on the Tasimboko Raid—that Kawaguchi had amassed over three thousand troops to reclaim the airfield. Even now, reports confirmed they were cutting their way through the thick jungles from the south.

General Vandegrift enunciated a summation of their precarious situation to his intelligence officer Colonel Jerry Thomas with bleak clarity: "We can't let this be another Bataan."

As the Raiders marched to the ridge, Lee still felt lingering effects of the Tasimboko Raid. Little sleep and scant food for the past several weeks left him wishing for a nice, hot meal followed by a long nap—perhaps a series of them. Once there, however, orders came down to begin to dig in. Training and dedication kicked in.

Lacking an E-tool (entrenching tool), Lee took off his helmet and began banging away at the coral ridge only covered by a couple inches of dirt. Ever the optimist, he encouraged those around him, who muttered a few choice names for their commander.

"I thought the ole man said we were going to a rest area," grumbled one to Lee, who just chuckled back.

"Well, I guess I'll need to have a talk with him."

Besides continuing the frustrating work of pounding out shallow depressions in the ground, Raiders strung what little barbed wire they had to bolster up their perimeter. Ammunition and hand grenades were distributed as evenly as possible among the front line.

Edson had positioned his front line near the southern end of the ridge, bisecting it roughly from a westerly direction toward the east. At his rear closer to the airfield, General Vandegrift had stationed the 2nd Battalion of his 5th Marines (sometimes written as 2/5) as a backstop. Another critically important element Edson felt fortunate to have behind him were the howitzers of Colonel Pedro del Valle and the 11th Marines. Colonel del Valle and his officers spent much of September 11 with their artillery teams surveying and plotting. Then, finally, they moved three batteries of 105-millimeter howitzers into supporting positions.

If any Raider needed additional proof that this would not be a time of rest, the 26 Japanese Betty bombers that bypassed Henderson Field and headed straight for the ridge put the matter beyond a reasonable doubt. The planes delivered a shellacking of 500-pound bombs inter-mixed with daisy cutters. Samuel Griffith said later, "Marines who clawed a few inches deeper into their holes or flung themselves behind logs emerged shaking but safe. Those who stood, or ran aimlessly...were killed or wounded by flying splinters.... [I]n the aftermath, men silently brushed dirt from their dungarees [and] suddenly knew that the Japs would—this night, or some night soon to come—swarm screaming out of the jungle...."

During the night of September 11, every Raider was on high alert. The surrounding jungles seemed alive with all sorts of noises—crackles and clicking sounds, chattering between all sorts of creatures and var-mints. It required steady nerves to remain calm and discern if a noise was man-made or natural. Sleeping, if there was any, was sporadic as the dark hours crept on. When would the attack begin? Nobody knew, and the thought of a Japanese horde emerging from the tree line at any moment kept the Raiders up all night.

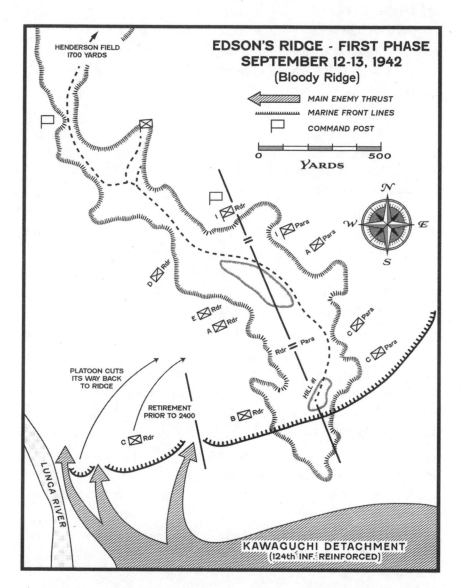

7. Edson's Ridge (Guadalcanal)—first phase of the battle, September 12–13, 1942

A Sleepless Night

Nobody came that night, and the morning of September 12 arrived with blistering heat atop the ridge. Lee spent part of the day trying to deepen his foxhole, which never really was more than a shallow depression.

He used his bayonet to clear a semblance of a pathway through the kunai grass, waist-high in spots. Others who manned machine guns did the same. The cleared paths would give them a more direct line of sight for firing into any oncoming enemy.

But it was exhausting, slow work. More than once Lee wondered how much he would be willing to pay for a mower right about then. The tall grass cut through cloth and skin with its sharp, serrated edges and was so dense that it wrapped around his legs completely when he tried to move forward. At ground level, the roots formed a tangled, emerald-green mat that was easy to trip in.

Four additional bombing raids marked daylight hours, during which all work would stop—except for attempting to find cover. Everyone generally agreed that this coming night might be when the attack would commence. But there was no way to know for certain.

However, something else happened on September 12—a completely unexpected event, but much welcomed by all. Major Ken Bailey, one of the Raider company commanders who had been severely wounded in the thigh during their invasion of Tulagi, suddenly appeared on the ridge, to everyone's utter surprise. He had been hospitalized in Nouméa, New Caledonia, and had walked out unauthorized. Ken, along with another hospital escapee, Lieutenant "Spike" Ryder, hitched rides to Guadalcanal.

When Ken appeared at the ridge, those Raiders who saw him realized he was still weak, not nearly healed. His tenacious grit, however, boosted everyone's morale, especially in his old company.

His sudden return carried another welcome bonus. Ken brought back with him hundreds of mail bags. Quietly and quickly, mail was distributed—letters which had been held up for weeks. It was the first mail call since the campaign had begun. In between fortifying foxholes and four additional Japanese bombardments on this Saturday, in this far-off part of the South Pacific, Raiders read welcome notes from loved ones and friends. The mail couldn't have come at a better time.

Lee Minier received his letters eagerly. There were two from his mom, one from his sister-in-law, Ann, and twenty-five from his girl-friend, Marge. Carefully folded inside the letters were a couple of small, black-and-white photos, including one of Marge herself.

He had been away from home nearly ten months now. In a piercing rush of nostalgia, Lee suddenly wished he could be breathing the cool, mountain air of the Adirondacks in Upstate New York with Marge at his side. He took off his helmet and tucked these small treasures under the webbing inside. It was the only place that might be somewhat "safe" during battle.

The Raiders on the ridge endured four more bombing runs during the day of September 12. Before dusk, battalion cooks made every effort to provide a bit of a hot meal to the troops in their positions across the line. They heated and distributed cans of Vienna sausage and small potatoes along with coffee as hot as possible under the circumstances. It helped boost everyone's spirits—that is, until a hard tropical downpour soaked the waiting warriors.

At approximately 9:00 p.m., a single Japanese plane flew overhead and dropped a green incendiary flare. Waiting Japanese warships off the coast saw the signal and adjusted their heavy, long-range guns. Almost immediately shells commenced from a cruiser and three destroyers. A short silence followed.

Lee knew what the noises meant: the attack was about to begin.

The Descent into Hell
September 12–13

Japanese troops initiated their attack with scattered small-arms fire mixed with intermittent mortar bombardments. The Raiders responded in kind along the line Edson had established as his forward position.

Behind this line of Raiders, del Valle's artillery unleashed preplanned salvos at selected areas in the surrounding jungles. Lee could hear the volleys whizzing over his head, even though he stretched out flat on his belly behind his machine gun.

"Keep your heads down, boys," he yelled to his machine gun team. "Let's not lose our helmets—or what's in 'em."

The din of battle ramped up, and Kawaguchi's brigade moved in earnest now. Lee could hear them crashing through the jungle. Then, suddenly, they came forth at a trot, slapping their rifle butts and yelling obscenities and oaths of doom at the top of their lungs.

It wasn't long before a jagged wave of enemy troops carried the slopes of the ridge, mainly along Edson's right flank. They were met with a hail of small-arms and machine gun fire from the Raiders. Then, just as suddenly, in several spots along the southwest section, Japanese soldiers met Raiders face-to-face in hand-to-hand combat.

At one point during the fighting, enemy troops broke through the Raider line in the lower-lying area between the ridge and the Lunga River. This swampy area, complete with a lagoon, was especially difficult to maneuver in. At one point, a group of Raiders was completely surrounded by enemy combatants. Under great duress, they were able to hold on. However, the melee resulted in seven missing Raiders, who were never found.

Close to daybreak, after a period of furious fighting on both sides, Raiders finally managed to reorganize in this section and contain the incursion of Japanese troops. The enemy broke off and retreated back into the jungle. But every Marine knew they would return. This night had just been round one.

Later that morning, Edson told his officers and unit leaders that Kawaguchi was simply testing the line to find weak spots. It wouldn't be until much later that Edson would gain information about his opponent's nighttime troubles.

The Japanese commander had been less than pleased with the performance of his men. The jungle had seemed to disorganize them, and for several hours all were in a state of disarray. Kawaguchi would later express his immense frustration at the troops' lack of organization in his field reports. And to add to the confusion of this initial advance, his communications suffered glitches throughout the night.

Years later, Samuel Griffith in his personal memoirs would also offer his own succinct opinion of that night: "The [Japanese] Army had been used to fighting the Chinese."

The Battle Continues

As the sun claimed the sky with mounting heat and humidity, the Raiders had no time to recuperate from the night's fighting. Carefully and ever mindful of random attacks or tree snipers, they did what they could to reestablish barbed wire and foxholes.

They also worked on what Edson planned as a "surprise" for the Japanese when they attacked next. It called for a gradual and systematic withdrawal all along the line back toward the northern end of the ridge. The Raiders would tighten up into a horseshoe-shaped line, the top of the curve pointing toward the oncoming assailants.

This would force the Japanese to follow the Raiders and parachutists across nearly a hundred yards of open terrain atop the ridge. Using this method, the Raiders could rain down a torrent of small arms, machine guns, mortars, and artillery as the attackers attempted to gain the crest.

At sundown the Raiders settled into waiting, surrounded only by the strange tropical jungle noises. Each man knew that any second could produce renewed hordes of Japanese, leaping and screaming from the surrounding dense foliage.

At 9:00 p.m. another lone Japanese plane flew over and dropped yet another green flare. Seconds later seven enemy destroyers from Sealark Channel initiated an hour's bombardment of explosive projectiles. On this night the enemy did not wait for that bombardment to end. The entire ridge suddenly erupted in fighting.

A red signal flare unleashed two reinforced Japanese battalions, over two thousand men against a total force of seven hundred men, mostly Raiders, along with a dwindling number of Marine parachutists.

At the same time, del Valle's 11th Marines again fired their howitzers into the oncoming mass of Imperial soldiers. Raiders lit up their machine guns and automatic weapons. Many of the adversaries that made it through this fiery wall of steel and mortar tumbled headlong into Raider positions. Some were bodily tossed back out of the shallow depressions used as foxholes.

Raider stilettos and blades flashed in retaliation to swords and bayonets. The fight was mortal combat, close-quarters, even hand-to-hand. No one escaped battle that night.

Edson had stationed himself immediately behind this secondary horseshoe line in order to relay messages as needed to the howitzers. Often during the night, he would move right up to the line to assess and determine ranges for himself. Those who saw him, often without wearing his helmet, would always remember how he seemed to display little regard for his own personal safety.

As the enemy pressed ever nearer, Red Mike would relay to the spotters: "Closer," then again: "Closer." Lee had thought the howitzers sent shells close to the top of his head the night before. But these were razor close. He had no idea how he wasn't hit with one of them—the booming sound was deafening.

Up and down the ridge, desperate calls of "Another belt! Another barrel!" could be heard. And all during the night, Major Ken Bailey, limping in pain from his wounds, made repeated trips into the midst of the fighting himself. Grenade after grenade was thrown, from one side of the line to another—sometimes at point-blank range of its intended human target. Without Bailey's courageous supply runs, the Raiders would have lacked the needed grenades and ammunition to keep the fight going.

Outnumbered three to one in the assault, the Raider line began to buckle under the sheer weight of superior numbers. At midnight, though

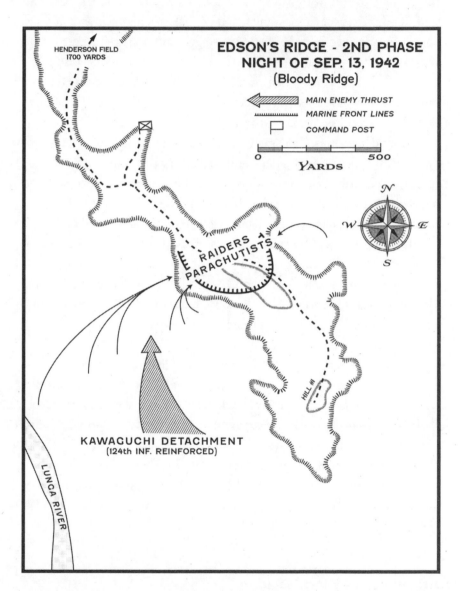

8. Edson's Ridge—second phase, night of September 13, 1942

the American line was still intact, it was strained. The Raiders had withstood two successive assaults, and both flanks had held, but at great cost. A few dazed troops happened to stagger into the area where Edson was positioned in order to direct the howitzers—in reality just yards back. Seeing them, he yelled out, "Get back to where you were! The only thing they have that you don't is guts!" It made the intended impression. The exhausted fighters stumbled back into the fray.

Around 2:00 a.m. Kawaguchi unleashed yet another screaming rush against the Raider line. Edson finally called for the planned "surprise" further up and back on the ridge. Here, the Raiders compressed and nearly back-to-back with each other, would be the final stand—every Raider knew it. Now was the time…a Raider "kills or is killed."

The attack was furious and vicious. A sudden flash of thousands of rounds of artillery; tracer shells arching though the dark of night; the crash of mortars; screams of men in anger and agony. The attack "was almost constant, like rain that subsides for a moment and then pours harder." But the Raiders and their courageous counterparts did not intend to move back anymore.

Shortly past 2:00 a.m., the enemy forces pushed to within a fifth of a mile of Henderson Field. In a total of twelve determined assaults, Kawaguchi's brigade tried to beat back the Raiders and parachutists from their brave defense of the airstrips. But, summoning it up from deep within, these courageous warriors stood the test—they would not be moved any further back on this night…*not on this night.*

Just before a fiery dawn, Red Mike Edson rang up Colonel Jerry Thomas back at Division Headquarters with a simple message: "We can hold."

Aftermath of Bloody Ridge

As a pale dawn broke, riflemen on both sides now had visible targets. The ridge became, if possible, even deadlier.

Edson hastily drew up a map of where Japanese troops remained. Thrusting it into Ken Bailey's exhausted hands, he sent the map to General Vandegrift requesting air support. As soon as daylight permitted, three P-400s (Bell P-39 Airacobras) led by Army captain John A. Thompson of the 67th Fighter Squadron headed for the ridge.

As Thompson flew over the trees, he saw the Marines on top of the ridge. A little further on, in a small clearing along one slope, hundreds of Japanese huddled together and were caught by surprise. The three planes, with toothy sharks' mouths painted on their noses, blazed away at the remnants of Kawaguchi's brigade. On their final pass, ground fire clipped all three planes. They limped back to Henderson Field for emergency landings.

But the decisive nail in the coffin had been delivered. The Japanese general knew it was over. Shortly past noon, he called for the withdrawal of his troops back into the forbidding jungle. His retreat would produce its own deadly conditions: a tortuous journey for the wounded and weakened troops. They hacked their way through tangled vines and thick undergrowth, soon without any food or fresh water. Many would die before reaching their encampment.

Now, the full light of day revealed just how truly dark the night had been. Dead bodies lay strewn all over the ridge: corpses of Japanese, sometimes piled high one on top of another, bloody and mangled. Interspersed here and there were fallen Raiders, many already unrecognizable.

By midmorning, Vandegrift had begun sending in his reserve troops from the 2/5 to relieve the Raiders and the parachutists. These fresh troops provided a much-needed boost to the bone-weary men who had had no break from intense battle for thirty-six hours. Small groups lurched back toward Edson's command post. By this time, however, they didn't have far to travel: the CP was located only a couple dozen yards behind the line itself. Most took only a few steps, collapsing against trees or fallen logs. Some stood around, weapons hanging from limp arms, staring out over the carnage.

One Raider recalled collapsing down beside a palm tree with legs stretched straight out. As he fumbled to light a cigarette, Edson himself, still without a helmet, squatted down beside him.

"I've got a real fighting unit here," the commander rasped.

The drained Raider could only stare and nod.

As the men trudged back to their bivouac area in the coconut grove, most were fatigued beyond hunger, even past their ability to sleep. The fighting had been so intense, it would take days to absorb the past thirty-six hours. Like film that plays at fast speed and needs to be rewound and watched over and over to make sense of it, this would take a while to process. They sat around in small groups, barely talking. Some smoked cigarettes; others just sat holding their helmets.

When Lee passed by the aid station, he ducked in to ask a medic to look at his left arm. During the first night, shrapnel had ripped flesh off it. He had yanked a strip of canvas from his helmet to tie it up and curtail the bleeding somewhat. But now it throbbed and needed attention.

A medic cleaned out the wound, then applied clean bandages. "If you want to stay here a while—you can," he told Lee.

"Naw—I'll keep up with my boys," Lee said, slowly rising. "Thanks for this." He held up his freshly bandaged left arm and trudged to catch up with his buddies.

As the weary troops sat around, Raider Jack Paulette from Tampa Bay, Florida, turned to Lee. "Sing us something, Lee," he begged. Several others looked up and quietly nodded their approval at the suggestion. Each one was dealing with the sights and sounds from the bloody battle in his own way. They were all aware of his beautiful baritone voice—he had entertained them many times before.

Lee sat down on a log and settled himself. After a moment, he began to sing softly: this time not the raucous and fun beer-drinking songs, but beautiful melodies and church hymns. That night after the battle on the ridge, he began slowly with "Ol' Man River," one of his favorite songs. The lyrics seemed apropos for the moment:

You and me
We sweat and strain
Body all aching
And wracked with pain...
But ol' man river
He just keeps rolling along.

Then, Lee paused and began a hymn he remembered from attending church back home with his aunt who raised him—"Nearer, My God, to Thee":

Nearer, my God, to Thee, nearer to Thee,
E'en though it be a cross that raiseth me.
Still all my song shall be, nearer,
My God, to Thee,
Nearer, my God, to Thee, nearer to Thee.

His mellow voice echoed through the darkness, a balm for their spirits. Later he would admit to his mother in a letter—"You need God out here."

Many Raiders testified in following years that hearing Lee sing that night helped them recover from the Battle of Bloody Ridge. One Raider friend said that Lee had the uncanny ability "to calm a person when they were afraid."

Another said, "When you're young and go through the things that we all did, you're scared. Day and night we lived with the thought of death, and it was pretty hard to take. But, I remember those evenings on Guadalcanal, when Lee would softly sing songs for us—and the sound of his voice would take us away from that fear for just a while."

◆　◆　◆

The casualties the Raiders suffered in the Battle of Bloody Ridge are still hard to count. Generally accepted numbers are 34 Raiders killed and 129 wounded. The parachutists under Edson's purview lost a proportionately greater number than the Raiders, as there were 128 casualties out of the roughly 200 men who started the battle. Total losses easily exceeded 20 percent of his command.

The lack of reliable accounting is also true for the Kawaguchi Brigade, which initially totaled as many as three thousand soldiers, perhaps more. (Most historians agree the Raiders were outnumbered at least three to one.) Over six hundred Japanese soldiers were counted dead that day on the ridge and along its slopes. According to Japanese reports after the war, another nine hundred were wounded, and untold numbers likely died on their harrowing return trip through the jungles. They retreated with no food, fresh water, or medical supplies as a result of the Raiders' successful Tasimboko Raid on the enemy supply depot the previous week.

When U.S. action summaries were later written, Raider unit leaders found it hard to distinguish one remarkable deed from another, as so many courageous and brave acts had occurred. Everyone knew what had been at stake. Had the Raiders and parachutists failed, the landing strip would have returned to enemy hands. As one Marine historian surmises, "…[L]ack of air cover probably would have led to the defeat of the 1st Marine Division and the loss of Guadalcanal. Such a reversal would have had a grave impact on the course of the war and the future of the Corps."

Both Edson and Bailey were awarded the highest honor of our country, the Medal of Honor. General Vandegrift cited Red Mike Edson's "cool leadership and personal courage." Of Ken Bailey, Vandegrift noted "his great personal valor while exposed to constant and merciless enemy fire and his indomitable fighting spirit."

The Navy Cross, second only to the Medal of Honor for esteeming courage and bravery, was awarded to fourteen men. This meant that over the 36-hour battle, individual Raiders merited Navy Crosses at the rate of one every couple of hours or so. Ironically, there were so many who displayed outstanding courage among the Raiders during their existence that the 24 ships named after individual 1st Raiders in the months and years to come didn't include any from this group except for Edson himself.

In short, valor was a common commodity among these men.

CHAPTER X

On the River of Death

M en recovered slowly from the battle for the ridge. Returning to their bivouac site provided much-needed rest. And Lee, like many others, benefited from the backlog of mail to sift through and from having the chance to write his loved ones back home.

In the following letter written to his mom back in Prospect, New York, Lee shows his sense of humor and easygoing manner even in the midst of a battlefield. In all his letters home, he tried not to include anything that might disturb his mother. He knew how much she worried about him and missed him. Always good-natured, he ends this particular letter with a humorous lexicon of Marine slang:

Dear Mom:

Your loving son is lying on his bunk recovering from a terrific battle with a huge rat that was trying to steal some of my gear from our tent. Rats here are as big as boar hogs in the corn belt. A few nights ago I heard a roaring sound and thinking it was an air raid, jumped up and rushed bravely out to open fire, only to be floored by the forward echelon of a mosquito attack. It was the night shift coming on. They put on a double shift that night or I could have held my own with them.

You can see that your son is leading an especially hazardous life. We have our moments of relaxation though. We have trained a centipede to walk on 99 legs and wave a baton with his other leg. He leads an orchestra made up of flies, ants, and other centipedes. But seriously though, I am having a pretty good time.

I received your letter with two dollars. Thanks very much. Don't send any money but you might send some other things sometime if you want to send something—Like a flash light with extra bubbles and batteries, some air mail stamps, a knife. Might also send aspirins, gauze, tape, and iodine for small cuts and bites. Things like this are hard to get.

I'm enclosing a list of expressions used by Marines that I thought would be interesting.

Definition of terms or sayings:

Secure—stop doing whatever your [*sic*] doing.
Belay—stop or change that.
No boats—no liberty or no way of going on liberty if allowed
    it
Going ashore—going on liberty whether you're on land or
    sea
Beat your molars or Chip your teeth—to complain or gripe
Snowing the troops—bragging or telling big lies
Head—toilet
Hear rumor or Scuttlebutt—rumors or unconfirmed talk
Boondocks—hiking or maneuvers in the jungle
Sick bay—hospital

Sick bay soldier—anyone who goes to doctor or corpsman
   with every little ache
Slop chute—tavern or bar
Skipper—commanding officer of company
Chow hand—big eater
Good or bad dope—good news or bad
The word—anything you're supposed to know or any order
   that's given
Get the word—know what's going on
Crap out—fall out or give out during a hike
Sack—bed or cot
Sack time—bed time
Pogey bait—candy
Dog face—soldier in Army
Swab jockey—sailor
Gook—native of tropical places where Marines are stationed
Ear banger or to bang ears—try to gain favor with officers
   or non-comers by talking
Own-way—a fellow that's selfish or stubborn
"Glad I found you out"—glad I know what kind of fellow
   you are
Sing'em or Sing the blues—complain or gripe
By the numbers—supply or regulation
Regulation Marine—a fellow that insists on things being
   just so

Love, Lee

Family members back in the States with loved ones off at war lived from one letter to the next. Lee's mother treasured the messages from her son and never failed to record in her daily journal that she had heard from him on a day when she received one. Like so many thousands of other mothers, she ended her day with prayers. "My boy is so fine. Please,

Lord, keep Lee safe"—a prayer that was no doubt repeated millions of times by mothers everywhere, just with different names.

The First Battle of Matanikau River

The Raiders had fought brilliantly on the ridge with Marine parachutists alongside. The toll, however, was staggering. Marine parachutists left Guadalcanal on September 17 to recuperate in Nouméa, having sustained casualties of over 55 percent. The 1st Raiders remained on the 'Canal, but with greatly diminished numbers, with over 33 percent suffering casualties. It is the old military adage: when you perform well, you are given more opportunities to perform well again.

After barely six days to rest and recuperate, Vandegrift called on the Raiders once again—this time to reconnoiter south of Edson's Ridge and destroy any Japanese stragglers.

On that same day, Vandegrift made several shifts in command positions. He placed Colonel Merritt Edson in command of the 5th Marines (not Raiders), a regular Marine line regiment, totaling at the time nearly five thousand men. Edson's name, nevertheless, would forever be associated with 1st Raider Battalion.

At the same time, Vandegrift named executive officer Lieutenant Colonel Samuel Griffith to replace Red Mike as commander of the 1st Raider Battalion. The men knew well the strengths of their new leader.

Griffith had come from tough fighting experiences in Nicaragua and China. In those matters, he was as respected as Edson. And he was an intellectual as well as a practical militarist. In later years, Griffith would receive a Ph.D. in Chinese Studies at Oxford and translate Sun Tzu's *The Art of War* into English with his own personal experiences in warfare providing a particularly unique perspective. Griffith continued well the tradition of interesting and accomplished men as leaders of the Raiders.

With the new mission of hunting down Japanese stragglers set, Lieutenant Colonel Lewis B. "Chesty" Puller departed the Henderson

Field perimeter at dawn on September 24 with his 1st Battalion, 7th Marines. He planned to go to the headwaters of the Matanikau River, cross it, and patrol from there north to Kokumbona village.

Two days later, on September 26, 1st Raiders were to proceed west along the beach road to Kokumbona. Once there they were to establish a permanent patrol base.

Puller ran into far greater numbers of enemy troops than expected. In fact, there was a veritable hornet's nest on the slopes of Mt. Austen. The 2/5 Marines were called in as reinforcements and shortly ran into trouble as well.

When Raiders arrived at the Matanikau, they were told to halt there and bivouac for the night. Unfortunately, when they arrived, 1st Raiders suffered two stinging casualties.

As a group of sergeants and unit leaders conferred on one side of the river in a small semicircle, a sniper's bullet whizzed throughout the tree leaves. Everyone in the group hit the deck. One of the sergeants looked to his left and saw Major Ken Bailey, who had just received news of his Medal of Honor award for outstanding courage and bravery during the Battle of Bloody Ridge, kneeling with his head bowed in his hands.

The sergeant called out to him, but Ken didn't answer. He pulled on Ken's ankle, and the fearless man tumbled over on his back. A sniper's bullet had pierced the lionhearted Raider squarely between the eyes, killing him instantly.

As word of this tragic event swept through the Raiders, no one could hold back his dismay. Ken Bailey was a Marine's Marine. He had come to them straight from the hospital to assist on the ridge. He had brought them the mail backlog and limped all up and down the lines throughout the two nights. After surviving the Battle of Bloody Ridge, to now be killed "with his hands in his pocket," as one Raider put it, was nearly too much for the group to bear.

To add to the general malaise, later that same afternoon, Commander Sam Griffith was shot through the shoulder and seriously wounded. Although in great pain, he refused to be evacuated until late in the day when the entire operation was called off and all units were ordered to report back to the Lunga position closer to the airfield. Lieutenant Colonel Griffith had been commander of 1st Raider Battalion for one week. To take over his command while his shoulder healed, Griffith turned over 1st Raiders to Captain Ira J. Irwin, the battalion supply officer and only senior officer remaining in the 1st Raider Battalion.

Four days they had been on the Matanikau River maneuvering up and down. During that short time, a total of sixty Marines had been killed, and more than one hundred wounded. And, though Raiders themselves suffered few casualties, they lost two of their superstars—one of them forever.

Second Battle of the Matanikau River

After two months of steady fighting in the extreme conditions of a tropical jungle, the 1st Raider Battalion was worn down. One Raider said it would have been "near impossible to see a sicklier, more bedraggled, miserable bunch of Marines anywhere." But they had one more battle to fight before they were given time off to rest and heal.

In early October, reports indicated the Japanese were once more building up for yet another attack against the perimeter around Henderson Field. The "Tokyo Express," originating from the Shortland Islands to the north, had been busy bringing Japanese replacements to the western shores of the island. These ferrying operations had been under the leadership of Rear Admiral Raizo Tanaka. This particular admiral has come to be considered one of the truly exceptional men to emerge from the ranks of Imperial Navy officers. His daring, resourcefulness, and clear thinking in combat were displayed several times over the course of the Guadalcanal campaign. Allied tacticians were both confounded and duly respectful of his prowess in reinforcing the Japanese garrison on the 'Canal.

At their command base in Rabaul, Imperial Army lieutenant general Harukichi Hyakutake of the 17th Army completed strategic plans for deployment of the famed "Sendai Division" on Guadalcanal under the leadership of Lieutenant General Masao Maruyama. Planned drops of troops, tanks, artillery pieces, and trucks for October 3, 8, and 11 would establish a combat-ready division to take back Henderson Field and restore dominance on Guadalcanal. Their intended goal: to establish a permanent base along the sandspit on the Matanikau River where it emptied into the ocean. The sandy area level with the sea made a perfect place for off-loading tanks, trucks, heavy weapons, and matériel to supply the invasion forces. The river provided a perfect transit deep into the jungles.

So certain were the Japanese of their plans that they even included a fixed surrender date for General Alexander Vandegrift: October 15.

Vandegrift had plans of his own. He wished to establish a stronghold close to Kokumbona. So doing, he could take command of the mouth of the Matanikau and thereby deny its use by the enemy. The general planned to use five infantry battalions with Red Mike Edson leading the tactical plan in battle. The attack date was set for October 8, 1942.

At daybreak on October 7, the American forces began their march toward the river. The first contact with Japanese forces occurred about a half mile west of the river bank. The enemy strongpoint, considered by the Americans to be a reinforced company, was located 150 yards upstream and only some 200 feet away from the river mouth on the east bank.

The Japanese began to withdraw to their prepared defense position around the sandspit. Division leaders were well aware of the enemy's intention to fight to the last man and felt that this force would try to hold on and even break out at any cost.

As fighting intensified, Edson felt the need to call upon his trusted Raiders, though battle-weary and decimated.

Edson's call-up of the exhausted Raiders gave way to one Raider's nicknaming Edson "Mad Merritt, the Morgue-Master." But there was also an inner pride in all of them that he would reach out in faith to his former Raiders. Once they arrived, Vandegrift and Edson felt they could proceed on the following day.

During the night, however, a torrential tropical downpour kept everyone hunkered down in whatever shallow depression could be found. The storm was so intense that Edson called off the multi-battalion sweep of the area for another twenty-four hours. The Raiders took advantage of the weather to settle in as securely as possible and wait. The next morning the other Raider companies arrived and were deployed along the river with skirmishes here and there. But the main Japanese force waited under pressure for the night and the darkness that suited their style of jungle fighting.

As darkness fell once more over the island, the Raiders remained in their foxholes, exhausted, many sick with various tropical illnesses— hardly combat-ready. However, when the Japanese made their move, the Raider lines displayed their valor once more, like cream that rises to the top, against superior numbers of enemy soldiers.

The attack came suddenly and without warning. The jungle erupted with yelling and sword-swinging combatants. The Raiders went to their knives, the wicked stiletto daggers and sharp Bowie blades. It was mortal combat in the dark of night.

One account describes a Raider surprised in his foxhole by a sword-bearing Japanese who slashed his back. The Raider caught part of the blow on his left arm and with his free right hand took the enemy down by the throat and tore out his windpipe. A few others, however, were jumped upon too quickly to even respond and were killed by sword in the onslaught. Gunfire, screams, and cursing filled the air as Japanese overran the Marine positions.

Raider Lieutenant Robert P. Neuffer, "A" Company commander, who had served under Edson since the beginning, reported the dire circumstances. Edson, in his now familiar way, said back, "Neuffer, you will hold your position." The Raider officer brought together some of those in the process of retreating, enough to form a secondary line. Slowly, the course of fighting began to shift to the Raiders' advantage.

At one point in the fighting, Lee Minier's weapon jammed. When he looked up, he saw three Japanese soldiers on top of him. He picked

Corporal Lee N. Minier, 1st Marine Raider Battalion. *Courtesy Minier family collection.*

Private First Class Kenneth "Mudhole" Merrill, 2nd Marine Raider Battalion. *Courtesy Merrill/Folsom family collection.*

Lieutenant Archibald Boyd Rackerby, 3rd Marine Raider Battalion. *Courtesy Rackerby family collection.*

BLOMBERG, EDwin R
Enl   19Aug42:
Taken   26Aug42,

3———————63
:)———————6'
9———————59'
6———————56'
3———————53'

4 4 2 7 4 0

Private First Class Edwin "the Swede" Blomberg, 4th Marine Raider Battalion. *Courtesy Blomberg family collection.*

Lieutenant Colonel Merritt A. Edson, commander of 1st Marine Raider Battalion. *USMC Archives.*

Lieutenant Colonel Evans Fordyce Carlson, commander of 2nd Marine Raider Battalion. *USMC Archives.*

Colonel Harry Bluett "Harry the Horse" Liversedge, commander of 3rd Marine Raider Battalion. *USMC Archives.*

Major James "Jimmy" Roosevelt, commander of 4th Marine Raider Battalion. *USMC Archives.*

The HMNZS *Monowai* was contracted for service during World War II, like many cruise ships from all over the world. The *Monowai* carried units from 1st Raider Battalion toward the Solomon Islands for D-Day, August 7, 1942, the invasion of Guadalcanal. Among those aboard was Raider Lee Minier. *Courtesy Reuben Goosens, ssmaritime.com.*

Dr. Lee N. Minier, Raider Lee Minier's nephew and namesake, standing atop Edson's Bloody Ridge on Guadalcanal. During the battle of September 12 and 13, 1942, this particular area provided an excellent view down the ridge and was the probable site of Raider Lee Minier's machine gun team. *Courtesy Minier family collection.*

Looking from the southern tip of Tulagi Island across Sealark Channel in the late '30s. The residence on the right, built in typical island style, was one of several used by British government officials of the Solomon Islands Protectorate. Once the Japanese invaded the Solomons, these buildings housed Japanese officers. *Courtesy Minier family collection.*

Ed Blomberg and his bothers during World War II, from left to right: John, Army, 30th Infantry, Regulation Company A, 3rd Division, France and Germany, shot in the stomach; Ivar, Army, 1945–1946, Field Artillery Training Center, Fort Bragg, North Carolina; Alan, Air Force, 1942–1945, bombardier, 15th Air Force, Italy, flew 35 missions; Ed "the Swede," 4th Marine Raider Battalion. *Courtesy Blomberg family collection.*

Members of 4th Marine Raider Battalion shortly after the New Georgia Campaign, fall 1943. *Courtesy Blomberg family collection.*

Sergeant Major Jacob C. Vouza, one of the courageous natives living in the Solomons who provided scouts, carriers, and valuable intel to Marines throughout the South Pacific campaigns. *Courtesy Blomberg family collection.*

Mudhole Merrill holds a Japanese flag removed from the rifle of an enemy combatant during the Makin Raid. *Courtesy Merrill/Folsom family collection.*

The Singing Eight Balls, mostly from 1st Raider Battalion, regularly performed for the U.S. troops serving in the South Pacific. Pictured here on New Caledonia in 1943 are (from left to right): George Ward, Rufus Rogers (partially hidden), Bill Vollack, Ed Dunn, Jinx Powers, Joe Kennedy, Eugene "Rebel" Fullerton, and Lee Minier. *USMC Archives.*

2nd Raider Battlion carefully patrolling its way up a river, always wary of its vulnerable exposure to Japanese snipers. *USMC Archives.*

1st Raider Battalion officers. Lieutenant Colonel and commander of 1st Raiders Merritt "Red Mike" Edson sits in the front row, second from the left. *USMC Archives.*
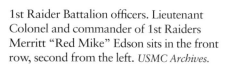

Raiders kneeling during Mass on Guadalcanal. Lee Minier attended early morning Mass, regularly writing home, "You need God out here." *USMC Archives.*

Raider scout and patrol dogs with their handlers on Bougainville. Raider dogs, from left to right: Jack (Dobie), Jack (German shepherd), Otto, and Caesar. *USMC Archives.*

Aerial view of Henderson Field, Guadalcanal, after the Seabees straightened the airstrip; originally the Japanese used circular strips. *USMC Archives.*

Mudhole Merrill wearing his leather jacket with a Raider death-skull patch on one side and a 2nd Raider Battalion patch on the other. Also shown is the newly designed 2016 Marine Forces Special Operations insignia for current Marine Raiders: an eagle with outstretched wings grasping a stiletto-style dagger. *Courtesy Merrill/Folsom family collection.*

Helen and Archie Rackerby attending a Marine Raider Reunion in 2016, a few years after their marriage. *Courtesy Rackerby family collection.*

Ed "the Swede" Blomberg celebrated his hundredth birthday during the writing of this book. The Swede served with 4th Raider Battalion on New Georgia in 1943. *Courtesy Blomberg family collection.*

up his Browning automatic rifle and used it to club two of the men in the face, then stripped away a bayonet from the third and dispatched all three with their own knife. The long hours of hand-to-hand combat training at Quantico paid off that night on the River of Death.

The thrust of the Japanese charge shifted toward the river mouth, where the Raiders had strung wire and emplaced heavy machine guns. These weapons, as at the Tenaru River and at the ridge earlier in the campaign, harvested their deadly numbers. The main attack was contained in a 45-minute firefight. Other smaller encounters punctuated the night.

At daylight the Raiders surveyed the carnage. They had destroyed the enemy force in the nighttime combat. Fifty-nine Japanese had died, many at the wire strung by the river's mouth. Twenty-two Raiders had been wounded and twelve more had lost their lives during the bitter fighting.

General Vandegrift and Colonel Edson had come to the advance area on the morning of the ninth to assess the situation. As Richard Wheeler relates in *A Special Valor*, the general asked, "Who did this job?" Edson looked around the scene. In a rare show of emotion, he choked out, "My Raiders, sir."

Vandegrift quickly responded, "They're my Raiders now."

CHAPTER XI

Paradise Lost

Sun, Sand, and Smiles

Mudhole's combat boots sank deep into the plush Oriental carpets as he strolled slowly down the long, ornate hotel gallery. Aromatic shops filled with toiletries, souvenirs, beach towels, and swim gear lined both sides. Here and there, large vases of plumeria and orchids adorned massive mahogany sideboards, adding their exotic colors and scents to the atmosphere. Everything breathed luxury.

The Royal Hawaiian on Waikiki Beach—the Pink Palace of the Pacific—lived up to its billing. After the Japanese bombed Pearl Harbor, the U.S. Navy Recreation and Morale Office leased the hotel for a massive rest and relaxation center for Navy personnel. For a couple of days after returning to Hawaii from the grueling Makin Raid, Carlson's Raiders would benefit from this arrangement.

"Good grief," thought Mudhole, whose handsome face and strong physique were still recovering from scratches and festering insect bites. He was in need of a long, hot bath, a haircut, and a close shave.

"Can you believe this place?" Mudhole said to Raider J. C. Green next to him. Green was the machine gunner Mudhole now worked with.

Both young men felt they were walking in a dream. Mudhole stopped in front of a shop with swimsuits displayed in the window.

"That's what I'm buying!" he announced. He walked in and purchased a brightly colored bathing suit with lime green palm fronds on a bright blue and purple background. He almost made it out of the store with his single purchase but saw a pair of large, dark sunglasses. "I'll take those, too," he looked up with his irresistibly charming grin. The young female clerk smiled back and added the sunglasses to his bag—but never charged him for them.

Upon returning to Hawaii, the 2nd Raiders discovered that their reputation preceded them. The spectacular welcome they had received while docking in Pearl Harbor testified to that. Americans were learning about who they were and what they had accomplished in the war. Magazines and newspapers continued to proclaim these special forces and their exploits. It made recuperating in Hawaii very pleasant for Carlson's Raiders. Mudhole Merrill and his buddies soaked in sun, sand, and smiles from admiring fans everywhere they went while recuperating on Waikiki.

Once back at Camp Catlin, training remained light. The time was primarily used to refit the battalion, since most 2nd Raiders had lost nearly everything they owned during the horrendous attempt to leave Makin Atoll. They had boarded the waiting submarines with little more than the shirts on their backs. Most needed new equipment, weapons, shoes, and uniforms. Many needed additional medical treatment. They all needed rest.

And always hanging around everywhere they went were magazine and newspaper editors from the mainland. These war correspondents found much to write about for an audience back home eager to learn more stories of the rising stars of the South Pacific: the Raiders.

Then, in fewer than two weeks, the war called again. Carlson and his 2nd Raider Battalion were about to get their chance to enter the main act—fighting to wrestle Guadalcanal from Imperial Japan permanently.

On September 6, 1942, Carlson and his 2nd Raiders boarded the USS *Wharton* docked in Pearl Harbor. The large transport bore the name of the third commandant of the Marine Corps, Franklin Wharton, who filled the command position in 1804. Ironically, the USS *Wharton* had originally been named the *Southern Cross,* apt nomenclature for its current mission.

Their initial destination was Espiritu Santo in the New Hebrides, a journey of over 3,500 miles into the South Pacific. This chain of islands lies 550 miles southeast of Guadalcanal and 1,400 miles east of Australia. It had become a primary jumping-off point for troops entering the fight in the southern Solomons and would be the Raiders' temporary training camp until they received their next assignment.

Zigzagging most of the way, the Raiders took over two weeks to reach their destination. They began daily doses of Atabrine to help ward off the effects of tropical diseases to whatever extent possible. Malaria, jaundice, filariasis, dysentery, and other illnesses endemic to Guadalcanal would prove to be as much an enemy as the two-legged ones.

Though a sizable transport ship, the USS *Wharton* was still suffocating below deck. Mudhole had developed claustrophobic feelings while he was on the submarines a few weeks before, and those only continued onboard the *Wharton.* He would go topside at night, finding the fresh sea air invigorating. Sometimes he would strap himself to one of the large mounted guns on deck, often sleeping there all night.

As the journey progressed, he could see the constellation of the Southern Cross begin to appear in the nighttime sky. It reminded him of his friend Joe Gifford and the times they had spent together topside on their way to Makin, talking and joking, feeling the salty spray on their faces.

While they were at Camp Catlin near Honolulu, Mudhole had searched through Joe's belongings and retrieved his wallet with ID and home address. He had placed it in his sea bag for safekeeping. If anything should happen, he intended to pay a visit to Joe's family.

At this point, there had been no word of the fate of the missing Raiders. Now he was facing another unknown—and without his courageous buddy. The Raiders realized—and hoped—they would soon be bound for Guadalcanal. Like everybody else, the young man had heard his fair share of the bloody battles and gruesome happenings there.

Mudhole prayed that the others would be found alive—and that he would never have to visit Joe's family alone.

Carlson's Raiders set sail from Hawaii bound for Espiritu Santo on September 6, 1942. The island in the New Hebrides archipelago brought them one step closer to his ultimate goal: Guadalcanal. Meanwhile, Edson's Raiders were carving out a name for themselves atop Bloody Ridge.

Carlson made no bones about his desires: he desperately wanted to join the fight on the 'Canal. He got his wish when orders came down from Vandegrift and 2nd Raiders were tapped to establish a beachhead on the northeast coast of Guadalcanal in the Aola Bay area. There, the Seabees (Navy Construction Battalions) would build a second airfield.

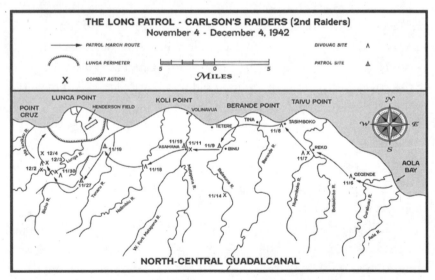

9. The Long Patrol of Carlson's Raiders (viewed lengthwise along the eastern side of Guadalcanal)

The hodgepodge of Army, Navy, Marine, and Allied aircraft, nick-named the Cactus Airforce after the code name for Guadalcanal, was expanding in the Solomons. The growth was tenuous, perhaps, but increasing nonetheless.

Admittedly, the mission didn't fit with the way Carlson had so passionately trained his men for months: to prosecute classic hit-and-run tactics with light, fast-moving raids behind enemy lines, echoes of his days traveling with Mao Tse-tung and the Chinese Red Army. But with this assignment, at least "the nose of the camel would be under the tent," so to speak. He had to first get his 2nd Raiders on Guadalcanal—then wait to see how things shaped up.

Carlson's desire for an opportunity to showcase what his Raiders were truly capable of came through an unexpected stroke of luck disguised as a glitch. On October 31, Carlson, with "C" and "E" Companies, had boarded the APDs *Manley* and *McKean* and landed unopposed at Aola Bay on Guadalcanal on November 4. It immediately became apparent that the area designated for a second airfield was unsuitable. The enormous, swampy jungle was thick and deep, filled with saltwater crocodiles, leeches, mangrove forests, and waterlogged vegetation. With a year-round water table at ground level, it would take weeks just to drain.

But Carlson was on the 'Canal with his Raiders. As continued evaluation of the area substantiated belief that it would be impossible to build an airfield at this location, Vandegrift airdropped Carlson with a change of instructions. He was to leave Aola Bay and march inland the following day. There was a large Japanese contingent, recently reinforced by the "Tokyo Express," moving toward the Marine perimeter around Henderson Field. Vandegrift wanted Carlson's Raiders to harass these Japanese troops from the rear.

This was perhaps an inauspicious beginning for an assignment but one that belied the heroics that would eventually punctuate it for all time. The new mission was straight out of Carlson's playbook: a raiding patrol in classic commando style—fast-moving and hard-hitting. The mission would last a grueling thirty-one days, through jungles and rivers, over mountains and cliffs, and create confusion among the enemy, with bitter fighting and hand-to-hand combat thrown into the mix.

It would come to be known as the Long Patrol. And those Raiders who were actually able to complete the exhausting journey would forever remember it with a sense of pride.

After unloading Carlson and two companies of Raiders at Aola Bay, the APDs *Manley* and *McKean* returned to Espiritu Santo. The remaining men of 2nd Raider Battalion, including Mudhole, saddled up for their trip to the place where fighting had reached its zenith—Guadalcanal. Imperial forces were dug in, and reinforcements from Rabaul arrived in a seemingly endless stream. Stories swirled about the bitter encounters and atrocities taking place. But nothing could really prepare them for what they would find.

Mudhole had spent nearly all of his seventeenth year training and fighting as a Raider. He celebrated his eighteenth birthday in the middle of the Pacific aboard the USS *Wharton*. Now, he was on his way to war once again. Midway had been an introduction; Makin, a fiery baptism. Now, the Long Patrol would bring Raiders face-to-face with demons capable of bringing a man to his breaking point.

The APDs, with their new load of troops, arrived back at Aola Bay on November 8. By noon, all the incoming 2nd Raider Battalion had off-loaded. Once ashore, a few native scouts met Raider officers with a message from Carlson: there had been a change in plans. They were to proceed the following morning up the coast fifteen miles. Then they were to head overland eight miles to Binu, where their commander was establishing a base camp.

At daybreak on November 9, platoon leaders and company commanders squeezed all their men and equipment into an improvised flotilla of Higgins boats, "tank lighters" (or LCMs, "landing craft mechanized"), and even a couple of native canoes. As they journeyed up the coast, Mudhole stared at the hulking island off to his left, the largest land mass in the Solomon Island group. At most places along the shore, a thick tropical jungle wall descended to water's edge and in some places met the sparkling, azure-colored ocean in one continuous line. The extreme density of dark green vegetation, though beautiful, gave the terrain a forbidding appearance.

Before long the assorted watercraft landed at a place where another group of native scouts appeared at the shoreline. Mudhole saw a half dozen ebony-skinned, mostly bare-chested natives. Their leader was a short, stocky fellow who quickly set about speaking to the officers. Occasionally, he would stop his conversation with the Raider leaders to issue instructions to other scouts with him. To these he spoke Pidgin, a wild assortment of words, sounds, hand gestures, and often whole-body language.

This particular native, however, held the rapt attention of all the company leaders. Mudhole noticed nasty-looking scars over most of his upper body, especially across his chest, arms, and throat. The wounds looked fairly fresh and in various stages of healing.

"Who's that?" Mudhole asked his platoon leader.

"That's Vouza," was the reply.

"So that's him!" exclaimed Mudhole. Stories regarding the scout's incredible commitment and heroism had already trickled through the Raider units.

The place the Raiders had landed turned out to be Tasimboko, a native village set back slightly offshore. It was also the vicinity of the birthplace of Jacob Charles Vouza, perhaps the most famous of all World War II scouts in the South Pacific.

Born in 1900, Jacob Vouza was educated at an evangelical mission school located nearby. At sixteen years old he joined the Solomon Islands Protectorate Armed Constabulary, the islands' policing authority under British jurisdiction. He retired in 1941 with the rank of sergeant major.

When the Japanese invaded his island home, they abused the women and young teenage girls. Vowing to get revenge, Vouza returned to active duty with British forces and volunteered to work with the Coastwatchers. During the U.S. invasion of August 7, Vouza rescued a Navy pilot who was shot down in enemy territory. He helped the pilot back to friendly lines where Vouza met the Marines for the first time. It was a fortuitous meeting—congenial on both sides. Vouza would become a most valued Marine scout, often behind enemy lines.

Mudhole learned more details that day of the native's story. Not long after the invasion, Vouza had been apprehended by the Japanese, who found a small American flag he had quickly tried to hide in his loincloth. They then tied him to a tree with straw ropes and tortured him for several hours.

The soldiers took turns hitting him in the face with their rifle butts and slashed him with swords in an effort to solicit information about the Marine troops and their plans. When Vouza wouldn't answer, they forced him to lie in a nest of red ants. Still he refused to speak.

Finally, when the Japanese soldiers planned to pull out of the area, they bayoneted him repeatedly and left him for dead. His chest bled from seven separate wounds, but his throat, worst of all, spewed blood from a large, gaping hole. After his captors departed, Vouza regained consciousness and gnawed the ropes loose. He then belly-crawled back through the jungle to American lines. Martin Clemens, a British officer who remained on the island as head of the Coastwatchers, found him. In Clemens's own words, he could hardly look at his trusted scout.

> Vouza, who had lost pints of blood, was in terrible shape. He fully expected to die, and before he passed out again, he gave me a long last message for his wife and children. I wrote with one hand and held his hand with the other. Once he had done his duty, the terrific strain told, and he collapsed. We carried him back (to the Marine hospital tents) and got the doctors operating on him. They pumped Vouza full of new blood, and amazingly it was expected that he would live.... What loyalty the man had!

News of his heroics had spread quickly. Vouza spent twelve days in the hospital recuperating from his ordeal, then immediately returned to the Marines as their chief scout. Raiders would come to be especially fond of the gutsy native, who accompanied Evans Carlson and 2nd Raiders throughout the Long Patrol. In later years, Sergeant Major Vouza would receive a Silver Star from Major General Alexander Vandegrift and the Legion of Merit for what he would accomplish on the Long Patrol, among many other awards. Perhaps the highlight would come when he was knighted by Britain's Queen Elizabeth II herself.

But all of that would be later. For now, Mudhole was thrilled to meet the hero who had persevered through what the Japanese had done to him.

"He's one tough SOB," was how Mudhole described Vouza, as the young Raider along with his unit, began to dig in for their second night on Guadalcanal.

The Patrol Goes On

At daybreak on November 10, the Raiders saddled up to join their commander and the two Raider companies with him at Binu. Vouza himself supervised the native scouts and supply carriers, who toted mostly ammunition. Mudhole counted about fifty or sixty of them, with an average height of about 5'9" or so.

Though Binu was fewer than ten miles inland, the trails were often faint and, in many places, indiscernible except to the sharp eyes of natives familiar with the terrain.

As the line of Raiders wove deeper into the jungle, Mudhole looked around. Every direction appeared the same. The tree canopy in spots towered to twenty feet and higher. Broad leaves and vines blocking out all but tiny, flickering pinpoints of light were mixed in at every level. In certain places the vegetation was so dense Raiders placed a hand on the backpack of the man in front to keep their line connected and moving forward.

In other areas, the jungle would open up into grassy fields full of the sharp-edged kunai grasses. These carried their own inherent dangers. A man could bury himself down into the grass and not be detected until stepped on.

The terrain of Guadalcanal—dense, tropical jungle mixed with swamps, sticky clay pits, and exposed areas of thigh-high grasses—was different from anything Mudhole had experienced on Midway, Makin, Hawaii, or even Espiritu Santo. The intense heat and heavy humidity were smothering once inside the walls of foliage. Within a few minutes of clawing through vines and bushes over decaying logs and branches, he was drenched in sweat, his shirt and trousers sticky with perspiration. His boots were filled with fetid water full of microorganisms, leeches, and bacteria.

At one point during the Patrol, Carlson saw Mudhole sitting down trying to adjust his wet socks and boots. "Hey, Mudhole, you keep those feet dry. They're going to get you home." He reached down and gave the teenager a slap on the shoulder.

"Yes, sir, Skipper," said Mudhole, using the affable term many Raiders called their commanders. But he wondered how on earth he could keep his feet dry in this environment.

Vouza moved the Raiders out, setting a good pace. By noon they had neared Binu and could hear machine gun clatter and small-arms fire coming from several directions. They found Carlson busy trying to keep in touch with his platoons, especially "C" Company, who had run into a large unit of Japanese and were in disarray.

Immediately, he told the Raiders just joining him to begin pushing the Japanese towards two stands of palm trees located in a large field of tall grass. Mudhole and his platoon, along with others, began a slow sweep to the right toward the sounds of battle.

After a couple of hours of skirmishes and firefights, the platoons had managed to funnel a number of Japanese soldiers into two copses. They received word from the Skipper to take T-shirts and form arrows in the grass pointing to these. Mudhole helped to round up about twenty T-shirts. Several others then began the dangerous task of laying these down to form crude pointers.

At 4:15 p.m. Carlson radioed Henderson Field to arrange an air strike. Soon dive-bombers came roaring in, tipping their wings. Then they circled up, gaining altitude, and began their descent.

"Here they come!" said Mudhole, nudging the gunner next to him. "Those T-shirts did the trick!" They watched as the bombers blew up sizable chunks of earth and palm trees guided by the makeshift arrows.

Near dusk he boiled a little rice in his helmet and threw in a few cuts of salt pork. Each man had a sock filled with rice and a sock filled with raisins, plus a small slab of salt pork—enough for a few days. Carlson had told them they would eat two meals per day, using rice with raisins in the morning and rice with a couple bites of pork in the evening. Sometimes, they would have rice "and whatever" depending on what they could forage. It was Carlson's favored way of fighting: commando-style, while living off the land.

◆ ◆ ◆

That evening, which happened to be the 167th birthday of the Marine Corps, Carlson held a brief, Gung Ho–style meeting with his officers: "My plan of operations is to fan out strong combat patrols to search for the enemy, each patrol reporting to the battalion CP (command post) every two hours. Once contact is made, I will concentrate the patrol as needed to destroy the enemy. As the enemy is cleared from our front, I plan to move the base forward and repeat the tactical cycle. One company will be retained at the base to provide security."

Afterwards, officers hastily returned to their units, where perimeter security checks were made, guards posted, and machine gun positions established. Men all along the lines dug in for the night, hoping to steal a few winks of sleep here and there.

Spending a night at the edge of a dense tropical jungle as Mudhole had done the first night on Guadalcanal differed from a night swallowed up by one. A cacophony of weird sounds assaulted him: shrill whistles, loud clacking and chirps, snapping twigs and rustling leaves. At every new noise, he jerked around, his eyes desperately straining into the hard dark of matted vines and branches. Everywhere was movement—if not from fauna, from hordes of mosquitoes, ants, spiders, caterpillars, rodents, and snakes.

Suddenly, Mudhole thought he heard scuffling sounds, maybe even muffled voices. Were they human?

"Listen," he whispered to Chappie, who crouched next to him. "Did you hear that? Sounded like somebody talking."

Mudhole could sense Chappie brace, stone-still. In a few moments, the other gunner simple shrugged his shoulders.

"Don't know," he whispered back. "Hard to tell."

Mudhole listened again. It was impossible to know—the jungle seemed alive. He closed his eyes, but sleep was elusive. His dungarees and shirt were saturated with sweat.

It was now deep into the night. Mudhole's head bobbed forward.

Suddenly, a blood-curdling scream somewhere in the jungle made him jolt upright. Then another agonizing cry. Chappie grabbed his arm. There was no mistaking this time. Someone, somewhere writhed in pain.

"Is that one of ours?" asked Mudhole. "Did somebody get left out there, wounded or something?"

Chappie shook his head. "Don't know. It's probably somebody left wounded from "C" Company—they got scattered the hell all over," he said.

Then they heard a gut-wrenching plea deep in the jungle.

"Please, God, please—no! Stop! Please don't!" It was a Raider pleading for mercy. The agonizing yelps continued, interspersed with heartbreaking moans. It lasted until just before daybreak, then silence.

The following morning a patrol found a private where the enemy had left him, staked to the ground. His face had been cut nearly past recognition and his genitals mutilated.

When Mudhole saw what had happened, he felt a strong urge to vomit. The young man was the same age as himself, barely eighteen years old.

As the Raiders silently filed past his body, their resolve turned to steel. The sight of their friend so brutalized left a mark they would never forget. It defined for many clarity of purpose and set a tone of cold rage for the Long Patrol. Though nobody said it, everyone knew they would take no prisoners alive.

The thirty-one days of Carlson's Long Patrol divided roughly into three phases: first, the Raiders established a base camp at Binu and utilized four patrols ranging out, with a fifth patrol remaining in defense at the base camp. During the second phase, Carlson moved his Raiders forward and established a new base camp at Asamana. Again, he employed patrols out from the base camp located several miles closer to the Marine perimeter around Henderson Field. In the third phase, once "A" Company finally arrived from Espiritu Santo, Carlson switched to deploying and moving forward the entire battalion in three prongs consisting of two companies each. Carlson would remain with the middle two companies to direct movements as needed.

For a month Carlson's Raiders harassed, disrupted, and chipped away at thousands of Japanese troops, who continued their attempts to reclaim Henderson Field. One large contingent of Imperial Japanese forces, led by Toshinari Shoji, had taken heavy casualties from U.S. Marine and U.S. Army forces in the Koli Point action. After being encircled by American forces, some three thousand enemy troops had managed to break out from the Americans. Carlson's Raiders pursued and attacked the runaway Japanese soldiers.

Each day Raider patrols fanned out to search for and destroy Japanese troops. Battle began as soon as contact was made. Though the numbers of enemy troops they encountered varied greatly, confronting them was always deadly, dangerous business.

The intensity never ceased over the 31-day period. A Japanese might be hiding behind any tree, within any brush—ready to kill. No one could ever let his guard down, day or night. To do so could mean death for them or their buddies. For most survivors of the Long Patrol, this had been the ultimate—and debilitating—challenge.

Despite all the dangers, 2nd Raiders constantly pursued their enemy; they were hunter-killers, finely tuned predators who showed no mercy, just as they knew beyond a shadow of doubt the enemy wouldn't show them any. Over the course of twelve specific engagements, plus numerous random firefights, the Raiders killed fifteen, twenty-five, fifty, or more Japanese troops at a time.

Enemy combatants were not their only targets, however. In mid-November, General Vandegrift directed Carlson to search for and destroy "Pistol Pete." This heavy artillery piece had allowed the Japanese to regularly shell Henderson Field. It had been a constant threat for weeks. Carlson and his men found the emplacement and dismantled it. Later, they found a 75-millimeter mountain gun and a 37-millimeter anti-tank gun and scattered key parts over the hills.

Mudhole Merrill slugged through the Long Patrol. The unbelievable second half of the month began shortly after a brief stay at an engineers' camp where 2nd Raiders were able to rest for a couple of days. The final portion of their trek was filled with almost unimaginable challenges and hardships.

In his own words, Mudhole Merrill remembers the ordeal he endured when he was eighteen years old on the dark island of Guadalcanal:

> We'd finished our original mission—patrolling that area between Aola Bay and Henderson Field. The 2nd Marine Engineers were building a bridge across a river so a road could be built to Henderson Field and the bay. At the same time this road would give a way to reach that flat area where the Seabees were already at work building a bomber strip.
>
> So, we rested up a few days at the Engineer[s'] camp. A lot of our guys were just plain ill from lack of proper foods and real feverish from malaria. Those unable to carry on were taken on back to Henderson Field. The remainder of us were lined up at sick bay.

Doctors examined us individually to decide who was fit to continue our pace. Many were left behind but under protest. After five days, there weren't but about 450 of us left. Those of us who remained [were] assigned the almost unbelievable task of entering the Upper Lunga River. We were going into a real mysterious part of the jungle which had never been patrolled.

I can say truthfully that we were going into the wilds where no white men had ever been. There were no maps or information concerning this area. Natives were ignorant about it too because they had no reason to go in there.

One thing we did know for certain, and that was the fact that there was considerable Jap activity up there. We also knew that large guns were hidden in caves. How in the world the Japs had ever managed to move these [8-inch] guns into these positions, Lord only knows. It's beyond my ability to explain.

There was one gun in particular which lobbed three or four shells into Henderson Field every morning. This became such a regular event that the gun was soon dubbed "Pistol Pete" by the Marines. This gun was more of a nuisance really, and the damage was actually next to nothing. Three out of four of the shells proved to be duds anyway—that was a common occurrence in Jap ammunition.

But we were to locate and destroy these gun emplacements. Our other mission was to secure data and information concerning the Great West Trail, which the Japs were using as a supply route.

So the gear we carried was cut down—we had a damned hard task ahead of us. Normally, we would carry [two thousand] rounds of ammo between the four of us per each machine gun team. This was cut to about [five hundred] rounds. Our rations still consisted of the old stand-by: bacon (salt pork), rice, and tea. Our clothes were the same old Marine dungarees.

It was early one morning when our force finally saddled up. We kept on the move for about two days without finding any signs of the Japs. We did run across many dead ones rotting along the trail. The majority of these probably had died from malaria.

The third day, we entered the large swamp area. For an entire day, we waded through the water up to our knees. Now and then we would brush aside the bodies of dead Japs, partially eaten by maggots. Them insects were terribly bothersome. We had to keep a sharp lookout for crocs, but mostly for Japs. The whole thing seemed like a nightmare.

At the end of the third day, we reached the foothills of the mountains. Those jagged cliffs looked like they rose straight up to heaven. It started to rain again, for we were in the middle of the rainy season of the tropics, and we didn't have no supplies. Mud was up to our knees. Traveling became really difficult.

We were a long way from Henderson Field. We had no way of getting supplies, and we depended entirely upon the planes that would drop us stuff by parachute—if and when they could locate us. At one point our patrol went three days without eating. All we had was what we could find in the jungle itself—we ate these little bananas and roots from the plants the natives pointed out to us. This went on until we were able to get some rations in a drop.

We finally got to some even steeper places of the mountains. In some cases we had to tie lines around each other so that the stronger Raiders could help the weaker ones up them sharp mountain sides. It was really something.

In my boyhood days in Arizona, I'd never seen mountains as rugged and jagged as these. I personally carried a [32-pound] machine gun, and I'm willing to admit it took all the stamina and courage in me to keep going.

Many times I would slip and fall into the slimy mud. Somebody's hands would grasp me by the arms and help me to my feet again. I would stumble along like a helpless drunk, forcing my aching body to keep going. It was torture. Sometimes I couldn't help it, but tears would roll down my cheeks, and a couple of times I'd just burst out crying.

Days passed—they were a blur. We were all suffering intensely from dysentery and malaria. Our corpsmen tried to help us best they could with the little medical supplies we had on hand.

Men too weak and tired to continue would drop out and had to get back to Henderson Field the best way they could. They would drift back into the main lines in such deplorable condition that the doctors were stunned by their appearance. How human beings could undergo such hardships—the doctors didn't know. Neither did most of us. It was beyond our ability to comprehend. The Docs, helpless to do much, did their best.

My condition wasn't so favorable either. I had large sores on my legs all the way up to my groin. Some were as large as big ringworm circles—maybe three or four inches or more across. They would bleed constantly, and pus would form. I had to scratch them because they itched terribly, and if I brushed too close to an object, the wounds would ooze pus out.

My socks hadn't been changed since we left our camp. They would stick to my wounds. I was more fortunate than some, though, who had these sores all the way up to their armpits. We were all in a horrible mess.

Yet someway, somehow, we doggedly carried on with our appointed task—to find Japs along the upper Lunga River.

Our clothes were almost torn from our bodies—our beards were matted with sweat and mire—men's eyes were turning yellow and looked like sunken holes in their foreheads.

The ranks were really thinning. There wasn't a man among us that feared death anymore. We all felt that when the Great Creator called, we would surely deserve everlasting peace—because in our own minds, we had seen hell already.

During the nights—which got really cold—we would keep warm by lying close to each other. I could hear stifled sobs of men. Yeah—men would cry like children. The toughest men in the Marines—Raiders—they would kill a man and never bat an eye—were crying. That was how tough it was back there behind them Jap lines. In the daytime, we would sit and stare at nothing, thinking of nothing, and knowing that soon we would maybe be nothing.

At last we finally made it up on the West Trail—we were so tired we could hardly move. We rested for a day and started to dig in and place our positions along the trail, and we found more evidence of close Jap activity.

We sent out short patrols to get as much info as to the larger Jap movements and the positions of their guns. We ran across a large Jap ammunition dump, which we promptly destroyed. I personally removed hundreds of bolts and firing pins from our captured rifles. We would throw those parts into the river to prevent the reuse of 'em. We found some small German-made carbines too with dum-dum bullets.

The next day a native scout came running into camp, saying that he had located a "Big Boom!" We knew immediately that he had probably located "Pistol Pete." It was up to us to destroy it.

Colonel Carlson picked [twenty-five] of the strongest men he had left and [ten] natives to do the job. The Japs were caught flatfooted. I guess they thought it impossible that the Raiders had guts enough to challenge something they had deemed impregnable. We killed all of 'em—about 90 [percent] of them were officers. We removed the breach out of the gun and threw it into the upper source of the Lunga. We pulled the pin out of a hand grenade and shoved it down the muzzle of the 8-incher. The firing days of that gun [were] over!

In the case there, we found a large amount of rice and canned pickled fish heads. Those Raiders brought that loot back to our bivouacked area on the West Trail. The pickled fish heads were good eating if you could get them past your nose. They went down like raw oysters. I was so hungry, I didn't care.

We'd accomplished about 50 percent of our task. The 2nd Raider Battalion had accomplished something that all the Marines had tried to do since the initial landing on August 7, 1942. The silencing of "Pistol Pete" was only one chapter in that campaign—the Long Patrol as it came to be called.

We had secured valuable information about the West Trail. This gave us one consolation, and that was the fact that soon we'd be headin' back to Henderson Field, medical attention, and "hot chow." This would truly be a Godsend. Our spirits were higher now than they'd ever been.

However, the "Old Fox" thought it wise if we would continue patrolling for a few more days to secure additional information. This added task cost me my closest friend at that time, [Corporal] J. C. Green.

Our patrol contacted about 150 Japs. We withdrew to better positions and called out our bivouacked area, informing them of our contact and asking for support. During our withdrawal, we captured three Jap stragglers.

We were again in a desperate situation. The Jap prisoners worried us because we were so near the Jap lines that we feared their escape or that one might make an outcry, thus revealing our position.

We had only one alternative—that was to do away with our prisoners in the most quiet manner. The men were eager to perform this duty because their memories were still vivid with the scenes of our wounded buddy at Asamana, who had been tortured and brutally disfigured. The kid was even younger than me—just seventeen.

Three of us fixed our bayonets and at a given signal we finished our task without even as much as a twitch.

To some people this may appear ruthless and cold blooded, but to us, who had seen what them Japs had done, it wasn't. We knew the type of men we were fighting. Almost every Jap we stripped down for information. Each soldier carried three or four condoms, as if they were standard issue to the Jap soldier. The Raiders had a different use for them. They would inflate them and use them as water proof containers for their cigarettes and matches. This too may be doubted, but I swear to it and back it up with my word of honor as a Raider.

Quite frequently we found large sums of American money, which had probably been taken from our men at the Philippines, Guam, and at Wake. There was also quite a bit of Jap occupational money for Australia and New Zealand, showing clearly that they had a goal set a great deal further ahead. It was the matter of putting the cart before the horse—this was the reason we fought so hard on [t]he 'Canal. We swore never to allow these men to have the pleasure of using this money—or their condoms.

It was now getting late in the evening, and our reserves had not arrived as yet to give us support. Corporal Green and I were assigned to cover a certain area with our machine gun. We dug ourselves in along a small knoll, giving us a commanding view for a quarter of a mile or so. We sat there, checking our equipment and ammunition. Corporal Green had a hunch we should need more ammunition, so he sent me back to our bivouacked area about [two hundred] yards to the rear.

While I was gone I heard a few shots being exchanged. This occurred pretty regularly, and I thought nothing of it at the time. I returned carrying a couple belts of ammunition. Green was still sitting behind the gun as if he were checking it over.

I dropped the belts near the gun and said, "Here's that damned ammunition, Green."

I didn't receive an answer. Green didn't make a move.

Fear crept over me. Cold chills raced up and down my spine and a cold sweat poured out all over my body.

I was petrified. I stood spell-bound for at least a minute, until I finally gathered my wits about me and slowly knelt down by his side.

He was dead—shot through the neck, most likely by a sniper. His trigger finger rested firmly on the gun trigger, but not a round had been fired.

I tried to hold back my tears, but something within me seemed to say go ahead and let go.

Many things raced through my mind. Why was he struck down so viciously when I could have easily been the one? Green was older and was the head of our little group. He was priceless to our group.

Then I felt a feeling of having been responsible for it—it crept all over me, and I couldn't breathe. Why did I have to go back when I could have stood close by and maybe prevented this? Out of the four men that made up our crew at the Aola Bay landing, I was the sole survivor.

I finally gathered enough strength to dig a shallow grave for my brave comrade. I had to stop every few minutes as my mind wandered off and brought back priceless memories of unforgettable days back in the states together. I could see his wife's face before me. How beautiful she looked when Green first introduced me to her back in San Diego. She possessed the same blue eyes and blond hair that Green had.

In the early days of Guadalcanal, we would sit together in foxholes and Green would tell me of his plans after the war. He spoke so much of having a home in Indiana and of raising kids.

I refused any assistance in digging his grave and told the other Raiders to leave us alone together. Green and I had a compact. We had agreed that if either of us were killed, the other would see to it that he had a proper burial and that his folks back home would receive a letter telling them all about it. I was left alone and finally finished digging the grave.

It started to rain again. I rolled him slowly into his "poncho" and then lowered him carefully into his everlasting resting place. I looked into his face and spoke to him, as if he could hear. I told him how I'd carry on and never forget him.

I pushed the dirt over him until he was completely covered. A native made a crude cross. We placed his helmet at the top of the cross as a token of remembrance.

The Colonel read a few lines from the Bible. And I gazed around into the faces of the Raiders standing slightly bowed. Everybody was sorry. The Colonel's voice cracked a few times, for he too had known the great character of this Raider.

The Colonel closed the Bible, and I turned slowly away as the opening lines of a familiar poem raced through my mind:
"A clearing has been made beside that twisting trail;
A Raider rests in peace as his ship for home sets sail.
Each passing pair of eyes now lowered in sorrow,
Reaps vengeance as evening brings promise of
tomorrow.
That rugged cross, native made, may it be

A token of remembrance, their humble fee,
There it stands in a far off tropic land,
A moment placed within God's helping hand."

◆ ◆ ◆

Though the Long Patrol had begun with an aborted mission to search for a second airfield site, its ending didn't lack for high drama. On December 1, Vandegrift wanted Carlson to end the patrol and come inside the perimeter. Carlson asked for a few more days, much to the chagrin of his beleaguered troops.

That evening, however, he held a large Gung Ho meeting which turned into one of Carlson's highly-charged, signature rallies. He convened the meeting at the base of Mount Austen, the 1,514-foot hill that overlooked Henderson Field. He challenged his men to dig deep and climb to the summit with him before entering the perimeter. He released some of the more spent Raiders to enter early, while he led the rest up the mountain in one final effort.

The climb required extreme physical exertion. At some points, the grade was so steep that men had to grab and pull themselves upward on branches. Once they reached the summit, they saw an enemy platoon approaching from the other side. A two-hour firefight ensued. At its conclusion, the Raiders had killed twenty-five Japanese soldiers, while losing four of their own to injury—one of whom would die.

The night spent on the mountain was taxing. The men had no water, and nighttime temperatures dropped dramatically at the higher elevation. Some of the fellows in Captain Oscar Peatross's company begged him to allow them to build a fire. Many were shivering with malaria, and everybody was cold.

At first, he denied the request but later reneged. He thought they wouldn't be able to get a fire started. Much to his complete surprise, they not only were able to scrounge enough dry wood, they were able to get a flame going—one that soon became at least twelve feet high by six feet across, according to Peatross himself. The bonfire was the high-light of their time on Mount Austen, and cold Raiders huddled around it, enjoying the warmth as well as the camaraderie that campfires so often promote.

The next morning, Carlson's Raiders would return to Henderson Field. Spirits soared, and the entire party was filled with joy. When they were all back at the camp, they sat for one of their characteristic Gung Ho meetings—one of the first since they had left the Hebrides.

At the meeting, Colonel Carlson congratulated them on having completed the task so many had written off as impossible. All the people who underestimated them and their training were properly chastened now. The Raiders were highly respected by their friends and feared by their enemies.

After the meeting, the 2nd Raider Battalion set out for Henderson Field, footsore and weary but with spirits still high. The men were all suffering from worms and the bleeding dysentery. They managed to force themselves on because they knew that medical attention was waiting for them at the field.

In returning to base, the forces were divided into two groups, each traveling a different route. Mudhole's group went down to the beach while the other followed the Lunga River to the field. They had no con-tact with the enemy on their way back.

Mudhole's group, however, was ambushed, and the point killed. They killed about ten Japs, and four of their own men were wounded. They dispersed and mopped up the ambushers, moved up with a new point, buried their dead, and shoved off immediately with their wounded on stretchers.

One of their wounded had been shot in the abdomen. His nickname was "Chauncey." As Mudhole passed his stretcher, he grasped him by the arm and gave him a heartwarming smile.

Mudhole asked him how he felt. He answered cheerfully: "Well, Mud-hole, I know now just how a woman feels when she is going to have a baby."

The colonel offered Chauncey, a habitual drinker, a shot of brandy.

Chauncey only laughed and replied, "Hell, give it to someone else because if I drink it, it will only run back out." He died that night at the hospital.

Out of all their engagements—at Makin, Midway, and Guadalcanal—Chauncey was the only man buried in a military graveyard. The rest had been buried where they fell on the field of battle.

When the Raiders finally entered their own lines, they were overcome with joy. They were choked with emotions but threw out their chests and held their heads high.

The bystanders were simply awed at the spectacle they saw before them. Men with their clothes torn and looking like walking ghosts proudly marched into the camp. Now and then a Marine would ask, "How is it back there Mac?"

A Raider would reply modestly, "Just like shooting ducks on a pond."

They kept marching down to Henderson Field. Mudhole was feeling ill and black spots appeared before his eyes. His sores were worse than ever, and every step seemed like eternity. The group passed near a field kitchen, feeding hot chow to the Marines encamped there.

From that moment, it was a free-for-all as to who would be first in line. All the men temporarily forgot their ailments as they gorged themselves on the kind of food they hadn't eaten for months. But they found out pretty soon that their constant rice-and-raw-bacon diet had ruined their stomachs. They would throw up but would try to force the hot chow into their stomachs time and time again.

After most gave up on eating, they continued on to the field, a half mile away. The men could hear the planes coming in overhead. Members of the group kept falling out, too tired to continue, but knowing that they were safe within their own lines.

The successful battalion patrol, at least tactically, had seen nearly 500 enemy soldiers killed to 16 Raiders dead and 18 wounded. But the severity of loss of combat-ready Raiders was staggering. During the patrol, 225 men had had to be evacuated due to jungle illnesses, including debilitating malaria, dysentery, and ringworm, among others. The ones who had been able to endure the climb of Mount Austen were in terrible shape nearly to a man. Lack of adequate rations and clean water, plus the extremely rough physical conditions, had taken a high toll.

At the beginning of the Long Patrol, Carlson had held a Gung Ho meeting with the battalion. He had mentioned the distance from Binu, their first base camp, to Henderson Field, their final destination. "Twenty-two miles as the crow flies," he had told them. One Raider had quickly shouted out, followed by uproarious laughter, "Yea, but Colonel, we ain't crows!"

In fact, by the time the Raiders entered the perimeter of Henderson Field, they had covered approximately 150 miles with their serpentine patrols, fanning out then back to base camps, through rivers, over hills, all the while battling a determined enemy.

Despite the severity of their trials, on December 4, 1942, when the Raiders from the Long Patrol crossed over the American perimeter, they marched with heads held high singing the Marine Corps hymn. Army and Marine troops lined both sides of their column, cheering wildly. When they had finished the Marine hymn, one of their greeters shouted out, "Now sing, 'Onward, Christian Soldiers.'" The Raiders obliged with renewed shouts. For all who were there, it was a sight none ever forgot.

After several days at Henderson Field, Mudhole began to have dizzy spells and felt like his head was going to burst open. At one point, he began talking incoherently. Soon he was shouting.

A couple of Raiders saw what was happening and grabbed him by the arms. Slowly they led him over to the field hospital.

Once inside, the doctors made Mudhole lie down. He was covered with ringworm infections and jungle rot on both legs and was shaking from malaria. His knee had an open wound on it—the medics weren't immediately certain if it was from a shell or other shrapnel. Both feet were badly swollen. When Mudhole became delirious, one of the doctors suggested he might be suffering from beriberi as well. A subsequent urine test confirmed that diagnosis. They began treatment for the ills of his body. The mental wounds would be another issue.

On December 10, 1942, word was passed around to inform all Raiders that they should proceed to the beach immediately and prepare to board the first ship out.

On December 19, after having received the Presidential Unit Citation and the second blanket citation of the war, the Raiders boarded the barges that were to take them to the awaiting ship.

All of the men gazed back at the island. No one said a word. It was truly a happy moment, but there was sorrow too. Mudhole's mind raced sometimes, and he couldn't seem to stop it—so many things jammed through it. Thoughts of dead comrades lying somewhere in the jungles and back up in the hills seemed to take over him.

A lump came to his throat as he turned away and looked out towards the ship the Raiders were about to board. They were now leaving "The Island of No Return."

Kenneth "Mudhole" Merrill from Gila County, Arizona, had finished the Long Patrol. But the good-looking, spunky eighteen-year-old was about to start on another journey that would prove equally as challenging—and last much longer.

CHAPTER XII

New Siblings in the Raider Family

"Island-Hopping," More Airstrips, and the Code of *Bushido*

"Lord," remembered General Oscar Peatross of the fall of '42, "We [were] getting farther from home all the time and not a bit closer to Japan." After zigzagging all over the Pacific, 2nd Raider "Pete" Peatross decided to tally the mileage. By the beginning of 1943, they "had covered [fourteen thousand] miles of water and barely skirted the eastern edge of the Central Pacific, [to] say nothing of waters to the south."

What would be the game plan for a war played out on so gargantuan a stage?

Geography forced Navy Admiral Chester Nimitz and General Douglas MacArthur, along with Admiral William "Bull" Halsey, to devise a unique strategy. Nimitz would call it "island-hopping."

Essentially, it meant—at least in theory—that islands heavily defended by Japanese forces would be "skipped over" and allowed to "wither on the vine." A lesser-defended island would be invaded, subdued, and fortified. The U.S. military would then use it as a stepping-stone to the next island, drawing ever closer and closer to the Japanese homelands.

Once an area on an island was secured, the Seabees would then move in quickly to build an airstrip or reinforce an airstrip begun by the Japanese. Miraculously, out of jungle environs airstrips sprang up ready for planes within a few days. This allowed American military forces to advance island by island, closer and closer to the Imperial homeland of Japan.

Prosecuting this plan at all levels, however, would require both massive and complex maneuvers. It would be costly warfare.

Yet another aspect of "island-hopping, airstrip-building" surfaced, perhaps even more complex and subsequently more devastating to scores of American soldiers. The enemy was dedicated to the code of *bushido*, equally alien to most American forces. The Raiders had been schooled by their leaders who had been in China and observed firsthand the lingering effects of this centuries-old Japanese samurai code of honor, which taught that to surrender to an enemy was unforgivable.

As the war raged on, American troops came to see *bushido* in practice more and more. On Tulagi and Guadalcanal, Raiders experienced an extreme expression of the code of *bushido* with the nighttime *banzai* attacks. And it expressed itself in ruthless treatment of both POWs and any Allied forces found wounded during or after battle. Later, the code of *bushido* would express itself in the *kamikaze*, meaning "god-wind"— when pilots would dive their planes into Allied ships for Imperial Japan, in imitation of the historical winds that drove away Mongol ships from the Japanese coast in the 1200s.

As "island-hopping" progressed through 1943, the awareness of Japan's dogged and fanatical resistance to surrender grew. One thing became clear: the Japanese intended to fight to the last man, woman, and child.

Beyond Guadalcanal, the Raiders would perform to the extent that their weapons, their armament, and their numbers allowed. What they lacked in these critical factors, they always made up for with their immense personal courage and their stunning professionalism that was the result of extraordinary training. The Raiders understood honor as well as the Imperial soldiers.

And with the formation of two new Raider Battalions, it seemed the Raider concept was a permanent part of the Marine Corps landscape.

Without question, the fall of 1942 represented the zenith of Raider success. Their activities and notoriety filled newspapers and magazine articles back home, sparking widespread interest and support. Their battle exploits were recognized by many up the chain of command in the Corps.

And when the go-ahead was given to establish two new sister battalions, the 3rd Raiders and the 4th Raiders, it appeared the Raider concept had taken firm hold. Two officers and twenty-five enlisted, each from 1st and 2nd Raider Battalions, would be transferred to join the new sister battalions to lend experience. Added to the formation of two new Raider Battalions, the choice of two high-profile officers as their commanders seemed to underscore the Raiders' permanence.

To command 3rd Raider Battalion, the Corps formally selected Lieutenant Colonel Harry Bluett Liversedge, nicknamed "Harry the Horse," on September 20, 1942. Liversedge, an athletic superstar, had played football at the University of California and went on to receive a Bronze Medal in shot put at the 1920 Olympics in Antwerp, Belgium, while serving in the Marines. In early 1924, he was transferred to the Naval Academy and participated in the 1924 Paris Olympics.

His career feats in World War II would not end, however, with his commanding the 3rd Raider Battalion. In January 1944, as commander of the 5th Marine Division, he would lead the invasion of Iwo Jima and was given the flag planted on Mount Suribachi by the Marines who secured that summit. He displayed the flag in his home until the day he died.

Not to be outdone, 4th Raiders also received a notable commander, none other than President Franklin Delano Roosevelt's son, Lieutenant Colonel James "Jimmy" Roosevelt. The 4th Raiders would be the best outfitted unit in the Marine Corps—they would lack nothing in terms of weapons, uniforms, or equipment. But these would be merely the accoutrements. By the time the 4th Raider Battalion was formed and organized, the Raider concept and training had been perfected. The new commander, taught by Evans Carlson himself, knew it by heart.

Despite the positive signs, however, there were storm clouds on the horizon that wouldn't go away. Some senior Marines held the lingering belief that the elite units were costly and redundant.

Colonel Omar Pfieffer drafted a missive for Nimitz that contained this sentence: "The basic training of all Marine Corps infantry units is essentially the same as that of the Raider Battalions, and, therefore, all Marine Corps infantry battalions are potentially [R]aider units."

Many, especially those who had trained with the Raiders, such as General Oscar Peatross, disagreed with Pfieffer's assessment. Peatross and other Raider supporters shrugged off these claims as "ludicrous." For them, it was like saying an offensive lineman could perform equally well the assignments of a fast wide receiver. In many areas of training, the Raiders had reached peak performance: marksmanship, demolitions, hiking, climbing, swimming, boating, foreign languages, and others. But in his own account of debating the pros and cons of Raider training, Peatross himself admitted that many senior Marines had already made up their minds concerning the Raiders.

Nonetheless, at the beginning of 1943, two new Raider Battalions were breathed into life. These two new units, 3rd and 4th Raiders, gave many more young men the opportunity to fight with a special forces outfit growing in reputation. For both Archibald Rackerby and Ed Blomberg, this was precisely the chance they had been waiting for.

Raider Archibald Rackerby, 3rd Raider Battalion

In the first four months of the ground war in the Pacific, talk of war stateside laced nearly every suppertime conversation. *Life* and *Time* magazines, plus many others, carried detailed stories with double-page photos about American troops—where they were and what they were doing. Strange-sounding names of remote South Pacific islands became familiar household words. So too, more than a few of these stories centered around the Raiders, their commanders, and members.

Archie Rackerby, already in the Marine Corps for nine months, heard stories of Raider exploits with increasing frequency. It made banging away at an office typewriter less appealing than ever.

The ambitious young man was determined to initiate plans to change his status—plans that would change his life in ways he could never have imagined.

After an intensive letter-writing campaign that lasted several weeks, Archie finally got orders on November 17 to travel immediately to Quantico, Virginia, and Officer Candidates School.

After twenty weeks of hard and miserable training during the months of November 1942 through April 1943, he had finished ten weeks of candidate class (for commission) and ten weeks of advanced Officer Training. He was then transferred back to California to Camp Elliot with four days leave to visit his family in Marysville en route.

His first job was to train the men and officers in basic survival and weapons skills via an abbreviated boot camp. It was something many of the men had not bargained for when they joined the Navy, but the sailors and the half dozen Navy officers of VD-3 (Fleet Air Photographic Squadron 3) took pride in learning close-order drills and "showing off" to some of the other Navy units and even an Army National Guard unit stationed there on North Island Naval Air Station. He also taught them basic field tactics that a Marine recruit learns in boot camp.

After this, Lieutenant Archie Rackerby received a notice of transfer. In June 1943, he was assigned to the 22nd Replacement Battalion with orders to leave aboard the Dutch motor-ship transport, the SS *Bloemfontein*, later in the month. He was to join the 2nd Marine Division in New Zealand. Archie was headed off to the Pacific war zone, but not as a Raider—yet.

After a brief stop in the Kingdom of Tonga, Archie was off to Nouméa, New Caledonia, instead of New Zealand. Apparently, several units on New Caledonia needed replacements immediately to ready themselves to return back into the fighting. Among these units were 2nd Raider Battalion—a lot of people by now often referred to them as Carlson's Raiders—and a newer Raider Battalion, 3rd Raiders, that had formed up mainly in Samoa in late '42. This newer Raider Battalion was encamped in Nouméa at Camp St. Louis.

Early the following morning, they told all Marines aboard to disembark and fall into ranks in a huge, open field. Archie was with a couple hundred other second lieutenants.

As the men stood at attention, Lieutenant Colonel Alan Shapley, who was now the new commanding officer of 2nd Raiders, since Carlson had been moved to an executive officer position—they had heard he wound up hospitalized with severe malaria—and Lieutenant Colonel Fred Beans were temporarily commanding the 3rd Raider Battalion. Their first sergeants accompanied them as they passed up and down the ranks of replacements, stopping here and there before a lieutenant that they thought might be suitable for the rigors of troop leadership in the Raiders.

Occasionally they would stop and talk to one of the officers and ask if they would volunteer for the Raiders. Colonel Beans was the first to stop before Archie and ask if he would like to volunteer for the 3rd Raider Battalion.

"Yes, sir," Archie replied, honored to be considered to serve as a Marine Raider.

He had little time to dwell on it, because about that moment, a Raider Battalion doctor came up and asked to see his feet. So he complied, and the doctor confirmed to Beans that Archie had "good marching feet." Archie never forgot this encounter and, with his characteristic dry humor, was quick to tell anyone in later years that the reason he was admitted into the Raiders was that he had "good feet"!

Colonel Beans came up and said, "Welcome to the 3rd Raiders, Lieutenant," and shook Archie's hand. The first sergeant then came up to fill out his papers.

Raider command had chosen about a dozen second lieutenants and then directed them to climb aboard waiting six-by-six trucks. They were driven to the 3rd Raider Camp, about six or eight miles from the village town of Nouméa, where they disembarked from the trucks at a large canvas-covered mess hall and were fed a great breakfast of ham and eggs, coffee, and toast. After breakfast, they were assigned to a 3rd Raider company—Archie was assigned to "K" Company, where Captain Robert N. Page placed him over the weapons platoon.

So there he was, a twenty-three-year-old Marine second lieutenant, in charge of forty-four men in a Marine Raider weapons platoon, soon to enter war. For the next several weeks, Archie would train new Raider recruits for that eventuality. Nobody knew when and where they would fight, but for now that didn't matter. All that mattered now was the honor Archie felt to be a Raider.

Raider Ed Blomberg, 4th Raider Battalion

Just like Archie Rackerby, the young clerk who longed to be doing more, Ed Blomberg yearned to be defending his country. With three brothers already on active duty, he was ready to enlist and do his part. And like Archie, he had heard the stories of the Raiders—their courage and determination.

It was time to leave home and go off to war.

Ed had worked hard through spring and summer of '42. By August, he felt he had carried Uncle George through the most demanding part of the year for farming. In addition, there were now other family members who could help. He was ready to enlist.

He said goodbye to Ma and Pa, his siblings, aunts, uncles, and cousins and asked a friend to drive him to Wausau, Wisconsin—about an hour away from Ogema.

At the recruiting office there, they gave Ed paperwork to fill out, then directed him to the required physical examination. He passed with flying colors—in reality, Ed was in the best shape he'd ever been in.

The big, strong young man with clear blue eyes and straw-colored hair had sailed through the admissions process. Within a few hours, he was on a train to San Diego via Chicago.

For about a month, Ed attended boot camp on the main base of the Recruit Depot. He easily adapted to the rigors of Marine boot camp, since he was in stellar physical condition, and his quiet self-confidence allowed him to respond with ease to the demands of tough Marine sergeants.

One day, Ed noticed a small group of officers and men observing them as they worked out and accomplished drills. Occasionally they would stop to talk to one of the trainees. Word quickly spread that these guys were Raiders. They were from a new battalion of Raiders just now forming up. Its designation would be the 4th Raider Battalion, and the commander of this new unit would be none other than the son of the president of the United States—Lieutenant Colonel James Roosevelt himself. Ed Blomberg now saw the opportunity he had long been waiting for.

The next morning, Captain Anthony Walker stepped forward and introduced himself as the commander of "C" Company in the new unit. He then turned and introduced Captain Raymond Luckel, head of "B" Company. Both men were already well-known within Raider circles for their tough fighting ability and exemplary leadership skills. They asked some of the men if they might be interested in volunteering for the Raiders. Some said yes. Then they came to Ed—it was the chance he had hoped for. He immediately spoke up in the affirmative.

For the next few days, the group of volunteers worked their way through several test trials, including rifle range demonstrations, strength conditioning, and wrestling. On the second afternoon, the young men were paired off and told to spar.

Ed was chosen to go up against a young man from Iowa. He was shorter than Ed but obviously athletic. His agile footwork quickly revealed his familiarity with fisticuffs and sparring.

Others circled up around them as they began to face off, recognizing there was a good chance this might turn into something worth watching.

A few shouts of encouragement boomed out here and there, and the match was on. Ed thought it was supposed to be more friendly than consequential. But when the Iowan began to "get personal," as Ed put it, the farm boy from Wisconsin realized it was more serious than he had expected.

The group around them grew larger when they recognized this had degenerated into what was indeed worth watching—a lusty, full-fledged grappling match. Someone called out to Ed, "Hey you, big Swedish guy, are you going to let him get away with that?"

Ed eyed the young man before him, who obviously knew what he was doing. After several entanglements back and forth, both young men were red-faced, shiny with sweat. But Ed was determined. Ed lunged his shoulders into his opponent's mid-section, knocking him backwards. Quickly, Ed had him on the ground and pulled his arms backwards, pinning him with pressure on the back of his neck.

Everyone cheered while Ed helped the Iowan up with a friendly dusting off. As Ed walked away, one of the Raider officers who had observed the scuffle followed Ed to congratulate him on how he had handled himself. Ed thanked him and was about to shrug it off when the officer said, "Do you know who that was?"

"No, sir, I don't," replied Ed.

"Well, son, that was one of the members on the Iowa Hawkeyes wrestling team!" The information startled Ed—the Hawkeyes were considered a powerhouse in the Big Ten Conference.

"Why don't you come with me, and let's talk some more," said the officer, and he led Ed over to a table where several other Raider officers and sergeants were gathered. Before Ed fully realized what was happening, a sergeant directed him to a truck with several other young men already loaded in the open back. The truck cranked up and headed toward the distant hills of Camp Pendleton. Training commenced immediately upon arrival for these new members of the 4th Marine Raider Battalion.

Ed was where he wanted to be—he was a Raider now—due to his intense determination and rugged strength, but mostly how he handled himself. He was quietly proud—the best kind of proud. Along with his new unit, he had a new name. From this point forward, most everyone knew him as "the Swede."

Roosevelt and His Thousand Thieves

Once Ed and the other neophyte 4th Raiders reached the Raider Training Center, Jimmy Roosevelt began their extremely rugged training regime in earnest. Since he had trained alongside Carlson and been at Makin and on the Long Patrol, he knew what his men would be facing. He intended to have them ready.

A few struggled with the intensity and endurance requirements. But most of these young men in the newly formed Raider Battalion adapted quickly to the extreme physical exertion. At this point in the war, Roosevelt and his officers had many enlistees available from whom to choose. Also, many were apt to volunteer due to the high profile and publicity the Raiders had received. In addition, Roosevelt had tough, seasoned company commanders like Captains Luckel and Walker, among many others, to assist him. They helped with the selection process and, more importantly, with training and leading the new Raiders. In short, Roosevelt obtained at all levels the cream of the crop.

The president's son could also obtain other cream-of-the-crop amenities not available to his fellow Raider Battalion commanders. Several times while at Camp Pendleton, the likes of entertainers such as Bob Hope and Faye Emerson gladly came to personally entertain Roosevelt's Raiders—at his request.

And there were other customs not usually found in more traditional units that marked 4th Raider Battalion; many of these echoed Roosevelt's own experiences with Carlson in 2nd Raiders. Roosevelt conducted easygoing meetings. He didn't demand saluting. The men used first names and wore no insignias. He told them they were "jungle Marines." And they became notorious for scrounging—to the point they were dubbed "Roosevelt's Thousand Thieves." Admittedly, these energetic

Raiders relished being slightly outside the mainstream of Corps culture and walked with noticeable swagger.

As the Swede entered into the elite world of Marine Raiders, he flourished both in the physical challenges and also the mental toughness required. He showed promise and leadership capabilities from the start. In the months to come, after his squad leader succumbed to fevers and jungle rot in both feet, Ed would be tapped to lead. He enjoyed every aspect of his new status.

General Oscar Peatross, who had fought with 2nd Raider Battalion as a young captain, made several observations about the 4th Raiders in later years. When 1st Battalion had shipped out a year earlier, they carried what was on hand at the time: the 1903 bolt-action rifles with .30-caliber ammunition that occasionally failed to fire, vintage World War I bayonets, and individual equipment that had been obsolete for years. On the other hand, the 4th Raiders carried the best our country had produced. But Peatross goes on to say that the new Raider Battalion wasn't only the best equipped. "Roosevelt brought to Espiritu Santo the best-trained Marines our Corps had produced."

Over the next two months, Jimmy Roosevelt sharpened these young warriors through an intense jungle regimen. Peatross goes on to say that "although the 4th Raiders had not been tested in combat at this time it [may well] have been the best battalion in the Raiders and perhaps in the entire [U.S.] Marine Corps."

On February 9, 1943, 4th Raiders ("Roosevelt and his Thousand Thieves") sailed out of San Diego Harbor on the USS *President Polk*. Their ship, part of the *President Jackson* class of attack transports, would be their home for the next two weeks. It wasn't until they were well underway that someone noticed the addition of a piano on board. A few of the Thousand Thieves had "borrowed" the instrument from the base chapel—surely they would need entertainment on such a long voyage! The ship headed south packed with troops and equipment, then took an abrupt turn west toward the South Pacific. Ed, along with many others, slept on deck with a life vest for a pillow.

Late on February 26, the USS *President Polk* pulled into Espiritu Santo, the largest island in the island nation of Vanuatu, part of the archipelago of the New Hebrides Islands. The following morning men and cargo disembarked. Ed began to experience islands, jungles, and natives firsthand.

These islands had been discovered by Spanish explorers in the early 1600s. Their location, some six hundred miles southeast of Guadalcanal, made them a prime choice for an Allied military base. Their unparalleled beauty inspired James Michener's *Tales of the South Pacific*, and the region featured in the Rodgers and Hammerstein musical *South Pacific*.

By nightfall, the Raiders were encamped in their new surroundings. As Ed drifted to sleep, he thought he could hear singing in the distance. As he listened closely, he detected a chorus of natives somewhere farther off softly vocalizing spiritual hymns—he deduced that from the tonal quality of the songs. For the Swede, it was a comforting reminder that though he was thousands of miles from home, his faith had accompanied him.

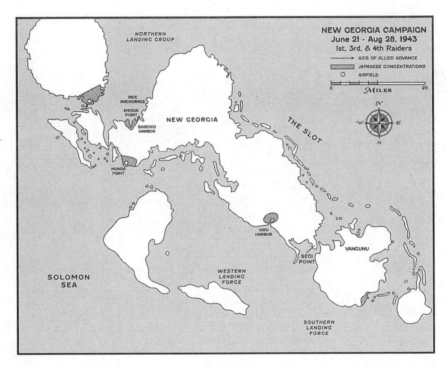

10. New Georgia Campaign, 1st and 4th Raiders participating, D-Day, June 30, 1943. Elements of 4th Raiders landed several days earlier.

CHAPTER XIII

Fourth Raiders Enter the Fray

O nce Americans secured Guadalcanal in early spring 1943, military strategists discussed what their next target should be. Since Rabaul on the western side of New Britain Island remained the primary base for the Japanese in the Southwest Pacific, American planners decided to drive farther up the Solomon Islands' "ladder." New Georgia, approximately two hundred miles from Henderson Field on Guadalcanal, seemed the most logical next island-rung.

Here, the Japanese had arrived in force during the second week of November 1942. By December 17 the Japanese had produced the all-important airstrip—a 4,700-foot runway—despite heavy air raids. If taken by American forces, this airfield, located at Munda Point on New Georgia's northwestern coast, would serve nicely as the next stepping-stone closer to Rabaul and one more island ever nearer the ultimate goal: Japan itself.

Before invading New Georgia, Admiral "Bull" Halsey proffered one intermediary stop—to invade the small islands between Guadalcanal and New Georgia known as the Russells. The plan was adopted, and companies from the newly formed 3rd Raiders were given the task.

The Russell Islands turned out to be unoccupied by the Japanese, but due to unexpected motor malfunctions, the small transports carrying organic supplies weren't able to off-load needed rations. Though 3rd Raiders weren't subjected to enemy hostilities, lack of substantive food and jungle conditions took a serious toll. Many 3rd Raiders, by the time they returned to Guadalcanal three weeks later, were severely weakened by malnutrition and disease. When Archie and the new replacements of 3rd Raiders arrived later in the summer of '43, they were welcomed as much-needed replacements for a Raider Battalion suffering severe non–battle related casualties.

The Swede on Patrol

Meanwhile, Ed "the Swede" Blomberg and 4th Raiders arrived on the 'Canal. Their appearance in the Solomon Islands marked an important milestone in Raider history: all four Raider Battalions were now either in the immediate war zone area or on island bases nearby. And soon two Raider Battalions would work together on a single objective: the invasion of New Georgia, another first in Raider history.

As happens in the uncertain ebb and flow of war, an unfortunate event transpired just prior to the arrival of 4th Raiders on Guadalcanal. Their commander, Lieutenant Colonel James "Jimmy" Roosevelt succumbed to malaria shortly before embarking for Guadalcanal and had to be evacuated back to the States. After being the executive officer under Carlson and participating in all the battles of 2nd Raiders, then training his own battalion of Raiders, bringing them to be what some called the finest group of fighting men ever produced by the Marine Corps, he would never lead his men in battle. None could say he had been anything less than a courageous Marine. With a score of ailments, including asthma, bouts of jungle fevers, such poor eyesight that, had he lost his glasses, he would have been near helpless, and flat feet that never allowed for wearing boots, he had stood the test.

To replace him, headquarters selected Michael S. Currin, known as "Mickey." He was a tough, dedicated Marine with fifteen years of service, beginning as a private until now as a lieutenant colonel.

Fourth Raiders also benefitted from outstanding company commanders—some of the best in the field. Ed's company commander, Lieutenant Ray Luckel, was "intelligent, big, strong, and durable." Starting his Marine Corps career as a private, he had served in every rank in line to first lieutenant and had excelled in each. "You could bet your life that every Raider in his company was expertly trained in all of the tools of the trade: pistol, rifle, machine gun, hand grenade, and bayonet[, and]was highly disciplined and physically fit. You could also bet that a company of such Marines under such a commander would be durable and could hike forever and a day."

Ed felt good to finally be on Guadalcanal. He wasn't afraid of going into battle; in fact he was ready to get to it. He had thrown himself into training and had worked really hard. All the men felt ready. They were good, and they knew it.

Once they settled into the large camp area on the 'Canal, they went out into the jungle every day to patrol and work together. Nobody ever let their guard down; even though they thought there were no Japanese left on the island, they could never be certain.

The Raiders hadn't been there long before their company commanders began briefing them on their first major combat campaign—New Georgia. Their company leader was Lieutenant Luckel—a big, strong guy who was a straight shooter. He told the Raiders that they would go in through the back door and work their way toward Munda Point, where the Japanese had an airstrip. The actual D-Day was scheduled in a couple of months.

In the mean time, the Raiders would undertake a series of night patrols in the Segi Point area. On one patrol, the Raiders were taken in, then let off in their rubber boats. Several natives in war canoes were waiting to guide them in. Ed had never seen anything like it—the natives were like ghosts in the darkness. They made no noise at all, though the canoes must have had at least a dozen paddlers each. They lifted their paddles in and out of the water with no noise whatsoever. The Raiders had trained for silence in paddling as well—and theirs were painted black to keep down reflections. But these natives were amazing. They were like a mirage. And the Raiders had to paddle like crazy to keep up with them. The mission went off without a hitch, and the Raiders were back on Guadalcanal in no time.

A few days later, Ed would receive another patrol assignment. The Raiders were called upon to rescue a Coastwatcher who needed help. His name was Donald G. Kennedy, and he had played a key role in assisting Allied Forces in the New Georgia area. Born in the village of Springhills, New Zealand, Kennedy spent much of his career as headmaster of several island schools for boys with a reputation as a heavy-handed disciplinarian. In the years leading up to World War II, he had joined the British Solomon Island Protectorate (BSIP) and been stationed first in Tulagi.

In mid-1942, he had moved his headquarters to Segi Point, organizing a large number of Solomon Islanders, mostly Australians, New Zealanders, and Brits, who regularly attacked enemy outposts and patrols in the area. Additionally, natives worked for him as spies and spotters.

Since Japanese planes on bombing missions from Rabaul to Guadalcanal had to fly over Segi Point, Kennedy was able to alert American forces. Major General Noboru Sasaki, recently appointed Japanese commander of all land defenses in the area, had had enough. Sasaki suspected, correctly, that many of his setbacks were due to the Coastwatcher system and considered Donald Kennedy a leader of the antagonists. The general sent units to advance toward the southern area of New Georgia. When news of the approaching Japanese troops reached Kennedy, he knew he would be overrun. He quickly contacted American forces and requested support.

A small group of Raiders including Ed was given the task of a night landing near Segi Point to assist Kennedy. Once they disembarked from their shallow-draft LCPs ("landing craft personnel"), Ed and several others from his platoon set up a defense perimeter with shallow foxholes on the beach. Their commander, along with the other Raiders, disappeared with guides into the jungle.

The night hours dragged. At one point, Ed looked over at a buddy in a foxhole nearby. He had dozed off with his finger on the trigger of his tommy gun.

Ed eased carefully over to him, crawling along, making as little noise as possible. He knew that, if he startled his companion, not only might he get shot, but if the enemy were in the area, they would certainly be alerted.

Ed began calling his friend's name real soft, over and over, attempting to rouse him. He moved slightly one time, and the Swede's heart jumped into his throat. Finally, after about fifteen minutes, Ed was able to get him awake enough to hear him.

The Raiders spent the following day lying low along the beach and just waiting. By nightfall, the men began to wonder what was happening. Sometime after dark on the second night, the other Raiders returned, making their way quietly through the jungle back to those waiting on the beach. With them was a wounded man on a stretcher, plus several other New Zealanders.

Before long the LCPs arrived, and the group boarded to go back to Guadalcanal. Someone said the wounded fellow was Kennedy himself. He looked like he had been shot in the leg. They made it back to camp without further incident.

The 4th Raiders now had experienced their first night landings. The campaign for New Georgia, code-named Operation Toenails, was about to begin in earnest. It would mark an important milestone in Raider history: the first time different Raider Battalions would fight during the same campaign. The intermediary step of invading the Russell Islands had been given to 3rd Raiders. Now, the Swede and other 4th Raiders would land at Segi Point in southern New Georgia to come in through the back door, so to speak, then go on to Viru Harbor and make their way to Munda Point, where the airfield was located. Shortly afterwards, 1st Raiders would land on the northern end of New Georgia Island at Rice Anchorage, then forge their way to Enogai and on to Bairoko Harbor, encircling the enemy from the north. It would be Lee Minier's first battle as a lieutenant and Ed "the Swede" Blomberg's first time in major combat.

No one can predict with absolute certainty what might transpire during a combat mission. What sometimes seems sure to end in victory has a way of tangling. Unfortunately, New Georgia would eventually prove to be a disastrous undertaking for the Raiders.

4th Raiders on New Georgia

Like most islands in the Solomons, the New Georgia island group lies roughly oriented northwest to southeast. Within this cluster, twelve larger islands stretch nearly 150 miles along that line between Guadalcanal to the south and Bougainville to the north. The island that gives the group its name—New Georgia—is an extremely convoluted, spiny clump approximately 20 miles wide and 45 miles long. An internal Marine Corps report on the Central Solomons described it as follows:

> . . . [A] tortuous, misshapen mass of volcanic cones, with cloud-obscured summits that reach [three thousand] to [five thousand] feet into the air. River-filled mangrove swamps, studded with coral outcroppings and matted with rotting vegetation, fill the surrounding valleys. An almost impenetrable jungle blankets most of the land area. Through this jungle natives have pushed a few trails or tracks, often passable only in dry weather, that skirt the swamps and pass along coral ridges or cling to the sides of precipitous volcanic cliffs.

Of the natives here, an official New Georgia history described them as mirroring their environment:

The dank, oppressive nature of the island characterized even the life of New Georgia natives. Theirs was a scrubby exis-tence.... Onetime headhunters, they were...excellent guides to the coastlines but almost completely ignorant of the interiors.

The campaign to take New Georgia with its existing airport at Munda Point would be submitted to the harsh realities of the island's foreboding and nearly impenetrable jungles. New Georgia made the jungles of Guadalcanal seem relatively tame. As one Raider later quipped: "New Georgia made Guadalcanal look like Hawaii."

June 30, 1943, was set for D-Day. However, on June 20, Admiral Turner ordered Lieutenant Colonel Currin and half of his 4th Raiders to move immediately from Guadalcanal to Segi Point to take Viru Harbor on the southwest coast, where the Japanese had a substantial build-up of troops. The enemy had made good use of the harbor's somewhat deep, protected waters. New reports had confirmed that Japanese troops were rapidly extending their coverage deep into southern New Georgia.

The Raiders landed unopposed in the Segi Point area the following morning. The next day they were joined by two Army infantry compa-nies and the first group of airfield construction personnel scheduled to build a landing strip at Segi Point.

Once ashore, after a couple days of reconnaissance patrols, Com-mander Currin decided the best route to Viru Harbor was from Regi Point then overland. He moved his Raiders by rubber boats at night on June 27 and arrived around midnight. After resting a few hours, the Raiders saddled up in single file and disappeared into the jungle interiors like a long black snake undulating along the narrow trail.

They had marched only a short distance before the column was forced to an abrupt halt. The scant path ahead had been swallowed up by an enormous swamp filled with smelly, thick mud that they had to drag their way through. The Raiders had sweat their way slowly along for about three hours when they heard shots coming from the rear. They guessed they'd met with a Japanese patrol along the way. They hurried up, got to a river, and crossed it. The current was pretty swift, but everybody got across okay. Then the men set up a perimeter. It rained all night, and everybody rolled up as best they could. They started out again the next morning and reached another river—only to have their rear attacked again by the Japanese. This time there was heavy machine gun and rifle fire. It sounded like they had been discovered by a larger patrol. The patrolling Raiders kept down, and after about three hours the firing stopped—and the rear guard rejoined the main column. They lost five Raiders in that, but the returning men said they counted eighteen enemy dead.

The battle against the elements was excruciating. The next day, the men would form a human chain to cross another river, much swifter than the last. After successfully making their way across, the men had to fight their way through another swamp, with mud waist-deep in places.

Finally, they reached the top of a ridge and stopped for the night. Everybody was pretty tired. Ed got the word that they would be attacking above the harbor the next morning. The Raiders knew it would be fortified and that the Japanese would be ready for them.

Early on July 1, the men headed out. Fairly soon, they saw American aircraft in the distance above the harbor. The bombing planes sent the Japanese inland towards the Raiders, who knew they were getting very close to enemy lines.

The Raiders began to work their way through an area where the foliage was less thick. Their platoon leader, Lieutenant Frank Anderwald—the men called him Andy—told Ed to lead his squad to the left, and he would lead right.

Once they moved a ways down the trail everything broke loose. All of Ed's men hit the ground and opened fire. In the distance Ed could see a machine gunner setting up and took him out with one shot.

Suddenly a machine gun nest opened up on them from somewhere off to the right. Ed's squad hit the ground and lay there face down. The machine gun kept them pinned for quite a while. Ed knew he had to do something; he motioned for his guys to stay put. Then he crawled and pulled himself along the side of the small, slightly raised outcropping where the machine gun nest was hidden—completely covered with foliage.

He took out the Japanese gunner with one shot from his rifle, but there were more enemy soldiers in the camouflaged defensive position. He crawled on his belly close to the enclosure, took out a grenade, pulled the pin, held it for four seconds, then lobbed it up into the enclosure. Then he lobbed in one more. The Swede pushed back from the nest slightly under the outcropping while it exploded before lobbing two more grenades in. After the dust settled a bit, he looked in to make sure the position wouldn't give his men any more trouble. There were three or four dead Japanese inside.

After securing the area Ed called to his squad and headed back to where they were. They had remained waiting face down on the ground in the bush. They started to cautiously move forward again, spreading out some to cover more ground. Ed took the point.

They hadn't progressed more than fifty yards when Ed felt a sudden, exploding, red-hot pain in his left shoulder. The force of a sniper's bullet nearly swung him completely around, but he continued to try to make his legs move forward. His entire left arm dangled, and he was bleeding heavily.

The others came to Ed's aid as he lurched forward from loss of blood and shock. When he came to, he was on a stretcher made from two large sticks stuck into the sleeves of a couple of shirts. Four of his guys hauled him back through the jungle and on down towards Viru Harbor, where PBY seaplanes took wounded back to Guadalcanal.

Once Ed "the Swede" Blomberg arrived back at Guadalcanal, the searing pain in his left shoulder rotated outward to every extremity, making his whole body feel on fire. He was transported from the PBY to the hospital tents at Henderson Field where medics assessed the wounded as they were carried in.

When they came to the Swede, they quickly cut away his blood-soaked shirt to get a better look. Though his wounds did not appear to be life-threatening, loss of blood had been extreme. He felt weakened and somewhat disoriented. With no feeling in his left arm, the shoulder was a mass of torn flesh, muscle, and tissue.

The medics cleaned and dressed the entire wound area. However, it was evident that if surgery was required to repair the shoulder joint, a specialist would be needed. At this point it was uncertain if he would regain full use of his left arm. He was marked for transport to a hospital in New Zealand, then his entire chest, shoulder, and arm were stabilized with heavy bandages.

In a couple of days, the Swede, along with other wounded, boarded a ship and departed for Wellington, New Zealand. There he was checked into a hospital ward filled with wounded Allied soldiers. Sleeping in a bed with linens seemed as foreign as big bowls of fresh fruit on every table. At any time, ice cream was available upon asking. In ten days, Ed gained ten pounds.

After his initial evaluation, the attending physician decided to stabilize his entire shoulder with a full plaster cast that covered most of his left side and arm down to his palm. The medical team then decided to send him stateside, where orthopedic specialists could better access and treat his shoulder wound.

Sailing back to the States, Ed felt deeply unfulfilled, even cheated. He had worked so hard to become a Raider, met every challenge with anticipation and excitement. He had shown himself capable; several times during training and then on a couple of raids, he had been placed in charge of small units, an augur of possible future leadership opportunities. After months of unrelenting effort, he had been stopped just as he was getting started. It was utterly disappointing.

CHAPTER XIV

First and Fourth Raiders at Enogai

The Swede and other wounded Raiders had been evacuated in PBYs at Viru Harbor on New Georgia's southwestern shore to return to Guadalcanal. Twenty-six Raiders had been killed, 42 wounded, and 150 or so more men lost to malaria and other tropical diseases. After their first major engagement, 4th Raiders were now about 200 men under-strength. They had six days to regroup before heading back to join the fight again, this time on New Georgia's northern coast.

Despite taking losses, they had successfully cleared the way at Segi Point for Seabees to follow. Within ten days, a fully functional airstrip allowed American fighter planes to begin their important operations of raining havoc from the skies.

Meanwhile, Lee Minier and 1st Raiders had been waiting at Camp Tetere on Guadalcanal, chomping at the bit to join the fight on New Georgia. These battle-tested Raiders had had to watch their neighbors, the untried 4th Raiders, and most of the Army units depart for battle while they waited for the Northern Landing Force to get going.

Time spent in camp between engagements was a great opportunity, however, to catch up on correspondence. In his longest and most powerful letter home, Lee Minier responds to a request from his mother to tell about his buddies. The letter yields wonderful insights into the men fighting to win the war. The tenor of this letter as a whole is more pensive than any other he wrote. His simple yet profound descriptions paint a picture of the Raider landscape, including Lt. Colonels Edson and Griffith, and hint at the deep bond among men who warrior together:

> May 15, 1943—Guadalcanal
> Dear Mom,
>
> Thanks for the snapshots and letter of March 30. I haven't had a chance to write for over a week but will catch up on my correspondence in a few days. Thanks a lot for arranging for *Life* and *Time* to be sent.
> You asked me to tell something about some of my buddies so I'll try.
> At present in my squad, I have only four men, although I formerly had more.
> My gunner is Cpl. [James] Morrison. His home is in Florida. Morrison is a typical Southerner, with a slow drawl and hasn't much to say. He has about three years in the Corps and recently was cited for bravery. He is tops as a machine gunner.
> Assistant gunner is John Karlik. His home is somewhere near Camillus, New York, between Utica and Syracuse. We have been together ever since joining the Raiders. He is quiet, unassuming, never complains, and always does more than his share of the work. He is about the finest soldier I have had the honor of knowing. Although he was badly wounded and could have gone home, he managed somehow to stay here. He doesn't say anything about it, but I know he feels he wouldn't be doing his share if he returned.

It makes me damn mad when I think of some guys I know going back for next to nothing while others like Karlik stick it out.

My No. 3 man is Andy Stevenson from Chester, Penn. Steve is about 5 ft. tall and 5 ft. wide. He is a natural-born clown and entertainer and a good Marine. He keeps things lively around here. He's either as happy as a lark and singing at the top of his voice or is mad at someone or something and is shouting his opinions in a voice that can be heard for miles. He is the tenor in our quartet. Also plays guitar.

My No. 4 man is "Red" Frazier from Pennsylvania. Red has been with us for only a couple of months but is going to be a darn good man. He is a huge red-headed giant and reminds me of Wallace Henry. Good-natured and easy-going but a good worker and conscientious.

That is my squad and it couldn't be better if I say so myself. I have had other men. Some good ones and some not so good. I try to get rid of a man if I think he won't make a good fighting man.

I have many good friends out here. Bill Groff and Cookie Grogan of Rome, N.Y., have been with this outfit since it started. Groff is a swell guy and one of my closest friends. Red Coleman of N.Y. City is another good friend. He is a red-headed Irishman and always ready for a good time.

For the last year I have lived with men like Gunnery Sergeant [Lawrence] Holdren of West Virginia, a real old-time Marine. Was in China, Guam, Nicaragua and etc. [*sic*] And Marine Gunner [George] McKain who is the closest to being the real Marine I have ever seen. Tall and rugged, he looks like Gary Cooper a little. He is really an efficient and intelligent man. And I learned what soldiering I know from McKain and Holdren and from watching them and keeping my eyes open.

Another real Marine is Cpl. [John] Simonich. Six years in the Corps and all over the world. He is a big bruiser and reminds one of a big clumsy bear. He can drink more liquor than any ordinary man can drink water and never bats an eye. He is the toughest man I think I've ever seen and, though full of holes, is still here.

And Sgt. [Alvin] Cline, my section leader, is another quiet, unassuming guy. His actions have spoken for him.

Oh yes, another fellow who is one of my best friends is Sgt. James Walsh of Syracuse, N.Y. He is short, stocky, and a true Irishman. A great lover of music. I want you to meet him sometime and also Karlik and Groff.

When it comes to good officers, the Marine Corps has more than its share. Lt. [John] Goulding of Brooklyn was my platoon leader for a long time and was the finest officer any man could serve under. He is a small guy and plenty rugged.

You may have read of Colonel M. A. Edson. He was the Bn. Commander. I never knew him personally of course, but I know that he is one of the ablest military leaders of the day and a very courageous man. He looks anything but a fighting man. Small and sort'a shriveled up. I never saw him really excited or nervous despite his great responsibilities.

Colonel Griffith is a real Marine officer. An Annapolis graduate, he is big, rugged and a real fighter. He is Bn. Commander now.

But I could go on telling of men I know or have known for quite some time. I am proud of having known and worked with these men. You probably won't hear or read of them— They don't drop bombs on cities or run great ships. They just lie in muddy foxholes, a cog in a machine. They live or die, just a name on a list. But they are the men that win wars. They are the men that must take and hold that which is fought for.

You won't see pictures of them in action because few photographers care to go there. You won't read the true stories of their adventures for most writers prefer to remain discretely [*sic*] behind the lines. Most of the trash written about battles and fighting men turn the stomachs of these men of whom I write.

These fellows go about their work much as a farmer or business man goes about his. Without the "glory road" technique or flag-waving heroism stuff. They are cool, efficient, and intelligent. Not homesick boys on a great adventure.

For example, tonight at the show we saw the picture "The Shores of Tripoli" about Marine recruit training. It was a terrible picture because it didn't show anything that was like the real "boot" camp training. While in "boot" camp a man is given a really tough and efficient training. You see no women, have no candy or drinks, have no entertainment or relaxation. A man going through "boot" camp is taught a real discipline and doesn't dare to act wise or smart. That is just an example of the kind of thing seen in newspapers, magazines, and shows that do not show the true side of things. *Time* magazine comes closest to the truth, but they as a rule report only on major events and don't go into details.

This is the longest letter I've written in some time but when I get to talking about some of these guys, I guess I get too enthusiastic and go on and on.

In short, they're a real bunch of guys.

Love,
Lee

Perhaps there was some nostalgia mixed in with his desire to describe his buddies to his mother on the 'Canal. Lee's status in the Marine Raiders was about to change. He had been recommended for a battlefield commission by his commanding officer.

Lee was clearly proud of receiving an officer's commission—and rightly so. Battlefield commissions were few and far between during World War II. A man had to establish a solid record of dependability, especially in battle, initiative, and leadership. Even so, many men with these characteristics were not awarded a commission. Lee had obviously displayed unequivocally his outstanding character and capabilities.

In a few weeks, the Raiders would leave Guadalcanal again. Lee would enter the field as a commissioned officer for the first time, and all the Raiders were battle-hungry after so much time at rest. As Raider Henry Poppell would write in his diary, "Each man knew his job, and we were eager to match steel for steel once again."

Darkness and Torrential Rains

The Northern Landing Force under Colonel Liversedge would consist of two Army Infantry Battalions from the 37th Army Infantry Division and all of 1st Raiders, with the remainder of 4th Raiders to join up after regrouping. Liversedge planned to land close to Rice Anchorage, then march on to attack Enogai and finally Bairoko on the Dragon's Peninsula.

The ultimate goal of all American forces was to take Munda Point with its airport, the hub for Japanese operations in New Georgia.

After the Japanese had sent one hundred bombers from Rabaul to help American troops celebrate July 4, the Northern Landing Force squeezed into eight APDs at Lunga Point under Commander R. H. Wilkinson, commodore of Transport Division 22. Wilkinson was a veteran APD skipper and was well-known throughout the Raiders. He and his crews were on a first-name basis with many. At 3:30 p.m., they headed up the Slot toward New Georgia at twenty knots, escorted by three light cruisers and four destroyers.

Anyone on deck the following morning saw the Russell Islands come into view off port side. But then, they lost most visibility. A sudden, heavy squall, though beneficial to help hide the invasion, would make off-loading equipment and supplies a tough, disagreeable task. The convoy cleared the northern point, then turned ninety degrees and began searching in the darkness for the mouth of the Pundakona River. Liversedge, in coordination with his advance search patrol on shore led by Raider Captain Clay Boyd, had chosen a sight some six hundred yards upstream to disembark and establish a supply base.

Lee and the Raiders had debarked many times in darkness and falling rain. But once in the Higgins boats, it was nearly impossible to spot the signal lights that Raider Boyd used to lead them to their landing spot up the dark, twisting river channel. The Higgins boats began to run aground on river sandbars and then had to wait turns at the narrow landing beach, since only four could nose up on the sand at one time. Each Higgins boat would off-load, then return to the waiting APD transports at the mouth of the river for the next load. Back and forth, back and forth it went, until over two thousand troops had landed and 90 percent of their supplies had been dragged up onto the beach. Confusion would have gotten the best of everyone if each individual Raider hadn't determined to continue slugging through ship-to-shore operations in the torrential rains.

In the midst of all this, the Japanese began firing artillery from the direction of Enogai. Understandably, the APD captains began to get antsy. Daylight would reveal their position, so close to shore that they would be sitting ducks for the heavy guns. Believing they had unloaded the lion's share of supplies, at around 6:00 a.m. Liversedge signaled for them to leave.

Then they made an unwelcome discovery. Though they had off-loaded around 90 percent of their equipment, rations, and medical supplies, the remaining 10 percent included a high-powered TCS (transmitter and receiver set) radio that somehow had been overlooked or else lost in the water. The misplaced radio might well prove to be, as one Raider would ruefully surmise later, "the horseshoe nail for want of which the Battle of Bairoko was lost."

During the grey dawn of July 5, rainfall had slowed to a sprinkle. Raiders shed backpacks, blanket rolls, everything except what could be carried in pockets or on their belts. Most had a small can or two of meat, a D-ration chocolate bar, and some K-ration crackers. They saddled up and began to march toward Enogai. It had been a long night. It would prove to be a longer day.

They had just set out when another tropical rainstorm began with tremendous force, intent on beating down to the ground anything standing. Quickly, the trail became a soggy mass of mud-slick slopes, jagged coral outcroppings, and lichen-covered banyan roots. Everyone, especially those toward the rear, was immediately plastered with sticky mud both on and in their uniforms, boots, and helmets.

Lee was thankful for a rest break an hour or so later. He had been fortunate to stay healthy for the most part since he had arrived in the Solomons. But for the last several days, he had felt feverish and experienced dysentery. Everyone suffered with dysentery to one degree or another. Along with most of the other Raiders, he decided to keep his meager rations until he couldn't bear the hunger any longer.

They took another break at noon, and once more most men fasted. Saddled up again, they inched their way forward mostly through mangrove swamps rather than on anything that felt solid. Finally, they reached a crest overlooking the Giza Giza River, although it was only their first objective. The Raiders had covered fewer than five miles in twelve hours. Though it poured most of the night and the rain was chilling cold, Lee felt sweaty. Thankfully, he was able to doze off that night and get some much-needed shut-eye.

The 1st Raiders were up again at daybreak on July 6 stretching their arms and legs, preparing for another day of slogging forward. During the previous evening, the Giza Giza River had been shallow, but the overnight rain and runoff had raised water levels to thigh-high depth. And to everyone's chagrin, once across the river, the faint trail gave way to complete swamp. The native guides did their best to keep the column on high ground, but there was nothing else to do but slog their way forward.

The next objective, the Tamoko River, came into view around noon. For Raider Boyd, who had led the advance scouting patrol on New

Georgia, the sight was dismaying. When he had scouted the area two weeks prior with a small patrolling party, the stream was easily fordable. Now he gazed upon a raging nine-foot-deep tide. He quickly sent native scouts in both directions along the shore, hoping against hope to find some way to cross.

One of the groups returned almost immediately with broad smiles. To Boyd's astonishment, they had discovered a huge tree fallen across the stream a little ways up that could be used as a bridge. It took a great deal of time and effort to get the entire column across, but the Raiders inched their way across the swirling waters on top of the tree trunk. Ropes tied together served as a safety to hold on to, with the strongest swimmers standing by as lifeguards in case anyone fell in—which some did, but fortunately these were rescued.

The Raiders continued struggling along, and finally the march was called to a halt for the day. Lee was exhausted. He was so tired, as were most others, that he couldn't think of digging a foxhole. He found some roots around a banyan tree and with his poncho tried to shield at least his face. He treated himself to a can of meat and a little rainwater. Most of the men had long since emptied their canteens and were easing their nagging thirst with whatever precipitation they could collect.

The next morning, a Raider advance guard met up with the enemy for the first time. There was a brief firefight, then later an intense encounter with a Japanese patrol moving around the village of Triri. By the morning of July 8, with Lee's company in the lead, Raiders encountered a strong enemy force along the trail to Enogai that took most of the morning to subdue. Lt. Colonel Griffith decided to return to Triri, where the Army now had control of the area.

Lee spent another restless night in drenching rain with only a little rain water and a bite or two from his K-ration bar. He felt flushed and dehydrated from diarrhea. Nearly everyone in his company struggled with it.

Early on the morning of July 9, the Raiders headed for Enogai back through the swamp using a slightly easier trail. However, Lee and "A"

Company soon met up with a larger enemy force defending the approach to Enogai. For the remainder of that day and the next, Raiders continued their attack. Though pinned down for much of the time, Lee was able to wreak havoc with his machine gun squads across a fairly low-growth forest floor. At nightfall things slacked off, but early the next morning, the Raiders pressed forward once more.

By July 10 there were many ambulatory casualties in desperate need of hospitalization. The only drinking water they consumed was what could be caught from falling rain. Their food was gone.

Freak accidents often add their own surreal tint to war's landscape. The command post had been established under a huge, sheltering banyan tree. It was chosen in an attempt to provide as much protection as possible for maps, papers, and sensitive communications equipment.

On July 10, one of its gargantuan limbs suddenly came crashing down without warning, killing one Raider and seriously wounding three others. In addition, the battalion TBX (transmitter/receiver radio) was destroyed. Those in the command post who had escaped unscathed rushed in to extract the Raiders buried under the massive weight of leaves and branches. It was a senseless accident that depressed everyone.

Lee couldn't believe what had happened. He thought back to the night just a few evenings before when he had slept beneath the branches of a banyan tree. It seemed the jungle was full of danger no matter where you were or what you were doing.

That same day, the Japanese began to pull out and cross a small spit of land next to a swampy area known as Leland Lagoon. A constant exchange of gunfire back and forth marked daylight hours, but by nightfall the Raiders had surrounded what few small pockets of enemy holdouts remained. Early on July 11, Raiders moved into these areas close enough to use hand grenades and completely subdue the remaining enemy.

Taking Engoai had been costly. American losses included 54 dead and 91 wounded. But Raiders and soldiers had killed 350 Japanese and seized 23 machine guns and four 140-millimeter coastal defense guns—remarkable results considering the handicaps. The terrain was so rough that supplies could not be transported through the endless, infested swamps. By the last day, Raiders had entered into the worst part of the engagement without food or adequate water for over 30 hours.

Also on that day three PBYs flew in to evacuate the wounded and sick. Lee himself was bent over with stomach cramps but refused to come off the line. "A" and "C" Companies had taken the brunt of the fighting and many of the casualties, plus the ones too sick to stand were from these units. They were mere skeleton units now and would be left behind to defend a perimeter around Enogai as the others marched onward to Bairoko Harbor.

After Liversedge reorganized his units, he issued an order to attack Bairoko on July 20. It would turn out that many more Japanese troops had now arrived than he knew. In addition, the Japanese main defenses consisted of four well-fortified lines along parallel coral ridges. These were supported by logs, and each held numerous machine gun placements. Furthermore, the Japanese had 90-millimeter mortars which would continually sweep the oncoming Raiders.

It would present a case study of what happens when light infantry meant for use in quick commando-style raids meets up with an entrenched enemy of superior numbers, densely fortified in fixed positions with heavy artillery and mortars.

Yet it would also present something else: a lasting testament to the audacious courage of the Raiders, who never had any intentions of withdrawing unless ordered.

CHAPTER XV

Disaster at Bairoko

Japanese headquarters at Rabaul and their leadership in New Georgia considered their situation carefully. The loss of Enogai hampered efforts to reinforce the air base at Munda Point to the south, but Bairoko Harbor was still in their control. This garrison was a valuable conduit through which troops and supplies could be funneled to Munda.

The Japanese were expecting an American attack. Their army commander, General Sasaki, had been advising Rabaul of the growing American pressure on New Georgia. The Raiders' swift capture of Enogai brought things into sharp focus. A delay in reinforcement would be nothing short of suicide, Sasaki reported.

To shore up the Bairoko defense, he ordered Colonel Tomonari of the 13th Regiment to transfer his men from nearby Kolombangara to Bairoko by barge. Tomonari was able to arrive there on July 13. In addition, elements of the 2nd Battalion, 45th Regiment, along with portions of the 8th Battery, 6th Field Artillery, arrived on New Georgia from Bougainville. While the United States' pre-landing estimate assumed about five hundred Japanese to be at Bairoko, the figure was now quite a bit larger than that. The Japanese guessed correctly that the next major push of the Americans' Northern Landing Group would have to be at Bairoko Harbor. They would not give it up without a determined fight.

On the other side, the Marines took a similar sober and realistic look at their position as well. The Raiders spent the days between July 12 and 19 consolidating the Enogai site and performing reconnaissance patrols. These probing maneuvers were designed to constantly assess enemy strength to the west near Bairoko. Battle casualties, disease, and exhaustion had all levied a toll on 1st Raiders.

When Lee retuned to Enogai, his fevers and dysentery abated somewhat. For the first time, he was really glad to be off the front lines for a while. He was tired to the bone, and Enogai at least had some supplies. Of course, high alert continued for all, especially on patrols, but it came with breaks.

With so many men down, Colonel Liversedge was compelled to request reinforcements. Accordingly, Admiral Turner released the already embattled 4th Raider Battalion under Colonel Micheal "Mickey" Currin to join with the Northern Landing Group.

Currin's Raiders had been in the fight on southern New Georgia for two weeks more than the 1st Raiders and were a full-strength battalion on paper only. Hard, fierce fighting had reduced the 4th Raiders to well less than full battalion force. Currin arrived at Enogai in the morning hours of July 18 with 701 men on APDs *Waters*, *Kilty*, *McKean*, and *Ward*. With them they brought 40 tons of supplies, in addition to 15 days' rations and 5 units of fire. It speaks well of the Raider reputation that Liversedge felt ready to assault a well-defended enemy position with a striking force of two understrength battalions. These Raiders had been trained for hardship of this type. They were ready to move again when called.

Liversedge consulted with Sam Griffith. 1st Raiders would be reorganized into two full-strength companies, "B" and "D," and two understrength companies, "A" and "C". These two smaller units would be held in position around Enogai while the Bairoko assault took place.

When Lee heard about the disposition of "A" Company, he accepted it with some relief. His fever continued intermittently along with his severe stomach issues. Yet his steady, good-natured attitude never dampened. And when he saw the other companies saddled up to push toward Bairoko, he was sorry he wasn't going with them.

On the afternoon of July 19, Colonel Liversedge released operational orders for the offensive. The attack would be a two-pronged assault by combined Army and Marine units. It called for a converging maneuver directed at the northeast side of Bairoko Harbor. The Army's 3rd Battalion, 148th Infantry, would march from Triri over the Triri-Bairoko trail; the Raider Battalions (1st preceding 4th) would move out of Enogai in column along the Enogai-Bairoko trail and thus unite with soldiers to compress Japanese resistance between the advancing pincers. As always, the Raiders would attempt to move swiftly, with concentrated, light weapons firepower, forsaking the heavy artillery support associated with regular line units.

However, Liversedge realized that heavy bombardment preparation was needed. He requested via the Navy TBW system at 5:00 p.m. that an air strike be mounted from Guadalcanal for 9:00 a.m. the following day. A staff officer confirmed the receipt of the message much later that evening, as atmospheric conditions had once more played havoc with transmission and delayed the message—but the request had been received.

In spite of receiving the request, the air strike order was shelved. No action was taken on the request. This seemingly arbitrary decision by others far removed from the scene of battle would prove to have tragic, heartbreaking repercussions for the Raiders.

The attack schedule proceeded as planned. Liversedge and the Raiders were unaware that the much-needed air support would not be forthcoming. The acting advance began at 8:00 a.m. on July 20 with the Army's "Dutch" Schultz taking his infantry troops down along the Triri-Bairoko trail. A half hour's time saw the Raiders saddled up and marching yet again as they left Enogai. The point unit of the Raiders from "B" Company led the companies in column order into the now familiar but still impassable New Georgia jungle. Swamps of mangroves interspersed among rugged hills covered with entwined roots, vines, and underbrush held the Raiders to slow but steady progress. But unbeknownst to them, the Raiders were marching into the jaws of death.

Just before 10:00 a.m. scouts from "B" Company sighted an enemy outpost of four soldiers approximately an eighth of a mile to the northeast of Bairoko. Rapidly dispatching the enemy sentries, the 1st Raiders arrayed themselves facing to the southwest with Lieutenant Frank Kemp's "D" Company on the left and Captain Wheeler's "B" Company on the right. Progress forward was made for about thirty minutes, but enemy return fire from the now alerted garrison steadily increased with each yard of jungle gained.

As Liversedge anxiously digested each piece of incoming information from the front, he soon realized that his Raiders were encountering stiff resistance. He knew that something must have gone wrong with his air support request of the night before, but he was powerless to do much about it. Still, he sent repeated queries asking for an immediate air strike.

At the front, Griffith called up the Raider demolition platoon under gunner Angus Goss to anchor the Raider line at "D" Company's position. The Raiders pushed forward against tree-borne snipers and deadly light machine gun fire.

Angus Goss was from Tampa, Florida, and had been a Marine for thirteen years. He was well aware of what they faced that day in their attempt to take Bairoko. During the invasion of Tulagi, Goss had exhibited extraordinary heroism when he cleaned out a nest of seven Japanese special forces single-handedly. During the bitter fighting on D-Day, Goss was wounded, as he had been several times since. Each time he would shake it off and continue on. Like so many other Raiders, he had attained a level of respect among his peers and was later awarded the Navy Cross and the United Kingdom's Conspicuous Gallantry Medal. He was a Marine's Marine.

His mission on this day, July 20, was of critical importance. As his demolition platoon came to realize, the Japanese had used the days since evacuation from Enogai to construct an interlacing system of coral and log redoubts. These were placed to afford the enemy avenues of cross fire against the Americans.

The deadly fire from these sites coupled with that of the snipers proved only too effective. The Raiders began to absorb heavy casualties. Had the original air strike Liversedge requested materialized, many of these defensive deployments might have been destroyed. As it was, the Raiders all too keenly felt the consequences of that error.

Nevertheless, the Raiders continued to push forward. Their training and accurate firepower allowed them to continue in the face of withering resistance.

By noon the Japanese had fallen back to their prepared line of defense, four parallel lines on ridges running north and south. From here they unleashed a deadly mortar attack against the Marines. This enemy weapon, classified as a 90-millimeter mortar, was far more powerful than the relatively light 60-millimeter mortar carried by the Raiders. The guns were fired from cleared areas surrounding Bairoko with telling accuracy. The Raiders, meanwhile, could not mount effective counterfire due to the jungle canopy directly over their heads. The American staff officers readily realized that the Raiders had been thrown against an enemy defense for which they were neither properly armed nor supported.

Yet the Raiders continued to push ahead, just as they had done at Tulagi and Guadalcanal. Shortly past noon, the Raiders had, by sheer concentrated and disciplined firepower, broken the first line of the Japanese defenses. Yet as the movement continued ahead, the rate of advance began to slow. More than one Marine present at this battle felt the rate and sound of gunfire was even greater than what they had experienced during the battles on Guadalcanal.

The Raiders needed the compressing effect of the Army's drive from the south, but this did not seem to be forthcoming. Where was "Dutch" Schultz and the 148th Infantry Battalion? Unbeknownst to Liversedge (communications having once again broken down for the Northern Landing Group), Schultz's Army battalion was enveloped in a heavy fight along the Triri-Bairoko Trail and was not able to carry through their half of the planned pincer movement.

Liversedge sensed trouble. He reacted swiftly and sent Currin's 4th Raiders to help Griffith's men and to provide the momentum necessary to carry the day. The 4th Raiders deployed southward to shore up the left flank. Colonel Currin sent "P" Company of his battalion through Goss's platoon with orders to push forward and then swing forth, acting as a substitute for the Army in the original operation plan. Captain Anthony Walker of the 4th Raiders did just that, taking the heat off "D" Company in the process. "N" Company under Captain Earl Snell protected the rear. To complete this complicated maneuver, Goss's platoon shifted to the right to fill in a potentially dangerous gap between "D" and "E" Companies.

The Raider advance came to be measured in yards as the men found themselves pinned down by the cross fire from enemy machine guns. Despite serious wounds to company leaders Walker and Snell, the 4th Raiders managed to punch through to a ridge within two hundred yards of the main line of enemy resistance. The 1st Raiders suffered heavily too, and the early afternoon hours found them with only "D" Company barely able to inch forward. "B" Company, still under Wheeler, was temporarily stopped.

At about 2:00 p.m., "D" Company had neutralized the first two of the four Japanese defensive lines in front of them. They moved to a high position within three football field–lengths of Bairoko Harbor.

The cost was great. Withering return fire by snipers abated as concealed machine guns tore at the Raiders' line. Liversedge directed Currin to commit Lieutenant Luckel's "O" Company (Ed "the Swede" Blomberg's company before he had been severely wounded) to a point between "P" and "D" Companies. The all-Raider line, from left to right, was then constituted by "N," "P," "O," "D," and "B" Companies, with the demolition platoon now anchoring the extreme right. Goss's group had shifted earlier to that far side.

Against a determined enemy well-entrenched in stoutly constructed earthworks; against the combined fire of snipers and machine guns; against superior mortar fire nearly twice as deadly as their own; against all odds, they were poised to make the final assault.

Outgunned and outmanned, with two weeks of jungle subsistence sapping their strength, these Raiders remained ready to take it to the Japanese one more time.

With supreme effort all along the line, Raiders continued to bear down and succeeded in two local breakthroughs against the Japanese defense. "D" Company initially reeled under the weight of an enemy counterattack, but Lieutenant Kemp drew his men together and routed the attackers shortly before 4:00 p.m.

Similarly, the 4th Raiders' "N" Company broke through on the far left. The combined effect of these successes caused many of the Japanese defenders to turn and run for safety, leaving their guns behind. Griffith saw this development and decided to send fresh reinforcements, at Liversedge's request. They both saw the moment of opportunity and were resolved on taking it.

But those reserves that Griffith had expected never arrived on that July afternoon in New Georgia. Liversedge had nothing left to throw at the Japanese. All available Raiders that could safely be drawn from "A" and "C" Companies had already moved forward; any further draws would seriously weaken the defensive perimeter of Enogai. The Army units were still engaged to the south; sounds of gunfire attested to that.

What remained of the 1st and 4th Raider Battalions would have to go it alone.

By late afternoon, with their backs to the sea, the enemy unleashed another devastating round of heavy mortar and machine gun barrages. Those deadly mortars did serious damage, killing and wounding scores of Raiders. Deafening explosions of shells at treetop level rained down branches and tree limbs of all sizes, large and lethal splinters crackling through the air. Often the concussion of the blasts was more deadly than the flying shrapnel.

That afternoon, having inched forward with his platoon against all odds, Raider Angus Goss, an undisputed hero of Tulagi, was killed during one of the heavy mortar explosions. Only a few days before, he had penned a letter home as if with an uncanny premonition: "...[I]f I can't get back this year, I'll see you next, I hope, and if not then, well, you can't live forever."

Liversedge decided to try his last ace in the hole: "Q" Company of the 4th Raiders. This group, under Captain Lincoln N. Holdzkom, moved to the left of "N" Company. They advanced straight into the same intense fire which had succeeded in stalling the other Raider thrust. A relatively quiet stalemate, punctuated by short volleys, settled over the jungle.

At Liversedge's request, Griffith took the time to speak with all his company commanders, then conferred with Mickey Currin. Opinion was unanimous that an advance could only be made if additional troops were committed to the line.

The attack was at a standstill.

Colonel Griffith and Lieutenant Kemp moved to a ridge that "D" Company had wrested from the enemy defenders. Both men looked down at Barioko Harbor no more than about a quarter mile away. There, they would have to make a final assault against a tenacious enemy with far superior numbers and firepower. Without proper air or artillery support, the Raiders might take the objective, but only at unbearable cost.

Reluctantly, Samuel Griffith knew what had to be done.

He returned to the regiment command post shortly after 5:00 p.m. and gave Liversedge his sober and realistic assessment. Liversedge concurred completely, and the necessary orders were issued…to withdraw.

Of this decision, Griffith would later write: "I feel that the decision to withdraw was entirely sound and the only sensible one to have made." Though filled with regret, Griffith knew that retreat was the only sensible option.

The evacuation itself was broken up into two phases, the first being made during the later afternoon and evening hours of the twentieth. All companies were instructed to withdraw in succession and retire to set a defensive cordon for the night on higher ground. The 4th Raiders' "O" and "P" Companies covered this initial withdrawal.

At the same time, litter carriers and medical personnel attempted to round up the wounded for subsequent removal to Enogai. The first of the ambulatory wounded, eighty in number, left before 6:00 p.m. over the Bairoko-Enogai Trail. Shortly thereafter, an Army relief unit from the 145th Infantry reached the Marines with water, food, and medical supplies, then joined the defensive perimeter for the night. All medical personnel worked through the night to relieve as best they could the suffering of so many.

At daybreak on July 21, the second phase of the withdrawal began. Colonel Liversedge radioed over Navy lines a cryptic message:

> Request all available planes strike both sides of Bairoko Harbor beginning 0900. You are covering our withdrawal.

These words must have struck a chord at Guadalcanal as planes delivered a virtually ferocious pounding—133 tons of bombs—to the enemy at Bairoko. The planes hammered the area all day long till dusk. Had these strikes been delivered when originally requested, the outcome would certainly have been different. To the wounded and exhausted warriors, the sounds of the bombing and strafing must have been bittersweet indeed.

More walking wounded began the trek back to Enogai around 6:00 a.m. Lee and other members of "A" Company were tasked with going to Leland Lagoon to meet those wounded who couldn't walk and help transfer them to waiting Higgins boats and rubber boats for the trip back to Enogai. Lee and his fellow Raiders could hardly believe what they saw of the remaining members of their battalion. Many of these warriors, for the first time that Lee could remember, looked despondent.

By 1:00 p.m. all wounded were safely in medical hands. Then those Raiders who could still hold weapons were set in defensive positions around Enogai in case of a Japanese attack.

Once the withdrawal was complete, activity along the Dragon's Peninsula became stalemated. Each side issued forth probing patrols to monitor the other's activities and deployment, but aside from relatively minor skirmishes (which nonetheless caused some casualties) no major actions developed…and no immediate plans were laid for another attempt to seize Bairoko Harbor.

Aftermath of Bairoko…and a Glimpse of the End

Unbeknownst to anyone at the time, the fighting of the 1st and 4th Marine Raider Battalions was essentially over once the evacuation from Bairoko was complete. Colonel Griffith and his company commanders were involved in planning and evaluating reconnaissance patrols and in the placement of trail blocks in the peninsula region. After supervising further evacuation of wounded personnel, he flew to Guadalcanal to fill out intelligence and action reports. The Raider Battalion, or more properly what was left of the battalion, formed part of the regimental reserve at Enogai.

Responsibility for the capture of Bairoko transferred to other hands as the first days of August passed. Two Army regiments, the 27th and the

161st of the 25th Division, used their preponderance of manpower to roll over the Japanese defenders remaining at Bairoko. Over a month after the embattled Raiders made their assault, Army commanders radioed the Northern Landing Group that the harbor was finally neutralized.

"Harry the Horse" loaded his tired men on the ships of Transport Division 22 on August 25, and the Raiders sailed for the shores of Guadalcanal. The fighting was over for the Raiders on New Georgia.

It had been an unfulfilled mission for them, with more than 25 percent casualties in each Raider Battalion—17 killed and 63 wounded at Bairoko alone. In addition, disease, malnutrition, malaria, exhaustion—no new hardships to the Raiders—claimed an even greater number. The 1st Raiders now had just 245 effectives; the 4th Raiders only 154. Yet the men of Edson's Raiders left New Georgia with their heads held high and their special sense of pride untarnished.

And well they should, for later critical evaluation of the New Georgia Campaign indicated that the Raiders were thrown against a heavily armed and determined foe entrenched in massive bunkers in numbers far greater than their own. Against this bristling array, the Raiders carried only light automatic weapons, grenades, and sidearms.

Yet the Raiders nearly carried the day through strict fire discipline and raw courage. Had artillery or air support been available, they would almost certainly have captured Bairoko Harbor during this initial siege, but just a few brave men would have lived to fight another day.

The 1st Marine Raider Regiment Special Action Report, filed by Colonel Liversedge on October 6, 1943, critically addressed the manifold problems the Raiders encountered while fighting for the Dragon's Peninsula. The report details the specific problems of preinvasion intelligence and jungle communications. But Harry Liversedge succinctly stated the cardinal issue which underlay the Raiders' experience on New Georgia:

> Raider Battalions are not properly equipped or trained for
> defensive warfare. Their whole indoctrination, training, and

organization is based on its being a highly mobile, hard-hitting outfit that will be replaced by [a] regular infantry battalion when the objective has been obtained. Situations such as existed at Enogai did much to lower the morale of these special troops.

Though they did not know it at the time, the 1st and 4th Raider Battalions would never fight under their same colors again. Reorganization as the nucleus of a reborn regiment awaited them in the coming months. But no heads hung low over New Georgia. The Raiders probably remembered the same verse of a song they sang as they had readied for the campaign earlier in 1943—a song that Lee Minier and the Singing Eight Balls had performed many times for the troops:

Right now we are rehearsing for another big affair;
We'll take another island and the Japs will be there,
And when they see us steaming in they'll take off on the run;
They'll say, "Old Pal from Guadalcanal, you didn't come here
for fun."

There did remain, however, one final invasion and battle for World War II Raiders. That dubious honor would go to the 2nd and 3rd Raider Battalions.

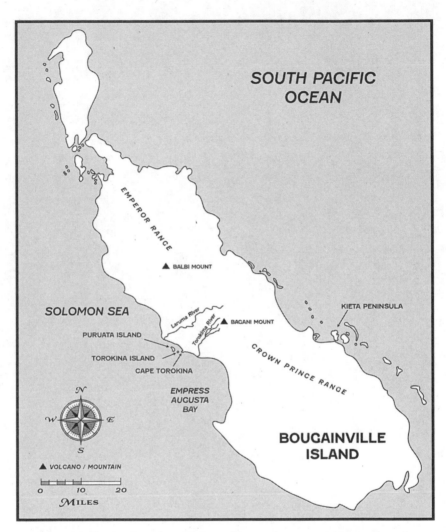

11. Bougainville Island, 2nd and 3rd Raiders participating, D-Day, November 1, 1943

CHAPTER XVI

The Beginning of the End

The fighting on Bougainville would mark the last time any Raiders entered combat designated as Marine Raiders during World War II. Several events had conspired to end their meteoric rise to fame and glory.

First, the nature of the war in the South Pacific was changing. The necessary strategy would require ever-increasing numbers of men, equipment, and ships to accomplish the island-hopping objectives. And the seemingly inevitable invasion of the main island of the Empire, Japan itself, always loomed on the minds of the top brass.

Expanding Pacific objectives resulted in an unprecedented expansion of the Marine Corps. By late 1943, there were a half million Marines organized into four regular line divisions, with two more divisions in the planning stages. (A division was comprised of roughly nineteen thousand men, which included infantry and support personnel.)

As American forces climbed the island-ladder leading to Japan, each rung seemed to be more heavily fortified than the last. These entrenched enemy troops would need to be matched by equally heavy firepower moved by large-scale amphibious assaults.

The Raiders, on the other hand, were designed and trained to be fast, hard-hitting commandos, lightly armed to ensure their supple maneuverability. They were to perform commando-type raids, ideally at night, to strike deep into the heart of enemy territory and withdraw just as quickly, to create bedlam and chaos along the way. These were the attributes that Holland Smith and Merritt Edson had envisioned, but they were no longer needed or required.

More than once the Raiders were given the same mission as any infantry battalion yet at an extreme disadvantage for the reasons listed above. Even so, their disciplined—and accurate—firing and superior conditioning overcame much of the extreme disadvantages.

Another development in the war effort surfaced by mid-1943—the introduction of the *Essex*-class carriers. These supercarriers became the backbone of U.S. naval strength from mid-1943 through the end of the war and beyond. Twenty-four of these ships that could carry as many as thirty-six fighters, thirty-six dive bombers, and eighteen torpedo bombers were built. Though places like Henderson Field, Segi Point Airfield, and the runways at Munda Point had been key elements in the early war effort, the all-important airstrips, though admittedly scaled-down versions, were now afloat.

One final factor, however, perhaps outweighed all others. Some members of Marine leadership were opposed to the hyper-elite force, viewing the Raiders as redundant.

The preferential treatment given the Raider battalions, especially at the beginning of the war, fueled enmity towards them. When two Marine traditionalists were advanced to positions of authority, the writing was on the wall for the experimental force. On January 1, 1944, Vandegrift became the commandant of the Marine Corps. He immediately made Gerald Thomas the director of plans and policies.

They wasted no time dismantling the Raiders. After receiving a memorandum that suggested "any operation carried out by Raiders could have been performed equally well by a standard organization," they got to work retasking the crack troops. By January 8, 1944, Vandegrift had set in motion the specific steps required to disband the Raiders. Lieutenant Lee Minier, now a *former* Raider, would write home in early February 1944 with crushing simplicity, "The Raiders are no more."

Before then, however, these commando-style units would participate in one final invasion, one closing battle as special forces on the largest island in the Solomons—Bougainville. And like a shooting star which seems to burn brightest moments before its demise, the World War II Marine Raiders would be sure to end their service in a blaze of glory.

3rd Raiders Prepare for War

As the month of August 1943 progressed, Army troops in the Southern Landing Group had secured Munda Airport on New Georgia's west coast. Later in the month two Army battalions moved cautiously toward Bairoko with little opposition. They discovered that the main enemy forces had escaped by the sea the night before their arrival. Army troops took control of Bairoko Harbor on August 24.

Now, Allied command turned their full attention to the Japanese command base at Rabaul on the northern tip of New Britain. After deliberation it was decided that Marine and Army forces would first land on Bougainville while MacArthur's command would assault Cape Gloucester on the western end of New Britain. Once these two sites were secured, Rabaul would be within range of Allied land-based fighter aircraft from both directions, its isolation assured.

D-Day on Bougainville was planned for November 1, 1943.

While these events unfolded, new members of 3rd Raiders readied themselves for assignments as replacements in the war zone of the South Pacific. By this time, everyone knew the general area where they would be shipped—the Solomons—but not the specific island. American forces were getting the job done, but it was costly. Preparation was key.

After being chosen as a weapons platoon leader in 3rd Raiders, Lieutenant Archie Rackerby spent several weeks in New Caledonia training the men in his new command. He organized them into smaller units in charge of different weapons and deployment tactics, always pushing them along.

The 3rd Raider Battalion camp and training area on New Caledonia was similar to the lower Sierra Nevada foothills in Northern California—where Rackerby was from. The training itself was not too physically hard—most of the men had already survived Marine boot camp, and Archie had also been through Officer Training. But the days were long. Dozens of times the men ran training "problems" at night until about 2:00 a.m. Reveille would still sound at 5:00 a.m., so they only got two or three hours' sleep those nights.

The night training consisted of paddling out to an island in the ocean about a mile offshore after dark in 8-man rubber boats. Archie would take his 40-man weapons platoon out to the island about an hour before the three rifle platoons would paddle out and attack the island from several sides. No live ammunition was used—naturally. There were no flashlights or other lights used. It was good training to prepare the new and old Raiders alike for the combat on Bougainville soon to come.

Archie Rackerby took his duties as platoon leader seriously. He had a smart leader's intuition, knowing when to push his men and when to ease up. As the rigorous training days continued, all the platoons would paddle back to the mainland around 1:00 a.m., then hike to camp to catch a couple hours of sleep before starting all over again the next morning. On the way back to camp, things were generally more relaxed. The men were permitted to walk rather than march, and smoking was permitted. They were all dead tired and quiet—all except the men in Archie's weapons platoon. He noticed that each night his men were in good spirits and conversed noisily as they hiked along.

After about three weeks, a sergeant in Archie's platoon made a confession. Each of Archie's men carried "raisin jack" in their one-quart canteens instead of water. "Raisin jack" was an alcoholic brew Marine Raiders made from their scant rations of raisins. The men were brewing the beverage in 20-gallon metal cans discarded by the camp cooks. "If they're willing to give up their socks of raisins in order to have a little libation after a hard training day, well, that's okay with me," thought Archie. He never let on to the other officers in the battalion. His men appreciated the minor leniency and worked all the harder for their lieutenant.

On October 6, the Raiders broke camp and saddled up to hike to the harbor. They left Nouméa for Guadalcanal, boarding an old former Dollar Line ship that had been acquired by the U.S. government. Arriving at Guadalcanal four days later, the Raiders would board another transport ship—the USS *Fuller*, an ancient tub of a transport that would take them to the New Hebrides Island of Efate. At Efate, the men practiced unloading the ship, going ashore, and reloading the ship. Two days later they would sail for Bougainville, an island occupied by the Japanese.

For the new Raiders, the war was about to begin.

Volcanoes and Earthquakes

The Solomon Island group, much like the Hawaiian archipelego, consists of islands with a wide range of features. Over the course of their island-hopping campaign, American forces would come to learn an often over-looked geographical fact: cookie-cutter islands don't exist. This was never clearer than it was to the men approaching Bougainville.

Bougainville boasts striking, unique features. As the island came into view, the Raiders were taken aback by the majestic Mount Balbi rising above the cobalt-blue ocean waters. Wispy clouds surrounded the mountain's 10,000-foot peak and floated across its jagged ridges. To its south lay Mount Bagana, not as tall as Balbi, but noteworthy nonetheless. An active volcano, it smoked continuously. Bagana would make its presence known through minor eruptions while American forces were on the island, as if to warn them against trespassing. Additionally, five weeks after landing, troops experienced an earthquake strong enough to disrupt the transmittal wire they had laid for communications. These seismic events made Bougainville formidable enough without considering the enemy soldiers who were keen on repelling the invading force.

Mount Balbi and Mount Bagana are part of one of the island's two mountain ranges. The Emperor Range, which contains Balbi and Bagana, is complemented by the Crown Prince Range, a smaller range, but still boasting a highest peak of eight thousand feet. Both ranges have active volcanoes and in 1943 remained largely unexplored. Even the forty-four thousand natives, whose ancestors had lived for centuries on the island, knew little of the interior.

These Melanesians, rumored to continue the practice of head-hunting, lived scattered among a hundred or so villages and weren't friendly to Japanese, American, Spanish, or any other foreign visitors. Communicable diseases were rampant among them, including acute poliomyelitis, tuberculosis, and leprosy. Fortunately for American forces, the natives lived across the island from the planned landing site on the southwest beaches.

But while the mountains caught their eye when they first saw Bougainville, the Raiders would remember something very different about the island's strange features: its heavy moisture. Come nightfall, temperatures and humidity would remain high—with the latter often reaching 90 percent at night. Four-hour rain squalls with roaring thunder and crackling lightning were not uncommon and could easily dump ten inches of water in an hour. These gulley-gushers swept mud and silt down the mountainsides at respectable speeds, blocking the mouths of rivers and sometimes shifting them as much as a mile. These moving targets made mapping a constant challenge.

Bougainville's downpours also created yawning mud pits, sometimes as deep as six feet. To keep troops from tumbling to death by drowning in sludge, patrolling Raiders tried to mark off these hazardous areas with wire or vines. The constant state of being wet and in mud 24/7 took a mental and physical toll on the men. No wonder that most of the men who fought on Bougainville remembered this pernicious aspect of the island above all else.

To help select a landing site, clandestine patrols had scouted several surrounding islands, including Shortland and Treasury Islands, Santa Isabel, and Choiseul, the least documented place on earth. These patrols were accomplished at night from submarines, PT (Patrol Torpedo) boats, and even by amphibious aircraft. Coastwatchers met patrols with guides and canoes when needed.

After determining that these other sites were ill-suited for building an airstrip or were occupied by too heavy a concentration of enemy troops, military planners had selected the Empress Augusta Bay–Cape Torokina region on the southwest coast of Bougainville for capture. Plans were then hammered out for thirty-three thousand troops, mostly Marines, and twenty-three thousand tons of cargo to land there beginning on D-Day and extending through November 13. Two hundred ships and landing craft would participate in the invasion.

Since the 1st and 4th Raider Battalions were still recuperating from their debilitating engagements on New Georgia, the invasion of Bougain-ville would include the 2nd and 3rd Raider Battalions. In the lives of these World War II Marine special forces units, it was only the second time two Raider Battalions had fought together in the same battle. Their

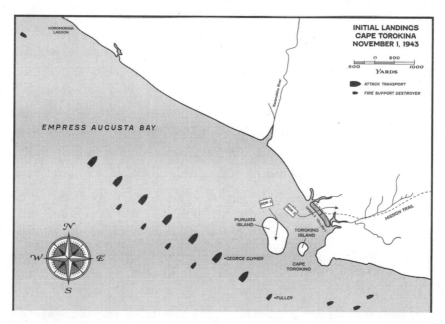

12. Initial Landings, Cape Torokina, 2nd and 3rd Raiders. The last engagement for Raiders in WWII.

participation marked a watershed event: the final time any Marine would fight as a World War II Raider.

As soon as plans for the invasion came down, most Raider leadership saw the writing on the wall. It wasn't hard to guess that their days as an independent force were limited, since the battle plans stated that the Raiders would be employed as "regular infantry in an amphibious assault: at arm's length apart, advancing straight inland a given number of yards and stopping; repeating the same routine day after day." The military command didn't have a need for the Raiders' unique skill set—or if they did, they weren't keen on using it.

Assault Landing on Bougainville

At 5:00 a.m. on November 1, 1943, general quarters sounded abroad the transports carrying the assault battalions. Even before the alarm, there had been a frenzy of activity, with men scrambling to get their equipment and the landing crafts ready.

The cacophony of sounds woke up the twenty-four young Marine Raider privates first class who were asleep topside on the USS *Clymer*. And they did what came naturally—they barked and barked and barked! The group of mainly Doberman pinschers and German and Belgian shepherds were members of the 1st War Dog Platoon, led by Lieutenant Clyde Henderson. They would add yet another unique aspect to the growing list of distinct characteristics marking the Marine Raiders—the first war dogs to be used in combat during World War II. And if there was any Raider that morning who may have looked at these four-legged invaders with cynicism, the hours, days, and weeks ahead would completely alter their opinions.

Heading toward Cape Torokina, the transports turned to port and opened fire with their three-inch guns onto the beaches. Next, the four destroyers started firing, followed by bombing and strafing from the Marine aircraft flying out of the recently taken airstrips on New Georgia.

The 2nd and 3rd Raiders watched the spectacle of explosions from the decks of their ships. Dirt and debris, tree limbs and plumes of water blasted upwards, scattering in all directions. The booming noise was deafening and welcome at the same time, as naval gunfire before an invasion meant a softened enemy—mostly.

Before disembarkation Colonel Alan Shapley, commander of the Raider regiment for Bougainville, gave a briefing to the troops over the ship's PA system. Shapley was no stranger to the noise and chaos of an active attack. He had been the senior Marine on the *Arizona* during the bombing of Pearl Harbor. When one of the first bombs hit, he had been thrown some one hundred feet in the air, plunging back down into burning water. Somehow, he had then managed to swim to Ford Island, pulling a wounded sailor along with him to safety.

His speech that morning contained more information than prebattle briefs normally give the rank and file. He noted that the 3rd and 9th Marines, assisted by the 2nd Raiders, would land to seize a swath of coast from Cape Torokina to the northwest, while 3rd Raider Battalion would invade Puruata Island. He described the naval support the landing force would receive and the diversionary tactics currently underway to misdirect Japanese attention from the actual landing site. After explaining that this was the largest amphibious landing endeavored in Marine history, Shapley ended by wishing Godspeed to all.

As the transports continued across the bay toward the Bougainville beaches, troops on board could see the 3rd Raiders landing on Puruata Island. One Raider observed, "Those guys are busy, busy, busy over there."

Puruata was a small jungle island about 300 yards long and 150 yards wide located about a half mile off the shore of the Bougainville mainland. Despite the island's size, the fighting on Puruata was intense. Archie's platoon and the two other accompanying rifle platoons sustained over two dozen casualties. It would take the 3rd Raiders two full days to secure the small island in the bay.

As soon as he and his men took the island, Archie was ordered to lead the machine gun section of four squads to a speck of an island called Torokina across from Puruata. There he would set up a defense against an anticipated Japanese counter landing from the sea that night. After seven days of waiting, the counterattack still hadn't materialized, so Archie led his Raiders over to Bougainville, where fierce fighting was in progress.

During the initial landing on Bougainville in the Torokina area, the Marines were met by a small Japanese force who defended their positions well. During the initial charge, Lieutenant Colonel Joe McCaffery, commander of the 2nd Raider Battalion, was caught in the cross fire and hit several times in the abdomen. Though he was successfully evacuated back to the transports, he died later that afternoon.

Second Raider company and platoon leaders quickly adjusted both to the loss of their battalion commander and the confusion that typically defines an opposed landing. They proceeded to establish a beachhead with a reinforced perimeter. By noon they had moved to a position some 1,500 yards up the Piva Trail, the primary way into the beachhead from the surrounding jungles.

On D-Day, the Dog Platoon also went ashore in two landing craft following the Raiders and immediately began to impress the experienced warriors. On the very first day, a company of 2nd Raiders was assigned to push up Mission Trail to its roadblock position. Two war dogs accompanied them, a Doberman pinscher named Andy and a German shepherd named Caesar.

During the hectic invasion, both dogs performed in amazing fashion. As Raiders pressed forward away from the beach, Andy led the way about twenty-five yards ahead of the Raider on point. Three times along the trail, Andy stopped frozen in his tracks while slowly turning his head in the direction of danger. Each time, Raiders hit the deck and took cover, giving them time to locate and eliminate enemy positions, including a machine gun nest.

Like Andy, the German shepherd, Caesar, also performed brilliantly that day, hence his legendary wartime career began. Obeying the commands of his handlers to carry written messages attached to his collar, Caesar would race off through the jungle, enemy sniper bullets popping. Several times that same day, the dog dutifully repeated his runs, keeping open critical communication between Raider positions. That first night on Bougainville, Raiders dug their foxholes larger to welcome the dog handlers and their charges. Word had spread fast. Among the many talents two-legged Raiders possessed was their ability to know a good thing when they saw it. War dogs had established their place in combat and at night made catching some shut-eye much easier. Second and 3rd Raider Battalions grew to love the war dogs and their handlers.

Over the course of the next several days, Raiders maintained the roadblock and engaged stubborn enemy resistance along the trail. They then picked their way forward on the Piva and Mission Trails to where these meet the Numa Numa Trail. Elements of the Japanese 23rd Infantry, seasoned soldiers from Rabaul, were defending the entire area.

The fighting was heaviest on November 8 and 9 in what would later be called the Battle for Piva Trail. At dawn on November 9, Raider Henry Burke and a fellow Marine with a BAR semiautomatic rifle occupied a two-man foxhole holding off a fierce onslaught of several Japanese insurgents. When one enemy soldier got close enough to drop a grenade squarely into their position, Burke made a split-second decision. He threw his fellow Marine aside and covered the grenade with his own body. The North Dakotan had just "celebrated" his twenty-first birthday three days before.

Archie and other Raiders fought alongside regular Marine Regiments to push back the Japanese. The combat took place in the terrain of the short hills, jungle, and swamp for several thousand yards to gain enough territory for the Seabees to build a bomber strip. The 2nd Raider Battalion was on the offensive line at the one end. Archie and other 3rd Raiders were at the other end, attached to units of 3rd and 9th line Marine Regiments. Third Raider Battalion and 9th Marine Regiment were awarded the Navy Unit Citation for outstanding achievement in battle during this part of the fighting.

As the weeks progressed, fighting ebbed and flowed in intensity. Several engagements, including the capture of an area Marines called Hellzapoppin Ridge required considerable force to subdue. Towards the end of November, Army's 37th Division came ashore, and the Raiders were placed in reserve. The new assignment would hardly make the most of Raider talents, as they were largely tasked with working the airfield or carrying supplies to the soldiers stationed on the front.

Like other Raider leadership, Archie saw their new position behind the main line of defense as "more or less permanent." The engineers and Seabees now had enough ground to begin building the bomber airstrip. As a result, Archie instructed his weapons platoon to dig more substantial foxholes large enough to sleep in.

However, foxholes weren't their only project. Archibald Rackerby had always been a young man of many interests and talents. Now he added feats of engineering to the list. "My weapons platoon dug by hand a well about [fifteen] feet deep—not to drink, but to provide water for a shower made up of a [rectangular] 5-gallon can with holes punched in the bottom," recalled Archie in later years. Together the men constructed a *fale*, a type of Samoan shelter, from tree limbs, with roof "tiles" made of slices from the trunks of a banana tree. Since the jungle was full of all kinds of tree specimens, his men also made a rough table of small-diameter limbs. Just a few weeks later when Christmas arrived, everyone used the table to place packages from home. They shared their Christmas candy and cookies. "We really had a very compatible group of guys in our outfit," Archie would always say.

And during this position that lasted about six weeks, an old friend resurfaced—"raisin jack." Somehow the two Raiders who had created the brew for Archie's platoon during training exercises procured an empty bean can from the Seabees' bakery. All the Raiders in Archie's platoon saved the sugar and dried fruit from their meager rations and contributed it to the "raisin jack" makers. Then they set up their still out in the jungle. After a few days, one of the brewmasters, Sergeant Maney, asked Lieutenant Rackerby to sample it. After Archie caught his breath again, he instructed the sergeant to dole it out no later than 3:00 p.m. in the afternoon. "I want the men to be alert and sober at night," Archie razzed his sergeant with a hearty slap on the back.

Fighting and Training under New Colors

When the Raiders returned to Guadalcanal after the Battle of Bougainville, they knew things would never be the same. The Raiders were being formally disbanded and were folded into the newly reestablished 4th Marine Regiment. By February 1, 1944, the 1st, 3rd, and 4th Raider Battalions became, respectively, 1st, 3rd, and 2nd Battalions of the 4th Marine Regiment. The 2nd Raider Battalion filled out the regimental weapons company.

If the Raiders were to be no more, at least there was consolation in becoming part of a reactivated division with its own storied past. The 4th Marines had garrisoned Shanghai in the interwar years and displayed their fighting spirit on Bataan and Corrigedor. Many of them were known as the "Old Breed" and were not unfamiliar men to the Raiders who had trained at Quantico. In the following months, the Raiders now fighting as members of the 4th Marines would lead the assaults on Guam and Okinawa.

Training, however, continued. Archie and others in 3rd Battalion went ashore at an area of the 'Canal known as Tassafaronga and set up camp. It became home for the 3rd Raider Battalion, which then transitioned to 3rd Battalion of the 4th Marine Regiment on February 1, 1944.

Archie had escaped without a scratch during all the fighting of the invasion of Bougainville, including the intensive struggle for Puruata Island. However, he would soon learn that grave wounds could come beyond an active battlefield—from friendly fire.

When Archie and his men arrived back on Guadalcanal, they immediately began training in the jungles and grassy hills in the designated combat areas where live firing was done. During one of these sessions on March 9, 1944, Archie was injured by a chunk from an antipersonnel grenade. It had been fired into a coconut tree some seventy-five to a hundred yards from where he stood with his mortar section.

The shrapnel hit Archie in the neck on the right side, severing the external jugular vein and paralyzing the vocal cords. The impact knocked him to the ground. Luckily, his corpsman, Bill Janssen, was near to stop the severe bleeding from the open vein with two gauze compresses.

The company commander sent a runner back through the jungle to camp several miles away, ordering a vehicle down a jungle trail about a mile away to pick up the wounded Rackerby. His men carried Archie on an improvised stretcher to the vehicle, which took him back to the sick bay at camp. There, Dr. Bob Painter of Grand Forks, North Dakota, carefully lifted the gauze bandage that Bill Janssen had tied over the spurting vein.

Dr. Painter immediately saw the seriousness of the wound and ordered a cot placed in the back of a Dodge power wagon from the battalion motor pool. Archie was loaded in the back of the truck. Dr. Painter got a pan of chipped ice and sat on a wooden box beside the cot. The driver drove as fast as he could over the dirt trails the twenty-five miles to Guadalcanal's U.S. Navy MOB (Mobile Offshore Base) 8th Hospital.

During the drive, the doctor kept putting chips of ice in Archie's mouth to keep it moist—so that he wouldn't cough, reopen the neck wound, and bleed to death. Archie was operated on that evening by the chief of surgery, Dr. Deaver, a Navy captain. The next morning, the chief surgeon apologized for the 5-inch incision in his neck—the medical team had needed to get to the ruptured vein immediately and tie it off before their patient bled to death. He also told Archie that he had removed a chunk of iron from his neck the size of two serrations of an antipersonnel rifle grenade.

After four weeks Archie was transferred on a hospital ship to the base hospital in Nouméa and examined by a team of surgeons there. After another three weeks, the team of doctors declared Archie unfit for combat and ordered him transferred to Oak Knoll Naval Hospital in Oakland, California. "Besides the need for healing of the deep neck wound and incision, my vocal chords were paralyzed—I couldn't speak above a very faint whisper," recalled Archie afterwards.

CHAPTER XVII

The Weight of Glory

"Greater love hath no man than this, that a man lay
down his life for his friends."

—The Lord Jesus Christ, John 15:13

(The Message Bible says it thus: "This is the very best
way to love. Put your life on the line for your friends.")

Lee Minier Makes a Decision

By spring 1944 Lee Minier had been a Raider for nearly two years and fought in the South Pacific for over a year and five months. He had participated in some of the most distinguished engagements in Marine history, such as Tulagi, Matanikau, and Bloody Ridge.

Now, he had a decision to make: Would he stay on as a Marine, or return home a Raider?

His letters to his mother shared his eagerness to return to Prospect, New York. There was no more important reason than the recent decision he and his girlfriend, Marge, had made—they were going to be married as soon as he returned. He teased his mother with obvious exuberance: "Guess Marge has told you we're figgurin' on gettin' hitched. Great day a-coming! La' me! Marge is going to make me a mighty fittin' wife," Lee wrote in one of his letters. Their engagement and wedding plans were announced in the Prospect newspaper.

Then, completely unexpectedly, in a letter dated May 11, 1944, Lee told his mother he had decided to stay in the Pacific for one more invasion. "My last letter to you said I was coming home but I changed my mind and am staying on for another campaign. I wrote Marge some time ago. This next one should be most interesting and I didn't want to miss it."

Lee found the new mission exciting—too exciting to pass up. He wanted to be a part of the push towards Japan. He wanted to be a part of the effort to take Guam. Perhaps only those who have experienced combat together can truly understand why Lee would want to stay for one more campaign. The camaraderie, brotherhood, and commitment to one another become overwhelmingly strong—so strong that shed blood does not seem too great a price to pay.

On July 21, 1944, Marines landed on Guam at 8:00 a.m. Despite the preceding heavy bombardment from both sea and air, the landing forces were met with stiff resistance. Lee began leading his platoon inland soon after landing, by 9:00 a.m. Around noon, his unit reached an area thought to be heavily occupied by enemy troops. Lee suspected that an enemy machine gun nest was nearby and gave orders for his men to hold back while he moved forward to scout the area ahead of his platoon. Suddenly, without warning, a sniper's bullet found its mark. Lee Minier was killed in action.

Besides the usual official letters Jolette Minier received about her son's death, she also received several from his buddies who took the time to write her, a testament to how much everyone respected the affable lieutenant. One letter called Lee a "wonderful leader." Another said, "He set an example which is an honor for any man to follow." Another Raider who had served beside him from the start said, "Lee will never be forgotten by those of us whom he left behind to carry on for him—for men of his caliber are very few and far between."

These letters must have offered, perhaps, at least a small degree of comfort to Lee's mother. But no diary entries were ever found in her personal journal—in which she wrote daily—past that summer of 1944. She passed away in 1949 at her home in Prospect, New York.

Lee's fiancée left Prospect and attended nursing school in New York. Eventually she met a young man who had served in the Navy during the war, and they soon married. Her husband possessed one gift she cherished deeply: a gifted baritone voice that brought back sweet memories of a Raider who hadn't returned home.

A Promise Fulfilled

Mudhole left Guadalcanal in bad condition. After the Long Patrol, the 2nd Raiders had boarded their APDs and made for Nouméa to recover. Those needing extra medical attention, which was most of the battalion, were sent to a base hospital in New Zealand for additional treatment.

Mudhole wasn't in great physical shape, but his mental condition was the main concern. The slightest noise would cause him to jump out of his skin. He began to tremble violently. Headaches, tremors, heavy sweats, and nightmares all indicated to the medical staff that Mudhole probably needed additional counseling.

Orders were cut. By April 1943, the young Raider was bound for the Naval Medical Center in San Diego. After a thorough examination and evaluation, Mudhole was admitted to the psychiatric ward for further observation and treatment.

Once there, it was obvious to doctors that Mudhole Merrill would not be able to return to battle. A knee injury required two separate surgeries and never healed properly. Several lesions continued to fester and reoccur. Nightmares plagued him. He dreamed often about the man he had killed in the tiny wooden church on Makin Atoll.

And soon he would also learn the fate of his buddy from Arizona, Joe Gifford. Along with the other Raiders who weren't able to get off Makin, the group had been captured by the Japanese and taken to Kwajalein. There, all of them had been beheaded. And often he would later dream of that event, though he hadn't been there or seen it in person. Then there was Green, a close friend, who had been shot in the brief period of time when Mudhole had gone to get more ammo for their machine gun. Mudhole could still see him just sitting right where he had left him in their foxhole, and when he called to Green, he just wouldn't answer. Sometimes he would awaken yelling for him.

Mudhole had physical ailments, but mainly he needed to heal mentally. When the spunky young man pleaded with doctors to allow him to return to the Raiders, one said to him, "Son, you've seen all the war you're going to see."

When Mudhole returned to Arizona, he fulfilled his promise to his father: he went back to high school. He wasn't Mudhole anymore; he was Kenny again. Since he had finished half of his junior year, Globe High School allowed him to enter as a senior. But there were many days of frustration ahead.

The first few days seemed to go fairly smoothly. But the substantial obstacles Kenny would have to overcome soon became evident. He would lose his temper with typewriters, get agitated by doors closing, and had a hard time controlling himself in the classroom. He needed help, and some at the school were more than eager to give it to him.

Though he struggled, Kenny not only made good on his promise to his father, but also one he had made to himself. He had made a commitment that if he got back to Arizona, he would try to locate Joe Gifford's family. By this time, Kenny was aware that, more than likely, Gifford and the other missing Raiders had been captured by the Japanese. The rumors circulated, to be proven true only later, that the group had been beheaded on Kwajalein. He still had Joe's wallet with an address.

One Saturday afternoon not long after he returned, Kenny went by car to a small community outside of Globe. He remembered that Joe had told him that his mother owned and operated a small grocery–dry goods store there. He found the place and walked through its front screen door.

As soon as he entered, a weathered-looking woman glanced up from behind a large cash register. Before he could say anything, she said with a broad grin, "You must be Mudhole!" This was all Kenny needed to let him know he was doing the right thing.

They spent a long time talking together. At one point the wrinkled, small woman suddenly stopped and looked Kenny in the eye. "Do you know the story about where Joe was from and all? I mean about where he came from?" she asked him.

"Just that he was from here and had spent time in the Marines before the war," said Kenny.

"Well, Joe was full-blooded Apache," she said.

"No kidding," said Mudhole. He had always noticed that Joe had high cheek bones and strong features but didn't think much about it.

"Yes," she went on. "Years ago, my husband and I were taking a shortcut one day on a road that led close to the Indian Reservation. We stopped to add some water to our car and thought we heard a baby crying in the distance. We were just about to leave when we heard it again. I followed the sounds, and we found a baby wrapped up in a blanket underneath a cactus tree. We took him with us and went to the Indian Reservation office. They said that he had probably been a twin and that they usually kept only one. I couldn't have children of my own, so we took Joe in and raised him as ours. Since my husband passed away a few years ago, Joe was all I had. I sure do miss him."

As the bright Arizona sun began to drop into the horizon, Kenny decided it was time to go home. He hugged Joe's mother and thanked her for being so kind to him. It had been a therapeutic visit for both of them.

Mudhole finished high school and after a few years went into partnership with his father and brother. They were successful owners of two popular bar-and-grill establishments. Mudhole proudly displayed his Japanese flags and pictures and was always eager to share wartime stories about Carlson's Raiders.

Gradually, the nightmares and angry outbursts grew fewer and fewer over the years. And as he himself would say much later in life, "I don't think too much anymore about the Japanese man in the church." In later years, he became a hit at Raider reunions, especially with the young Raiders in attendance. They loved being entertained by Mudhole, who always wore flashy clothes with his infamous bracelet and necklace that dangled with gold nuggets. He would thrill them with the best Raider stories from 2nd Raider Battalion—Carlson's Raiders—and he could still shout "Gung Ho!" with gusto.

Kenny "Mudhole" Merrill died on Veteran's Day, November 11, 2018, at the age of ninety-five. And those who attended his funeral swore they could hear him say as he had many times during his senior years, "If I had known I was gonna live so long, I would have taken damn better care of myself."

Archie: A Year of Convalescing...and Beyond

Archibald Rackerby was released from Oak Knoll Naval Hospital and sent to Marine Barracks, Naval Ordnance Plant, in Pocatello, Idaho. Once there, he was assigned to numerous different jobs.

Archie kept requesting a return to active combat duty with the 4th Marines. But the Navy doctors there wouldn't pass him as fit for full duty due to his very coarse whisper. It took him about a year to get his voice back to sounding anything like normal and would remain raspy-sounding for most of his life.

Though tremendously disappointed not to return to combat, Archie would eventually become the commanding officer of the Sun Valley Naval Hospital's Casual Company, where he would meet his wife Bobbie.

Archie left active duty on December 5, 1945. He and Bobbie purchased a 30-acre farm covered with orchards, primarily peach trees. Archie built a home for his family himself with the help of a carpenter who lived on the property while they worked. And at the end of two years, their first child entered the world, a son they named Tom.

But in 1949, a series of tragedies befell Archie. Close to the end of Bobbie's second pregnancy, undetected health issues caused her death and the death of their unborn child. Archie took on the mantle of single parenting with all the dedication he had done everything else in his life.

Then, two years later, the area where his home and farm were located experienced one of the worst floods in decades. His house sat in two feet of water for nearly two weeks and ruined most of his 2,200 peach trees.

A few years later, however, fortune seemed to smile once more. Archie met another single parent, named Gladys. After a brief courtship, the two married and enjoyed forty-five years of marriage together before her death.

Throughout all these years, Archibald Boyd Rackerby maintained his optimistic and committed outlook on life. That outlook included an abiding loyalty to the Marine Corps. For thirty-nine years, Archie remained in the Marine Corps Reserves, attaining the rank of colonel in 1966. It also included continued contact and support of those special forces from World War II that he had been so proud to be a part of—the Raiders.

Over the years, he kept in touch with his old Raider comrades, those men with whom he had served in the Pacific theater, putting his life on the line for his country, just as they were.

And it was at the 1978 Raider Reunion a few years after his wife had passed away that he reconnected with Raider Philip Anderson and his wife, Helen. Raider Anderson had served under Archie in his weapon's platoon during the invasion of Bougainville. On one occasion Philip had received a photo of Helen, his then girlfriend back home. Proud to have such a beautiful sweetheart, he had shown it to Archie some sixty years before. The three of them enjoyed sharing memories and stories, and the two Raiders renewed the unique bonds of those who have been in combat together.

Tragically, six weeks after the Raider reunion, Philip Anderson died suddenly of a massive heart attack. Many years passed. In 2008, Helen's son convinced her to accompany him to another Raider Reunion. Archie Rackerby attended the reunion as well and afterwards began calling Helen. The rest is history as they say. Archie proposed on bended knee in an airport as Helen deboarded her plane. The airport waiting area erupted into shouts and cheering. They married in December 2009.

The couple spent ten wonderful years together attending Raider functions, supporting Raider groups and causes, and sharing their story. Helen had the unique distinction of having been married not to just one World War II Marine Raider, but two! Archie did calisthenics early every morning, a holdover from his training days in the 3rd Raider Battalion. He continued this routine until just two months before he passed away on March 9, 2019. Former World War II Raider and Marine Colonel Reservist Archibald Rackerby was ninety-eight years old.

The Swede Returns to War

After Ed "the Swede" Blomberg had been hit by a sniper's bullet, a large plaster upper-body cast covered his left side and arm for nearly a month. At the Naval Medical Center in San Diego, orthopedic specialists removed the cast. Immediately the most putrid odor the Swede had ever smelled filled the room. But his arm and shoulder were frozen stiff.

"Just relax," the surgeon said as he proceeded to grab Ed by the wrist and elbow and jerk the entire arm straight up over Ed's head. The Swede did his best not to react, but the pain was excruciating. He moaned out loud. The wound was infected and oozing pus. At least it wasn't frozen anymore.

In the weeks that followed, physical therapy helped the Raider regain use of his arm and shoulder. Just as Ed had worked hard before the war in order to join the Raiders, he labored now to climb back up the ladder to top physical conditioning.

Eventually, once Ed had healed, he received his new assignment. It was then that he learned that the rumors were true: the Raiders were in the process of being disbanded.

Ed's second tour of duty would be much less glamorous than his first. Rather than serving with an elite troop of warriors, Ed was assigned to drive a dump truck. Though he was desperate to join in on the fighting, Ed's superiors wouldn't let him switch roles despite his talents in marksmanship and combat. They needed men in transportation, and that was the end of it.

When he and others in transportation were taken to San Diego Naval Harbor to embark once again to the Pacific, Swede couldn't believe his eyes. There awaited the USS *President Polk*, the same ship that had carried him and 4th Raiders—Roosevelt and His Thousand Thieves—off to glory many months before. Ed was swamped with memories of the exultant spirit and justifiable pride that had accompanied him and his fellow Raiders during those early days. He was returning to war, but not as the Raider he'd been trained to be. It was bittersweet.

When the Swede reached Guadalcanal, it was unrecognizable from a year and a half earlier. Americans occupied it unopposed. The Swede's group sailed on to the Admiralty Islands, Palau Island, and finally to Peleliu, bringing in supplies and equipment not long after the fighting was over in each place. While on Guam, Swede got word that two atomic bombs had been dropped on Japan. Shortly thereafter, the transportation group loaded up on a tank landing ship and headed for the big island of Japan itself.

As the Swede stood on deck with other Marines, several of them former Raiders, the convoy glided past smaller islands through waterways leading up to Sasebo, Japan. These small islands rose straight up from the water with no beaches to land on—just rock and cliffs. In some of the huge granite cliffs, the Swede could see large, hollowed-out caves, big enough to park airplanes inside. And in fact, he thought he spotted several Japanese fighter aircraft in the dim light.

"Thank God we didn't have to invade these places. It would have been a bloodbath. No telling how many would have died trying to get on those islands," the Swede said to those standing around him. They all nodded in somber agreement.

Finally, after some time stationed in Japan driving a garbage truck, Ed was discharged. With the help of friends, he got a job as a park ranger in Yosemite National Park. His first assignment was at a ranger station in a remote area of the Tioga Pass region. It was some of the most beautiful country he had ever seen—at an elevation of about ten thousand feet, with clear, spectacular lakes and mountains all around. He could imagine no better place to think and sort some things out.

The Swede had the same question that pierces the heart and soul of many warriors who return home after leaving so many fallen brothers behind: Why did I survive when so many others fell?

> I'd been at the ranger site for a few days when an unexpected snow blizzard descended—trapped me inside the ranger cabin for over a week. There I was alone with nothing to do, and I had only my Bible to read. That week was to become a pivotal experience.
>
> In the back of my mind now, really for many months, I had kept thinking about my previous experiences—all the training I had undergone as a Raider, how hard I had worked, how much I liked what I was doing in the Raiders: the men, the camaraderie, the missions we had together, Guadalcanal, jungle living, and patrols into New Georgia. Then getting shot, my shoulder being smashed so early in the war. Driving trucks and landing vehicles for over two years after that— never being allowed to return to the Raiders.
>
> But the overriding question that kept spinning around in my mind was, "Why, Lord, was I allowed to live?" I knew so many Raiders who had been killed over there. And I'd heard of many, many more I never knew. Yet, here I was still alive with only a gimpy shoulder. The Bible became my source for healing and revealing truth.

After several months of contemplation, Ed believed he knew the answer to the question that had haunted him. For the next thirty years, he found his life's purpose: serving others as a missionary in the rainforests of Belize. Together with his wife at his side, he established churches, elementary schools, orphanages, and a Bible school that later transitioned into a high school, King's College.

One day, after they had been living there about twenty-five years, Ed was chopping and trimming lumber to help build a bridge for a rustic summer camp. The work was extremely difficult physically. The following day, Ed discovered he couldn't move his left arm. When his condition rapidly worsened, he flew to Oklahoma City, Oklahoma, for surgery. During the operation, surgeons found two pieces of bullet fragments remaining in his shoulder—a reminder of the day during the Second Great War the 4th Raider had taken a sniper's bullet on New Georgia while protecting his unit from a machine gun nest. The old wound served to remind him of an important chapter in his life—and how it had served to lead him eventually to an even "higher calling," as the former Raider expresses it.

Ed "the Swede" Blomberg, member of 4th Raider Battalion, which some say was the finest fighting battalion ever fielded by the Marine Corps, turned one hundred years old during the writing of this book.

CHAPTER XVIII

Echoes of Honor

In 1945 the Second Great War was over. American businesses returned to peacetime production: car companies slid easily back into producing cars again instead of airplanes, shipyards started laying keels for cruise ships rather than warships, and steel mills and factories hammered out products for popular consumption, not just weaponry and wartime equipment. The country as a whole returned to peaceful pursuits.

It wasn't always so easy for those who came home, the ones who had "seen the elephant," so to speak. Adjusting to some kind of normalcy challenged even the most stouthearted. Their individual war narratives would take years to unwind, much less share—many who survived would never speak of their wartime experiences again. And some stories, though astonishing, were often overlooked or perhaps even relegated mostly to footnotes. To some extent, the deeds of the Marine Raider battalions of World War II fell into that category. Numerical facts, unadorned with platitudes, help pull back the curtain from the reality.

The percentage of medals to numbers of World War II Raiders is extraordinary. In all, Marines who served as Raiders in World War II were awarded 7 Medals of Honor (4 posthumously), 142 Navy Crosses and Army Distinguished Service Crosses (60 posthumously), and 308 Silver Stars (63 posthumously). Thus, of all the three highest U.S. decorations for valor (the Navy Cross and Army Distinguished Cross are equivalent) awarded to Marines in other divisions, almost 7 percent went to Raiders. Why is this so remarkable? Because as a group Raiders comprised less than 1.75 percent of the approximately 500,000 men who served in the U.S. Marine Corps during the war.

Not surprisingly, their casualty rate was also extremely high. One out of every ten Marines who ever served as a Raider was killed in action, died of wounds, or went missing in action, presumed dead. This represented a fatality rate two-and-two-thirds times that of the Marine Corps as a whole.

Their memory as heroes was further commemorated when the U.S. Navy named twenty-nine ships after Raiders, including one Navy physician and one Navy corpsman serving with the Raider Battalions. Twenty-two of these ships were named for men from 1st Raider Battalion for their contribution in the critical battles of Tulagi and Guadalcanal. According to Major General Oscar Peatross, as nearly as can be determined, no other battalion in the history of the United States Naval Service has ever had as many ships named for its fallen heroes.

In late 1943, as evidence mounted that the Raider Battalions would soon be officially dismantled, they refused to "slink away into the night." Folded mostly into the 4th Marines, former Raiders continued to give evidence of their remarkable fighting skills. They participated in every major Marine Corps battle in the Pacific, including the bloody fighting on Guam, Iwo Jima, and Okinawa. These former Raiders who now fought under the colors of other units continued to accrue an amazing number of medals awarded for valor: formerly of 1st Raider Battalion, Corporal Richard E. Bush received the Medal of Honor, as did Lieutenant Colonel Justin "Jumping Joe" Chambers (1st Raider Battalion) and Gunnery Sergeant William G. Walsh (3rd Raider Battalion). An additional 49 former Raiders received the Navy Cross in later engagements, and 158 former Raiders received the Silver Star. However, maintaining their reputation came at great cost. During the successive engagements, 620 former Raiders died, and approximately 2000 more were wounded.

The Marine Raiders of World War II walked daily in the halls of glory. Their deeds inspire, motivate, and challenge. This has been a story about that glorious past. But it does not end there...

Though glory may dim with time, it can never be extinguished. Given one small spark, it can flame again, often with an even greater brilliance. More than sixty-five years after the demise of these special forces of World War II, the memory of their unique place in Marine Corps history received just such a spark.

In 2006, Secretary of Defense Donald Rumsfeld, along with former commandant James L. Jones, proposed policy changes that laid the groundwork to establish a small Marine Corps detachment (Det One). It was to be a pilot program for integrating into Special Operations Command or SOCOM. This command is made up of all existing special forces from other branches of service. The Marine Corps was the only branch not participating at the time—an ironic situation considering its history.

By 2013 these developing special forces units in the Marine Corps were being deployed on missions and reconnaissance. They utilized the title of MARSOC, Marine Special Operations Command.

When surviving World War II Raiders got wind of all this, they began as a group led by the World War II Marine Raider Association to lobby the powers that be for a name change. They proposed one that hearkened back to the unique heritage of special forces in the Marine Corps—to rename them "Raiders."

In 2011 General James Amos, the Corps commandant, denied that proposal to rename MARSOC personnel "Marine Raiders." He made it clear that the tie, the connection to the Marine Corps past was absolutely important to him, but he said, "...[W]e're not going to name a unit by some naming convention—any unit in the Marine Corps—because we're Marines first."

But these glorious yet humble former World War II Raiders, true to form, weren't going to give up. In August 2013, the Marine Raider

Association invited General Amos to appear as guest of honor for the annual Marine Raider reunion, celebrating members of the elite Marine units that conducted special operations missions during World War II.

After General Amos gave his address, the acting U.S. Marine Raider Association president, Andy Koehler, shook his hand before the attentive audience, then slapped the iconic Raider patch on the shoulder of the commandant's uniform. The unannounced gesture caused a stir among the guests and, of potentially more consequence, prompted the general's security detail to take an urgent step forward. The Raider old-timers, however, erupted into a standing ovation.

General Amos was a good sport about the "ambush," grinning while wearing the unmistakable death-skull patch with its Southern Cross constellation on his dress blues. Later, he admitted to his aides that the evening was one of the highlights of his four years as commandant.

In March 2014, General James Amos made it known that he was reconsidering—perhaps—a request from Marine Corps Forces Special Operations Command, or MARSOC, to revive the Raider name for its special forces units.

Then, in August 2014, more than four hundred people attended the change of command ceremony at Stone Bay, Camp LeJeune. On that occasion, General Amos announced a final directive before leaving his post as outgoing commandant. "MARSOC will be named Marine Raiders, as [an] homage to the Marine Raider Battalions of World War II. Today, the Marine Corps continues this proud legacy and commitment to special operations through its Marine Corps Special Operations Command (MARSOC)," Amos said in a proclamation read aloud. "Like the Marine Raiders of World War II, our MARSOC Marines are trained and equipped to conduct special operations and thus [serve] a unique and critical role on the battlefield."

Today, the Marine Raider regiment stands with three Raider battalions. Although they no longer wear the iconic death-skull patch of their predecessors in World War II, a special new insignia has been created for them.

Heritage is important. And if the heritage happens to be a great one, it can be transformational. The Marine Raiders of today stand on the broad shoulders of Raiders past—brave, young warriors who were innocent yet magnificent, strong yet vulnerable, idealistic yet unsentimental. Marine Raiders of World War II laid a foundation, rock-solid and powerful.

While serving on the 'Canal in World War II, Private First Class Jack Blair wrote a poem titled "The Raiders of Guadalcanal"—were he here today, he might be amazed at the prophetic nature of his words:

> When the sands of time are sifted,
> And glowing tales of heroes spun,
> The legend of the Raiders
> Will have its day in the sun!

And if we listen closely, somewhere softly in the distance, we might hear an echo from glory—a chorus made up of former World War II Raiders, most certainly led by the Singing Eight Balls, joyfully crooning again a favorite Raider drinking song—if such songs are allowed in the hallowed places...

> Bless 'em all! Bless 'em all! Bless 'em all!
> The long and the short, and the tall.
> Bless all the sergeants, and officers too;
> Bless all the corporals, and above all bless you!
> For we're saying goodbye to them all,
> The Raiders who've answered the call,
> They'll all get promotions for Gung Ho devotion,
> So cheer up my lads, bless 'em all!

The new Marine Raider insignia worn by current Marine special ops, the resurrected Raiders.

Acknowledgements

To God, who once more graciously has provided an avenue to feature narratives of men and women during World War II. Their deeds stir the soul and implore us to reflect on what it truly means to face hardship, to commit to service, to sacrifice all.

As for Marine Raiders specifically, one would be hard pressed to find more spectacular examples of young warriors, trained to knife-edge preparedness and willing to place everything on the line. Their heritage is unparalleled for the Marine Raiders of today.

My research began in an unexpected way some four years ago when I was the keynote speaker to a military history club in The Villages, Florida. One of the attendees came up afterwards and asked if I had studied the Raiders of World War II. At that point, I'd only heard of them but never done specific research into their story. He said he thought I would really enjoy learning about them, then slipped away. I returned to signing my previous World War II memoir.

A little while later, I looked up to see the gentleman had returned. He handed me a well-worn video tape and said grinning, "Watch this."

It was the 1943 movie *Gung Ho!*, about World War II Marine Raiders. I did watch and thoroughly enjoyed it.

Afterwards, in the weeks to come, I was planning a trip to Washington, D.C., for research on another military history project. I decided to contact the Marine Raider Association for recommendations as to someone who might help me with information about World War II Raiders. The reply was straightforward: "Lieutenant Colonel Joe Shusko at Raider Hall, Quantico, is who you need to talk to."

And so it happened that I contacted Joe "Marine" Shusko, who graciously invited my husband and me to visit with him at Quantico. Once at Raider Hall, a modest brick building located amid the vast acreage of Quantico, I was formally introduced to the extraordinary world of Marine Raiders of the past. Housed there were artifacts from all over the world donated by World War II Raiders and their families. Joe graciously showed us around, then pulled out stacks of loose-leaf binders with original letters, photos, and testimonies from these World War II warriors. It was a veritable treasure trove for a researcher/historian.

My husband and I spent hours looking at the photos and poring over these pieces of history while my interest in this extraordinary heritage grew. I knew this story was something special—and so compelling.

One of the documents I came across was a lengthy research paper by a certain Lee N. Minier, Ph.D., who had donated the manuscript to Raider Hall prior to his death in 2007. The treatise told the story of his uncle and namesake, World War II Raider Lieutenant Lee N. Minier, and the 1st Raider Battalion. It was too lengthy to read while there, so I asked Lieutenant Colonel Shusko if I could have a copy of the first few pages. He asked his gunnery sergeant to help me. When the gunny returned, he had xeroxed the entire treatise! This meticulously researched paper provided a wonderful starting point for my own journey exploring the incredible story of World War II Marine Raiders, especially Dr. Minier's outstanding depiction of the events during the New Georgia campaign.

Since that day at Quantico's Raider Hall, I've had the privilege and joy of interviewing many surviving Raiders, their families, adult children, and other historians who recognize the heritage and significance embodied in these former Raider Battalions. When I attended my first National Raider Reunion in 2018, held in Washington, D.C., I met face-to-face many of these warriors from the "Greatest Generation." One evening my husband and I had dinner with Raider Ed Blomberg and his brother, George. It was mesmerizing to hear Ed relate his Raider experiences.

In the following months and years, I was honored to interview Ken "Mudhole" Merrill, Colonel Archie Rackerby, and Ed "the Swede" Blomberg, among others. Through more telephone conversations than I can even count, they shared their stories with me—the more I talked with them, the more certain I was I wanted to write the story of the Marine Raiders of the Second World War—to showcase a glimpse of each of the remarkable four battalions.

I offer my utmost thanks to these Raiders and their families, who combed through old papers, photos, and memorabilia to provide the splendid new material presented in this book: to the Merrill/Folsom family, the Rackerby/Anderson family, the Blomberg family, and the Minier/Cannon family, especially Meredith Minier, the widow of Dr. Lee Minier. All of you have been so gracious and always so willing to help me when I had a question or needed additional information or materials. In every way possible, this book belongs to each of you.

Regrettably, after interviewing extensively both Mudhole Merrill and Archie Rackerby, both men have passed away. Mudhole died on Veterans Day, 2018, and Archie Rackerby on March 9, 2019. I am so thankful for the time I was able to spend with these amazing people. It was my honor and privilege to be the last writer to interview both of them. As for Raider Ed "the Swede" Blomberg, he celebrated his hundredth birthday on December 22, 2020.

A work such as this requires a team. For all of the books I've written thus far, special thanks must go to a few professionals who help me continue to do what I love. First, to my agent, Greg Johnson, for his expertise in the publishing industry. Next, to my dear friend and personal editor, Brenda Holder, who reads every line I write and makes wonderful suggestions and corrections along the way. Her encouragement keeps me going. Bren, you are a jewel, and I count on your prayers! To Jim Wortham, a former IT expert who helps with all things related to files, photos, and computers. Jim, I couldn't do what I do without you. And to illustrator extraordinaire, Bret Melvin, who generated some wonderful maps of each of the important locales of Raider engagements. This is the sixth book these wonderful people have assisted me with.

But a story is only a dream until a publisher emerges. So, my heartfelt thanks goes to Regnery History with publisher Alex Novak for accepting this, my second book with them. Regnery History continues their commitment to print and produce these important stories with the most excellent quality. They play a critical role in seeing that in the years to come, these incredible heroic stories from our country's past will not go unchronicled and therefore will be preserved for the future.

This brings me to my final thoughts. I've often asked myself, "Who is my audience?" Naturally, people who enjoy military history will thrill to read these amazing stories; people who look for a great adventure story will surely find that here.

But when it's all said and done, I pray my grandchildren—and yours—will at some point read this true story from our great country's history...and utter a prayer of thanks for what the men and women who participated in World War II did for us.

May God continue to bless our country with freedom.

Bibliography

Author Interviews and Other Unpublished Primary Sources
(in order of appearance in book)

Blomberg, Ed "the Swede" (4th Raider Battalion). Interviews with author and personal notes. July 2018–present. (Raider Blomberg celebrated his 100th birthday during the writing of this book.)

Merrill family. Interviews, excerpts from original letters, and memoirs.

Merrill, Kenneth "Mudhole" (2nd Raider Battalion). Interviews with author and personal notes. July 2018–November 2018.

Minier, Jolette. Diaries, letters, and notes. Minier/Cannon family collection.

Minier, Lee N. (of 1st Raider Battalion). Letters, postcards, and notes. Minier/Cannon family collection. (The collection also includes nephew Dr. Lee N. Minier's work entitled "Raider: An Account of the First Marine Raider Battalion, 1942–1944.")

Morang, Joe (Marine Tech. Sergeant, Rifle Range Instructor, Quantico, Spring 1942). Testimony and observations of Raiders.

Rackerby, Archibald B. (3rd Raider Battalion). Interviews, personal notes, and memoirs. July 2018–May 2019. (Family members include his wife, Helen, who was the widow of Philip Anderson, 3rd Raider Battalion.)

Robinson, Marjorie. Poems and letters. Robinson family collection.

Published Primary Sources

Carlson, Evans Fordyce. *Twin Stars of China: A Behind-the-scenes Story of China's Valiant Struggle for Existence.* New York: Dodd, Mead, & Co., 1940.

Clemens, Martin. *Alone on Guadalcanal: A Coastwatcher's Story.* Annapolis, Maryland: Naval Institute Press, 1998.

Ford, John. "Recollections of Commander John Ford, USNR." February 9, 2001. Box 10 of World War II Interviews, Archives, Naval History and Heritage Command. https://www.history.navy.mil/research/lib rary/oral-histories/wwii/battle-of-midway/john-ford-remembers-filming-battle-of-midway.html.

Griffith, Samuel B. *The Battle for Guadalcanal.* Annapolis, Maryland: Nautical & Aviation Publishing, 1979. (First published Philadelphia: Lippincott, 1963.)

Groft, Marlin "Whitey" and Larry Alexander. *Bloody Ridge and Beyond: A World War II Marine's Memoir of Edson's Raiders in the Pacific.* New York: Berkley Caliber, 2014.

Lord, Walter. *Lonely Vigil: Coastwatchers of the Solomons.* Annapolis, Maryland: Naval Institute Press, 2006. (First published New York: Viking Press, 1977.)

McCormick, John. *The Right Kind of War.* Annapolis, Maryland: Naval Institute Press, 1992.

Peatross, Oscar F. *Bless 'Em All: The Marine Raiders of World War II.* 65th Anniversary Commemorative Edition. Irvine, California: ReView Publications, 1995.

Sledge, E. B. *With the Old Breed: At Peleliu and Okinawa.* Novato, California: Presidio Press, 1981.

Stratton, Donald and Ken Gire. *All the Gallant Men: An American Soldier's Firsthand Account of Pearl Harbor.* New York: William Morrow, 2016.

Sun Tzu. *The Illustrated Art of War: The Definitive English Translation.* Translated by Samuel B. Griffith. New York: Oxford University Press, 2005.

Tregaskis, Richard. *Guadalcanal Diary.* New York: Random House, Modern Library, 2000 (reprinted).

Tregaskis, Richard. "The Best Soldier I Ever Knew." *Saga*, February 1960.

Vandegrift, Alexander A. and Robert B. Asprey. *Once a Marine: The Memoirs of General A. A. Vandegrift, U.S.M.C.* New York: W. W. Norton, 1964.

Published Secondary Sources

Alexander, Joseph H. *Edson's Raiders: 1st Marine Raider Battalion in WWII.* Annapolis, Maryland: Naval Institute Press, 2001.

Alexander, Joseph H. *Storm Landings: Epic Amphibious Battles in the Central Pacific.* Annapolis, Maryland: Naval Institute Press, 1997.

Blankfort, Michael. *The Big Yankee: The Life of Carlson of the Raiders.* Nashville: The Battery Press, 2004. (First published Boston: Little, Brown & Co., 1947.)

Crumley, B. L. *The Marine Corps: Three Centuries of Glory.* New York: Metro Books, 2012. (First published San Diego: Thunder Bay Press, 2002.)

Hoffman, Jon T. *From Makin to Bougainville: Marine Raiders in the Pacific War.* Washington, D.C.: History and Museums Division, U.S. Marine Corps, 1995.

Hoffman, Jon T. *Once a Legend: "Red Mike" Edson of the Marine Raiders.* Novato, California: Presidio Press, 1994 (reprinted 2000).

Hoffman, Jon T. *Silk Chutes and Hard Fighting: U.S. Marine Corps Parachute Units in WWII.* Washington, D.C.: History and Museums Division, U.S. Marine Corps, 1999.

Hutton, Robin. *War Animals: The Unsung Heroes of World War II.* Washington, D.C.: Regnery History, 2018.

Rhody, Donald. *He Built with Stones: A Story of the Swedish Emigration Years of the Late Nineteenth Century.* Mustang, Oklahoma: Tate Publishing & Enterprises, 2016.

Shaw, Henry I., Jr., and Douglas T. Kane. *Isolation of Rabaul.* Vol. 2 of *History of U.S. Marine Corps Operations in World War II.* Washington, D.C.: Historical Branch, U.S. Marine Corps, 1963.

Twining, Merrill B. *No Bended Knee: The Battle for Guadalcanal: The Memoir of Gen. Merrill B. Twining, U.S.M.C. (Ret.).* Novato, California: Presidio Press, 1996.

Wheeler, Richard. *A Special Valor: The U.S. Marines and the Pacific War.* Edison, New Jersey: Castle Books, 1996. (First published New York: Harper & Row, 1983.)

Wukovits, John. *American Commando: Evans Carlson, His WWII Marine Raiders, and America's First Special Forces Mission.* New York: NAL Caliber, 2009.

Magazines, Articles, Papers, Etc.

Canfield, Bruce N. "The Remington M1903 Rifles." *American Rifleman*, November 2002. https://www.americanrifleman.org/content/the-remington-m1903-rifles/.

Daley, Jason. "The Dogs of War." *Reader's Digest*, November 2020. https://www.rd.com/article/the-dogs-of-war/.

Doying, George. "Red Mike and His 'Do or Die' Men." *Leatherneck*, March 1944.

LeFrancois, Wilfred "Frenchie." "We Mopped Up Makin Island," Parts 1 and 2. *Saturday Evening Post*, December 4 and December 11, 1943. *Life*, November 9, 1942.

Raider Patch: Magazine of the Marine Raider Association. Edited by John Dailey.

"War-time Production." *The War Series, American Lives II.* Film project, Washington, D.C., September 2007.

Index

263